Bringing the Sacred Down to Earth

Bringing the Sacred Down to Earth

Adventures in Comparative Religion

Corinne G. Dempsey

OXFORD
UNIVERSITY PRESS

OXFORD

UNIVERSITY PRESS

Oxford University Press, Inc., publishes works that further
Oxford University's objective of excellence
in research, scholarship, and education.

Oxford   New York
Auckland   Cape Town   Dar es Salaam   Hong Kong   Karachi
Kuala Lumpur   Madrid   Melbourne   Mexico City   Nairobi
New Delhi   Shanghai   Taipei   Toronto

With offices in
Argentina   Austria   Brazil   Chile   Czech Republic   France   Greece
Guatemala   Hungary   Italy   Japan   Poland   Portugal   Singapore
South Korea   Switzerland   Thailand   Turkey   Ukraine   Vietnam

Copyright © 2012 by Oxford University Press, Inc.

Published by Oxford University Press, Inc.
198 Madison Avenue, New York, New York 10016

www.oup.com

Library of Congress Cataloging-in-Publication Data
Dempsey, Corinne G.
Bringing the sacred down to earth : adventures in
comparative religion / Corinne G. Dempsey.
p.   cm.
Includes bibliographical references.
ISBN 978-0-19-986032-6—ISBN 978-0-19-986033-3
1. Religion.   2. Religions—Relations.   I. Title.
BL80.3.D46 2012
201'.5--dc22   2011016109

1 3 5 7 9 8 6 4 2

Printed in the United States of America
on acid-free paper

For Nick

CONTENTS

ACKNOWLEDGMENTS

The following pages draw from different disciplinary approaches as well as from far-flung fieldwork stints in southern India, upstate New York, and northern Iceland. As such they involve—as do these acknowledgments—a kind of reliving of my scholarly travels so far.

In Kerala, India, and in upstate New York I wish to thank those who continue to entrust me with traditions they hold dear, who have helped make these places feel like homes-away-from-home for me. In Bharanganam, Sr. Florence and Sr. Christie continue to lavishly welcome Nick and me, most recently on our 2009 trip to the shrine of the newly canonized St. Alphonsa. The hospitality and friendship of Fr. Abraham and Ammal Vellamthadathil, Sujatha Menon, Anil Krishnan, Elizabeth Jyothi Mathew, and Dr. Mathew Abraham likewise remain vital to our continued connection to the splendors of Kerala. At the Rush temple, Aiya's generously shared reflections and opinions seemingly know no bounds and devotees too numerous to name make return visits a true pleasure for me. I wish to especially thank Amma, Aiya's wife, whose kitchen encounters are unfailingly warm and Aparna Hasling, whose insights, occasionally from high atop tree forts, challenge me in the best of ways. I am eternally grateful to Susan Nowak and the Sisters of St. Joseph who welcomed me year after year when traveling from Wisconsin to Rochester. Mary Lee Bishop, strength and sweetness incarnate, made these visits especially memorable. She is sorely missed.

The final chapter of this book draws from my most recent fieldwork encounters in Akureyri, Iceland, where I met with a long list of Spiritualist practitioners who agreed, often multiple times, to share with me their experiences and reflections. I am grateful to those quoted in this book: Björn

Jónsson, Guðbjörg Guðjónsdóttir, Hrafnhildur Sigurgeirsdóttir, Jón Birkir Lúðvíksson, Ingibjörg Tryggvadóttir, Matthías Henriksen, Ragnheiður Ragnarsdóttir, Rósa Sigurlaug Gestsdóttir, and Þórhallur Guðmundsson. Thanks also to Pétur Péturson, who graciously offered me his valuable historical and theological perspectives during his brief visit to Akureyri. Most of those I interviewed in Akureyri are not included by name in this book, yet their wisdom and experiences inform my work significantly. Among those I wish to thank by name are Halldór Hannesson for welcoming me repeatedly into his trance medium sessions, Jóhann Rúnar Sigurðsson for his ongoing, unflagging enthusiasm and assistance, Anna Guðný Egilsdóttir for accompanying me to Hrísey Island, and Hulda Hrönn Ingadóttir, whose initial efforts and introductions opened a community to me. This volume contains the tip of a veritable Icelandic iceberg; those not featured here will likely find their voices in the book I intend to write next.

I am extremely grateful to Gunnar Karlsson for plying me with stacks of Icelandic articles and book chapters dated from 1916 onward, not to mention decades-old recordings of trance medium sessions that he worked so diligently to preserve. Kristján Jósteinsson, Minerva Björg Sverrisdóttir, Rannveig Magnúsdóttir, and Sólveig Hrafnsdóttir graciously helped in various capacities as translators. Hrafnhildur Sigurgeirsdóttir and Vilhjálmur Bergmann Bragason kindly alerted me to undetected misspellings in the chapter's final version. To Ragnheiður Ragnarsdóttir I owe a debt of gratitude for her countless hours of expert assistance, advice, and companionship. In Stevens Point, Pálmi Möller served as my ever-patient Icelandic tutor, to whom I am grateful. Finally, the Icelandic component of this book would have been impossible if it were not for Sólveig Hrafnsdóttir and Kristján Jósteinsson, who extended their Akureyri home and hearts to me and planted the idea of Icelandic fieldwork in the first place. It's hard to imagine greater gifts or dearer friends.

Colleagues in religious studies and beyond have helped pave the road for this comparative book. Among them are Maureen O'Connor and Tadgh Foley, organizers of the 2004 and 2007 Conference on Colonialism at NUI, Galway, that allowed me to dream up what became chapters 1 and 3. I thank John Cort for organizing a 2006 AAR panel on Hinduism and social justice that inspired what became chapter 2 and Karen Pechilis for organizing a 2007 AAR panel on ethnography and methodology that helped start what became the postscript. I am grateful to the Society for Hindu-Christian Studies for offering a context from which to think comparatively. I thank in particular members Chad Bauman, Kristin Bloomer, Frank Clooney, Eliza Kent, Reid Locklin, Brad Malkowsky, Brian Pennington, and Deepak Sarma for stimulating exchanges throughout the years. I am also indebted to ongoing conversations with South Asia colleagues and friends Loreilei Birnacki, Sudharshan Durayappah, Joyce Flueckiger, Karen Pechilis, Tracy Pintchman, Whitney Sanford, Robin Rinehart, Susan Wadley, Joanne Waghorne, Luke Whitmore, and Paul Younger. Conversations with dearly departed Selva Raj, although not ongoing with him, continue to live on in my head and in my work. Thanks also to Kimberly Patton for helping me get this book's introduction off the ground. At the University of Wisconsin–Stevens Point I thank colleagues Don Fadner, Alice Keefe, Sandhya Ganapati, and Karin Fry for suggestions and feedback at crucial stages of this book's evolution. Thanks to Teresa Cooper Jacobs for encouraging me to incorporate the neighborhood kids in my introduction. I wish to acknowledge especially Ann Gold and Bill Harman, whose formal and informal support and inspiration have been instrumental to the joyful twists and turns of my career so far.

Thanks to all the good people at Oxford University Press who have helped this book see the light of day. It has been a pleasure, once again, to work with religion acquisitions editor Cynthia Read, whose encouragement and excellent work I so appreciate. I also wish to thank Christi Stanforth for her careful copyediting, production editors Emily Perry and G. Hari Kumar for ushering this book to completion, and editorial assistant Sasha Grossman for keeping all bases covered and communicating. I am sincerely grateful for anonymous readers' assurances and insightful suggestions that helped create a better finished product. As always, I take full responsibility for any final shortcomings.

Closer to home, I proudly thank Jack Dempsey Garigliano for his stunning editorial insights that improved portions of this book. I offer my heartfelt appreciation for both of my sons, Jack and Sam Garigliano, for accompanying me in so many ways—logistically, emotionally, and intellectually—over the years. I am better for their fine company and so, I believe, is my work. My parents, Fran and Tom Dempsey, who raised me with a respectful fascination for all things spiritual, are true inspirations that no doubt laid the foundation for my comparative mind-set. Finally, I must humbly consider the many ways Nick Garigliano has supported my research and writing over the years. He has dropped everything more than once to move across the country and halfway across the planet and has endured, with grace, my extended absences and occasional hibernations. Perhaps most importantly, he seems to maintain faith in the value of my work even when mine flags and willingly marvels alongside me at each new tradition that crosses our path. The least I can do is dedicate this book to him.

ICELANDIC AND INDIAN
LANGUAGE NOTES

The Icelandic alphabet contains several letters not included in the (modern) English alphabet. I have chosen to keep original spellings of Icelandic names and words because letter variations are few and simple to learn. Furthermore, if (non-Icelandic) readers adhere to the following guide, pertinent to the Icelandic words used in the chapter 4, they will not only get the pronunciation right but also duly impress all their Icelandic friends.

á   *ow*, as in *cow*
é   *ye*, as in *yes*
æ   *i*, as in *like*
ei *ay*, as in *way*
ö   *e*, as in *bed*, but with rounded lips
ð   soft *th*, as in *father*
f   *v*, as in *vase*
j   *y*, as in *yes*
þ   hard *th*, as in *thick*

To accommodate readers not familiar with Indian languages, I have chosen to anglicize rather than apply standard transliteration to Sanskrit and Tamil words. Although this system is not foolproof, it manages to simplify while keeping proper pronunciation fairly intact.

Bringing the Sacred Down to Earth

Introduction

Adventures and Misadventures in Comparison

This book's comparison of religious phenomena will seem, to some, an innocent enough endeavor. To others, its juxtapositions of Hindu and Christian traditions, many of which exist on opposite sides of the planet, represent a leap, with faith, into a disciplinary minefield. One side of this debate has argued for decades that comparison is an outmoded, politically troubled approach to the human sciences. Opponents, represented by a growing number of religion scholars, are recently "writing back" in comparison's defense, both ameliorating and rejecting their critics' concerns, asserting the invaluable merits of a readjusted, new comparativism.

Just days before I started writing this introduction I overheard a passionate exchange that spoke to me about the ways this book, broadly speaking, engages the comparative religion debate. I was walking home from campus one afternoon and passed a solid wooden fence lining one of our neighbor's yards. I could hear voices just behind the fence belonging to two children I know to be around six or seven years old who seemed to be setting down ground rules for a freelance game. Just as I was opposite them on the other side of the fence, one of the children loudly established, with authority, "This here [which I couldn't see] is magic." After a brief pause, another voice said, rather indignantly, "*Everything* can't be magic." Seemingly having anticipated this complaint, the original voice shot back, "Oh yes it can!" I did not hear the rest of the argument as I kept on walking, chuckling to myself (although now I wish I'd slowed my pace).

It occurred to me as I neared my house, my mind switching back to this introduction, that this debate about magic, featuring the sticky issues of what is perceived as such and who gets to decide, could be extended and applied to this book on two levels: to the comparative method that gives it shape and to the topic of religion and the sacred that founds its substance.[1] Similar to the over-the-fence argument, current critique of the comparative method often rests on questioning the authority presumed in determining what will and will not (magically) be compared. At what point is the power conferred on those who perform seemingly whimsical comparisons overdetermining if not oppressive to those whose practices and beliefs she brings into her charmed circle? On the other hand, similar to the voice that insists that everything can indeed be magic, new comparison advocates argue that comparison is an intrinsic and inevitable part of human activity and thought. The question then becomes not whether we should compare but, in comparing, how we can do so transparently and responsibly. How do we choose among infinitely available points of comparison such that the process advances rather than predetermines or undermines our knowledge of religious phenomena? Depending on how comparisons are conceived and executed, the game need not be unfair, uninteresting, or over.

The second way this book echoes the over-of-the-fence argument has to do with the problem of religious (and other) authorities' designations of the category of the sacred. The following chapters investigate understandings of where and how the sacred resides, who has the authority to decide, and whether such decisions are fair—all written in the knowledge that definitions of and access to the sacred are eternally precarious, at best. Under scrutiny are official religious, political, and epistemological processes that keep the sacred at least partially out of reach from the general populace, abstracted and disembodied in ways that make them irrelevant to if not neglectful of earthly realities. Working at cross purposes, described in each of the volume's chapters, are religious contexts that attend to material needs, confer sacred access to a wider public, and imbue land and bodies with sacred meaning and power. This process of grounding the sacred is enabled by folklore figures, democratizing theologies, newly sanctified land, and extraordinary human abilities. Like the voices on the other side of the fence, this book narrates how the disposition and location of the sacred is not only hotly contested, given its potency, but can also shift depending on who is calling the shots.[2] For some the sacred must, by its very nature, be closely sequestered and beyond the solid grasp of all but a select few. For others, although *everything* cannot be sacred, neither should it be unavailable to or beyond the reach of those who faithfully wish, or need, to engage.

These dual debates—reflecting the method and structure of this book— emerge as a two-pronged rebuttal to two similarly constructed scholarly critiques. A complaint often lodged against the comparative approach, as I soon elaborate, is that it conjures and imposes abstracted categories that too often erase culturally embedded distinctions and realities. Likewise, critics of religion often note how religious systems impose on adherents spiritualizing abstractions that deflect and neglect material needs and realities. As both sets of critics have it, scholarly comparison and religion, imposed from above, easily lend themselves to imperialistic structures of oppression. It is no surprise that, as frameworks that name and claim varieties of power, both are often guilty as charged. Yet by working contextually—and perhaps brazenly—across religious and cultural divides, the following chapters demonstrate instances in which concepts and performances of the sacred, when brought down to earth, can dismantle such impositions and abstractions.

The horizontal and vertical leaps forming the weave of this book thus offer challenges to top-heavy power dynamics in purported spheres of anathema. Each chapter contains a comparative case study that turns on its own axis of discovery and analysis, exploring contests for naming and claiming the sacred from different angles and in a variety of settings. Working from a range of sources, employing a variety of approaches, each undertakes comparison to reveal instances in which religious expressions and experiences engage with rather than ignore earthly existence. Each chapter ultimately demonstrates comparison's potential to shed light on angles and contours otherwise obscured within particular religious contexts and, in the process, suggests possibilities for bridging human contingencies and perceptions across religious, cultural, and disciplinary divides.

COMPARATIVE RELIGION AND ITS CRITICS

In the beginning, comparative religion was synonymous with the field of religious studies.[3] From its inception in the mid- to late 1800s, one of the expressed aims of religious studies as a discipline was to bring all religions—including those outside Judaism, Christianity, and Islam, that is, those previously labeled "pagan"—on equal footing through the process of comparison. Contrasting what he understood to be the objectivity of this new discipline with the religious bias of theology, Max Müller championed a "Science of Religion" that was to be based on methods of comparison.[4] Müller considered it impossible to understand any religion's deities, myths, and rituals unless they were put in cross-cultural context, juxtaposed with other deities, myths, and rituals. In this spirit, he famously remarked about religion: "He who knows one, knows none."[5]

Although comparative religion set its sights differently than theology, its aim to be value neutral and non-Christian-centric seems to have missed its mark significantly from the start. Informed by Darwinian-Spencerian theories of evolution popular at the time, the comparative approach hinged upon classifying religions on an evolutionary scale from primitive to civilized, inferior to superior, in which Christianity, the normative template from which the category "religion" arose, typically fared well.[6] Furthermore, the data early scholars used for their comparisons were gleaned largely from interactions between European colonizers and the "pagan" or "primitive" societies they managed. Although these scholars of religion did not typically identify with colonial frontiers or imperial centers, the emerging understanding of global religious systems nonetheless was informed by sources and methodologies that reflected racist presumptions.[7]

Although Protestant Christianity managed well in the evolutionary ordering of early religion scholars, comparative religion was often accused of an anti-religion, anti-Christian bias. The rise of the field coincided with nineteenth-century scientific breakthroughs that, for many, threatened religion's validity, often putting religion advocates on the defensive. The fact that comparative religion identified itself, at the start, as a science that relied heavily on Darwinian methodology made it appear to some as though the field had positioned itself as an enemy to religion. Comparative religion's task of identifying shared patterns of belief and practice among all religions, including nonmonotheistic traditions, also challenged for some the uniqueness, and therefore the validity, of Christianity. This uneasiness held considerable sway up into the middle of the twentieth century, prompting Joachim Wach, founder of the History of Religions at the University of Chicago, to defend the comparative approach to religious studies in a 1935 address, republished in 1965 as the introduction to the seminal volume *The History of Religions*. Here, Wach reassures his audience of the merits of comparison for enhancing religious loyalties:

> To observe the multiplicity of religious life and of religious expression, to discover similarities and relationships, need not, as some fear, have a sobering or paralyzing effect on one's own religiosity. On the contrary, it could become a support and an aid in the battle against the godless and estranged powers; it ought to lead to the examination and preservation of one's own religious faith. (Wach 1965: 4)[8]

Wach's faith-friendly view was shared, but in a different form, by his successor at the University of Chicago, Mircea Eliade, one of the most influential comparativists of the twentieth century who received critique from the other side of the fence. Like Müller before him, Eliade felt that essential to the study and understanding of religion was the comparison of religious phenomena—the irreducible core of which, for Eliade, was the element of the sacred (Eliade 1958: xiii). Eliade categorized and organized a wide range of religious data into cross-cultural studies that, unlike some of his predecessors' work, were intended to be descriptive, not prescriptive; phenomena he identified as sacred were not meant to be ordered as superior or inferior, but could be investigated without resorting to judgment. Although Eliade's comparisons were designed to reveal the sacred as perceived by practitioners, colleagues criticized his purportedly "scientific" study for appearing to advocate for the recovery of sacred values. Eliade indeed believed that comparative religion had the potential to bring about a second Renaissance of sorts, allowing new, non-Western ideas to influence Western culture and self-understanding.[9]

The most recent charges leveled against comparativism arise from postmodern and postcolonial perspectives that, unlike earlier critiques, have threatened the very existence of comparison as a viable means for studying religions. At very least, these criticisms have altered the course of the field forever. Here, the list of charges against comparativism can be boiled down to accusations that it creates uncontextualized, abstracted categories that lead to essentialism and intellectual imperialism. In the wake of these accusations, comparative religion has often found itself on the sidelines, dismissed by scholars both within and outside the discipline, vanished from graduate programs in favor of more narrowly focused area-studies research into specific religious texts and communities (Patton and Ray 2000: 1, 3; Patton 2000a: 153).

Reminiscent of the fact that comparative religion's origins can be traced to colonial frontiers, a core critique of comparativism today is of intellectual imperialism, a process that imposes universal categories that distort or disregard locally embedded meanings and differences. Somewhat like the earlier religiously generated discomfort with what was felt to be comparativism's neglect of crucial religious differences, this more recent critique asserts an obligation to recognize cultural particularities.[10] As Wendy Doniger notes, contemporary critics who consider comparison to be politically rather than religiously problematic find that, in this era of "multinationalism and the politics of individual ethnic and religious groups, of identity politics and minority politics, to assume that two phenomena from different cultures are 'the same' in any significant way is regarded as demeaning to the individualism of each, a reflection of the old racist, colonialist attitude that 'all wogs look alike'" (Doniger 2000: 64).[11]

Mircea Eliade's encyclopedic rendering of similarities between religious categories and phenomena across space and time, most famously available in his *Patterns of Comparative Religion*, is particularly vulnerable to accusations of abstraction due to its scarcity of context.[12] Also bothersome to critics who view comparativism's organizing patterns as abstract impositions masking vital differences is the category of the sacred, likewise understood to be imposed from above by scholars of religion.[13] Eliade's work again emerges as particularly problematic in this regard, based as it is on his understanding that a transcendent "sacred" can be discovered cross-culturally in the rituals and myths of humanity, or *Homo religiosus*.[14] Attention to practices and beliefs that engage with an all-pervasive sacred is particularly vexing for many scholars who, according to today's academic trends, tend to associate religion and religious phenomena with social processes and constructions.

IN DEFENSE

Rather than overlooking comparative religion's checkered past and potentially checkered future, new comparativists promote a reformed enterprise committed to cultural specificity that may or may not assume shared inter-religious essences. Advocates of comparison argue that religious categories applied cross-culturally can become, when properly contextualized, a means for "understanding a tradition more profoundly, and paradoxically, more on its own terms." Departing from Müller, the process of comparison is seen less as a science than, admittedly, as "the scholar's own *inventio*—the 'magic' of creative insight and mutual understanding" (Patton and Ray 2000: 9, 18).[15]

On a more foundational level, many advocates argue that comparison is ultimately unavoidable, indispensable not only to the process of categorization but to the act of identification itself.[16] As stated by Robert Segal, "To understand any phenomenon, however specific, is to identify it and to account for it. To identify something is to place it in a category, and to account for it is to account for the category of which it is a member. Both procedures are thus inescapably comparativist" (Segal 2001: 352, 358). When applied to the study of religion, as William Paden describes it, we find that

> there *is* no study of religion without cross-cultural categories, analysis, and perspective. Knowledge in any field advances by finding connections between the specific and the generic, and one cannot even carry out ethnographic or historical work without utilizing transcontextual concepts. Like it or not, we attend to the world

not in terms of objects but in terms of categories. Wherever there is a theory, wherever there is a concept, there is a comparative program. (Paden 2000: 182)[17]

Practically speaking, the inevitability of comparison—and the futility of studying religion solely in search of particularities—arises from the realities of a globalized community that rarely experiences religion as simple, singular, or uncontested. Central to comparative study is the acknowledgment of ongoing exchanges between religions that share common economies, politics, and geographies and, moreover, of conflicts and multiple worldviews set within purportedly singular religious traditions. As Diana Eck notes, while these inter- and intrareligious dynamics may be keenly felt in today's world, they are not unique to our current historical context: "Indeed the challenge of studying the postmodern world with all its plurality should alert us to the difficulty of studying any historical period as if its religious life could be color-coded, boundaried, and studied in separate units" (Eck 2000: 132–133, 135).[18]

In the end, exclusive attention to either similarity or difference can be immobilizing to the study of religion. Recognizing the need to avoid both extremes, anthropologist Gananath Obeyesekere's comparison of reincarnation beliefs within Amerindian, Buddhist, and ancient Greek cultures rejects overarching, essentializing theories in addition to, as he puts it, "the contemporary fascination in my own discipline for ethnographic particularity and a rejection of theory unless it shows that no theories are possible outside descriptive specificity" (2002: xiv).[19] As described by Wendy Doniger, "Either similarity or difference may lead to a form of paralyzing reductionism and demeaning essentialism, and thence into an area where 'difference' itself can be politically harmful. For, where extreme universalism means that the other is exactly like you, extreme nominalism means that the other may not be human at all" (Doniger 2000: 65–66).[20]

A potential by-product of comparison that produces, for some, an ethical imperative to bring disparate contexts into dialogue is the ability of such exchanges to challenge set boundaries that artificially divide human communities and religions. This potential challenge suggests a course for contemporary comparative religion that veers decidedly from its founding commitment to "value-free" scholarship.[21] Literary theorist Terry Eagleton maintains that contextualized comparison can act as a counterforce to "vacuous universalism" as well as "myopic particularism"—positions that are, in their own ways, politically ineffective.[22] Particularly ineffective, in Eagleton's mind, is contemporary scholarship's overemphasis on particularity. As he puts it, "Differences cannot fully flourish while men and women languish under forms of exploitation; and to combat those forms effectively implicates ideas of humanity which are necessarily universal" (Eagleton 1996: 120–121).[23]

As I see it, the key to maintaining productive exchanges between scholar and subject, helping to deflect comparativism's imperialistic potential, is the resolve to take seriously the religious experiences and expressions of those we study.[24] Although this may seem an obvious suggestion, it appears that the current emphasis religion scholarship tends to place on power dynamics is precisely capable of diminishing this resolve, creating barriers between students of religion and the communities they study. As Patton describes it, Foucauldian analysis, a considerable force in the study of religion in recent decades, typically assumes that what "a religious tradition says it is about, that is, the mediation of the human relationship to the 'really real,' is not what it is actually about. What it is 'actually' (allegedly) about is power—political relationships: who is included, and who is not, and how, and why. . . . But is this all—or always—the story?" Patton points to a contradiction embedded in "this methodological condescension," which tends to ignore understandings of the sacred put forward by practitioners, those most dynamically engaged with the practices and expressions under consideration. This scholarly position is ironically "in direct and irreconcilable conflict with the new emphasis on 'context.'" To understand the sacred as an entity solely used as a pretext for power and as a socially constructed tool for hegemonic interests, "is arrogantly to disenfranchise those we purport to understand" (Patton 2000a: 164, 168).[25]

Mircea Eliade, whose pioneering work on comparative religion has risen and fallen in popularity throughout the decades, expressed what seems to have been his amusement at the ironies, inconsistencies, and ethereal nature of academic "fashion."[26] Watching trends in religious studies come and go, Darwinian-Spencerian postulations about the evolution of religion fade, and the stars of Freud, Lévi-Strauss, Teilhard de Chardin, and others rise, Eliade notes,

> Now, as we all know well, for a particular theory or philosophy to become popular, to be *à la mode, en vogue*, implies neither that it is a remarkable creation nor that it is devoid of all value. One of the fascinating aspects of the "cultural fashion" is that it does not matter whether the facts in question and their interpretation are true or not. No amount of criticism can destroy a vogue.[27] There is something "religious" about this imperviousness to criticism, even if only in a narrow-minded, sectarian way. But even beyond this general aspect, some cultural fashions are extremely significant for the historian of religions. Their popularity, especially among the intelligentsia, reveals something of Western man's dissatisfactions, drives, and nostalgias. (Eliade 1965: 23–25)

Seemingly impervious academic fashions—including extreme positions held with unshakable "faith"—eventually loosen their grip and give way, revealing not only their limitations but the perpetually shifting ethical, practical, and theoretical concerns of scholars who make use of them.

THIS BOOK AND ITS AUTHOR

The following collection of chapters—emerging through the current revolving-door world of academic fashion—provides one among many possible approaches to a new comparativism.[28] In the strictest sense of comparison, it reaches across "East/West" religious and cultural divides, juxtaposing particular Hindu and Christian, South Asian and European/American contexts. Another juncture, angled quite differently, explores competing conceptions and experiences of sacred meaning and power. Each chapter conducts a dialogue of sorts between established hegemonic systems (asserted through colonialism, nationalism, scientism, and institutional religion) and localized religious expressions (found in folklore figures, democratizing theologies, and embodied and landed sacrality) that, I argue, talk back.

My interest in localized, democratizing, and materially embedded religion has a history. Sifting through the layers of my academic training, this inclination began with graduate studies in systematic theology that focused on liberation theologies. Although over twenty years have elapsed since my study of Christian theology, the central impulse of liberation theologies—the analysis of religious systems in light of social justice concerns—has informed my ethnographical work ever since, often in unanticipated ways. Doctoral research took me to Kerala, where I investigated localized, shrine-based religion, culminating in a project largely informed by postcolonial and folklore theory. Subsequent explorations at a Hindu temple in upstate New York led me to a community that breaks with caste and gender convention, availing priestly roles to anyone willing to learn the temple's elaborate rituals, traditionally the preserve of male Brahmans. My most recent lessons in Icelandic Spiritualism have introduced me to a tradition that promotes body-spirit engagement, supported by a theology that largely humanizes Jesus and divinizes humanity. Although my Icelandic adventures have taken me a good distance from my primary emphasis in South Asian traditions, their espousal of a theology similar to liberation theologies that is furthermore influenced by modern Indian philosophical movements brings me full circle and beyond.

My investment in comparison also has a history. Given my chosen areas of study, religious juxtapositions have been fairly—and, for me, happily—unavoidable. I learned about liberation theology against the backdrop of the normative Catholicism with which I was raised. Research in south India introduced me to a Christian tradition culturally and theologically different than the (to me) more familiar Euroamerican and Latin American Christianities and similar in many ways to locally practiced Hinduism—distinctions that would be indecipherable, obviously, without comparison. Explorations of a Hindu temple in upstate New York were often framed by my exposure to south Indian Hinduism and with an eye to North American influences. My turn to Icelandic Spiritualism, viewed through an increasingly kaleido-scopic lens, was with the explicit intention of comparing understandings of extraordinary human abilities with those promoted by Hindu Neo-Vedanta, a tradition that, although founded across the globe, arose in similar histori-cal and political circumstances. These juxtapositions that shaped my un-derstandings of liberation theology, Indian Christianity, and American Hinduism and my more deliberate comparative explorations of Icelandic Spiritualism provide the point of entry into this intentionally comparative book.

Departing from past tendencies to analyze religious traditions existing side by side, their proximities creating mutual influences that naturally call for comparison, the following chapters juxtapose decidedly nonproximate conceptions and practices.[29] Here, fixed within a single frame, are sacred fig-ures from India set beside Irish counterparts, Latin and North American Catholic theologies in conversation with North American Hindu reflections, diaspora Hindu constructions of sacred land contrasted with similar attempts by Euroamerican New Age "Hindus," and extraordinary human abilities com-pared between Iceland and India. These "unnatural" pairings, often spanning giant geographical gaps, build from shared political, religious, historical, or material contingencies producing nongeographical proximities that, I con-tend, are no less instructive, interesting, or natural to consider.[30] Such match-making feats, instigated by my own well-informed imagination, are in accord with the adamant voice behind the fence who finds no good reason to out-right limit the sites where comparative "magic" can put to good use.[31] The remaining question for me is not whether but how to compare.

This question is central to Jonathan Z. Smith's long-standing critique of the comparative enterprise, one that rests on the view that religion schol-ars have tended to perform comparison as an afterthought, without a clear sense of purpose. Smith repeatedly states this reservation in his addresses over the decades, typically inserted in his concluding remarks for empha-sis. He finished a 1979 lecture with this observation about comparison:

> There is nothing easier than the making of patterns; from planaria to babies, it is done with little apparent difficulty. But the "how" and the "why" and, above all,

the "so what" remain most refractory. These matters will not be resolved by new or increased data. In many respects, we already have too much. It is a problem to be solved by theories and reasons, of which we have had too little. (1982: 35)

In 1988, Smith wrapped up another lecture with a similar appeal to comparativists: "Lacking a clear articulation of purpose, one may derive arresting anecdotal juxtapositions or self-serving differentiations, but the disciplined constructive work of the academy will not have been advanced, nor will the study of religion come of age" (1990: 53). In his essay "The 'End' of Comparison," Smith seems encouraged by new comparativism's resolve to attend to context and difference yet maintains his concern that the endeavor be sufficiently purposeful, advancing information and concepts that further the field. As he puts it, restating the title of his essay, "the 'end' of comparison cannot be the act of comparison itself" (2000: 239).[32]

In this more recent essay, Smith goes on to suggest the four components he considers necessary for comparison to be worthwhile to the study of religion: description, comparison, redescription, and rectification. By description, Smith refers to the historical or anthropological contexts that set the stage for comparison. Redescriptions are the new discoveries that arise in light of comparison, and rectifications are corrections made to earlier-imagined academic categories that are called for by these new discoveries.

Most broadly speaking, redescriptions and rectifications addressed in each of the following chapters—the "so what" or "end" of comparison—comprise the book's frame; they hinge upon the ways earthbound religious beliefs, practices, and experiences complicate and resist religious, political, and epistemological abstractions and generalizations. These redescriptions involve refinements of facile religious, political, and scholarly generalizations regarding religion and religious phenomena, complicating one-dimensional, spiritualized understandings. Theoretical rectifications also include, most basically, challenges to the view that the comparative endeavor necessarily creates and promotes universalizing, dehumanizing abstractions. Although concerns about the potentially abstracting and distracting natures of religion and of comparison cannot—and should not—be dispelled altogether, they can, I trust, dim and diffuse in light of earthbound religious beliefs and practices.

Also key to this book's substantive redescriptions and methodological rectifications is a retrieval of the category of the sacred that has all but faded from scholarly fashion. This fall from popularity emerges partly out of an effort to avoid mistakes of past scholarship that has uncritically assigned the term universalizing or exclusively transcendent significance, laden with cultural and political bias, rendering "the sacred" useless at best for the study of religion, and imperialistic at worst. A related critique has been leveled against the equally contentious category "religion" as traditionally conceived by religion scholars, narrowly associated with privately held, non-empirically-based belief systems. When applied universally, those traditions lying outside the fold, beyond designated belief-based "religions" (typically non-Western, non-Protestant ones), have been assigned an inferior status, linked with heathendom and immorality.[33]

A recent corrective to this problem is an approach known as "new materialism" that recognizes publicly performed material manifestations of religion, understood as embedded in worldly dynamics.[34] In such contexts the category of the sacred, when not dropped from use altogether, is often spoken about in relation to social, political, and economic forces, removed from the realm of religious experiences and understandings of transcendence. Although successfully sidestepping past mistakes, this framework, as I see it, stops short of allowing the category of the sacred to fulfill its interpretive potential.[35]

More recently, religion scholars indebted to new materialism have called for a revitalization, on new terms, of metaphysical and theological exploration. This both/and approach, described by philosopher of religion Hent de Vries, supports the idea that materiality is not the alternative to transcendent universality but "its filled and, as it were, incarnate form" (2008: 4, 11).[36] At the same time, de Vries makes it clear that he advocates not a return to transcendentalist metaphysics but a "(re)transcendentalizing movement" implicit to the process of interpretation, similar to the ways the "abstract and virtual global category, 'religion'" invariably emerges when scholarly studies compile and "connect the dots" between religious particularities (2008: 11–12).[37] This inclination toward universalizing theory recalls, as we have seen, advocates of comparison who insist that comparative categories are not only potentially enriching but inevitably manifest amid explorations of religious particularity.

In support of this both/and proposition—and of its implications for the method and structure of this book—I consider the category of the sacred, much truncated and neglected by recent scholarship, to be a vital component for comparing multilayered religious contexts. This stems from the broad applicability of "the sacred" as a category that implies ties to transcendent meaning and power yet is not limited to or divided against the unempirical or metaphysical. As a deeply contoured point of reference, I find that, for the purposes of this book, the sacred can be usefully employed to cast the wide net of comparison. Conversely, comparative frameworks can provide multifaceted scenarios from which to explore conceptions and experiences of the sacred in their complexity. In making good use of the category's impressive reach, the following chapters associate the sacred with religiously ordained power sources, manifest and interpreted in a variety of ways, from a variety of angles, emerging sometimes as forming and controlled by systems of authority, sometimes defying and superseding the same. By joining religion and politics, official imposition and individual agency, transcendence and immanence, this both/and approach to the sacred enables it to reconcile otherwise disparate spheres of influence or run at cross purposes.[38]

Aligning itself somewhat with new materialism, this book follows de Vries in distinguishing itself from recent scholarship that applies the category of religion—and, by association, the category of the sacred—warily and narrowly in an attempt to avoid the universalizing and perhaps irrational language of transcendence. Unlike de Vries, however, who casts "religion" broadly to include analyses of transcendence yet whose sociopolitical perspective prevents relapse into transcendental metaphysics, I aim also to convey the sacred more on its own weighty and often uncertain terms, labeled as such by adherents and practitioners. While the following indeed views the sacred as formed by worldly power structures, at moments it is simply left in the raw, examined in light of theological interpretations, metaphysical understandings, and reported experiences likely recognizable to a range of practitioners. These layers of "raw" description supply crucial details for bringing comparative panoramas into sharper relief, where sacred efficacies are revered and contested, jealously guarded and discarded, by those who name and claim them as their own.

Another substantive redescription and theoretical rectification collectively advanced by this book's chapters is its challenge to perceptions that religion and comparison, as universalizing entities and approaches, are necessarily dehumanizing and politically harmful. As I see it, not only can comparisons help bridge divides between otherwise sequestered human communities and experiences—confounding as well, in the case of this book, perceived Orientalist divisions between East and West—the process can also draw attention to ethical concerns and solutions emerging cross-culturally or interreligiously. In this way, the following chapters challenge normative expectation by highlighting cross-cultural instances when sacred figures do not bypass the material needs of their devotees, democratizing theologies widen possibilities for ritual participation, newly sanctified land coexists with rather than colonizes prior inhabitants, and modern systems integrate rather than separate body and spirit. The focus this book gives to religiously motivated humanizing practices is, I trust, sharpened and enhanced by comparison's layering effect, adding ethical weight and interest to its redescriptions and analyses.

I pave the way for the following chapters' redescriptions and rectifications through a variety of historical and ethnographical descriptions emerging from four very different settings. Although each chapter contains vertically construed conversations between authoritative discourses and earthbound religious expressions as well as horizontally aligned comparisons that cut across Hindu/Christian or South Asian/European American divides, the materials chosen to construct this grid represent an eclectic mix, to say the least. Each chapter incorporates portions of my own long-term fieldwork findings accompanied by and juxtaposed with a range of written sources, scenarios, and time periods. The logic of pairing what may seem, at the outset, such odd couples has to do with matching sets of authoritative discourses, whether political, social, religious, or epistemological. Each duo's response to its shared authoritative challenge steers each chapter's narrative, allowing for unlikely pairs to engage meaningfully within a comparative framework.

Chapter 1 draws from fieldwork in the state of Kerala, in southern India, and from folkloric and historical materials from northwestern Ireland to explore the heroic figures of the wandering priest and the suffering nun. When portrayed by their respective institutional churches, these Indian and Irish Catholic figures appear as inverted colonial stereotypes that act as antidotes to imperial imposition. In the realm of folklore and in response to more immediate human concerns, these figures offer sacred healing powers that require adjustments to their official portrayals, causing them to turn away from if not against institutional incarnations and prescriptions. This series of turns—in the service of nationalist Church politics and earthly human needs—demonstrate similar Indian and Irish religious responses to colonialism and to human suffering. At the same time the juxtaposed interplay between colonialism and anticolonialism, institutional prescription and popular concern, demonstrates ways in which Catholic Christianities in India and Ireland are layered and possessed of divergent realities, represented by both institutional and earthbound approaches to the sacred.

Continuing this juxtaposition of institutional and earthly religious dynamics, chapter 2 moves the conversation into the realm of theology and reaches across the Hindu-Christian divide. In what amounts to a comparison of liberation theologies set against the backdrop of religious orthodoxies, this chapter emerges from a series of conversations between Aiya, the head priest/guru of a temple in upstate New York, and me. Informed by the largely nondualistic tantric goddess tradition he leads at the temple, Aiya shares with feminist and Latin American liberation theologians a concern for those marginalized by traditional religious authority structures.

He also shares with them a rejection of the earth- and body-negating theologies that sequester the sacred to exclusive or transcendent realms and
that set the foundation for social marginalization. While the varieties of
discrimination practiced within Hindu and Christian contexts are far from
identical, the strategies Aiya and liberation theologians propose to combat
them, fed by shared understandings of divine immanence, hold some compelling similarities. In the end, an interesting conundrum faced by all par-
ties is that of building an earthly Utopia—a logical aim for idealistic
earthbound theologies but one whose attainment is not only impossible
but ultimately, as this chapter elaborates, undesirable.

Elusive Utopia resurfaces, although quite differently, in chapter 3's exploration of traditions that confer sacred meaning and power onto landscapes.
The communities I compare here—one largely Euroamerican and the other
South Asian—struggle to transplant their South Asian traditions onto
North American terrain during the late twentieth century. I contrast what
became an increasingly utopian Rajneesh community that briefly settled in
eastern Oregon in the 1980s with diaspora Hindu communities whose ongoing religiously informed settlements I refer to as heterotopian. I argue
that whereas the Rajneesh community's abstracted utopian vision enabled
settler dynamics reminiscent of colonial times, Hindu diaspora communities' sense of sacred terrain that is historically and religiously—and therefore more realistically—layered creates settlements that tend to steer clear
of colonizing impositions. Despite these differences that ultimately distinguish failed and successful settlements, a shared challenge faced by these
communities has been an ironic "indigenous" nationalism that likewise expresses itself in religiously laden, utopian claims upon the land.

In keeping with the theme of imbuing the material realm with sacred
meaning and power, chapter 4 juxtaposes Hindu and Christian strategies
for conferring extraordinary abilities onto human bodies. Here the traditions under consideration, Indian Neo-Vedanta and Icelandic Spiritualism,
were similarly formed by their countries' respective independence struggles during the turn of the last century as well as by global exchanges that
debated intersecting religious, political, and epistemological concerns.
Superficially speaking, the extraordinary abilities promoted by both these
traditions are nearly identical, as are the scientific frameworks they use to
validate them. The use of science in these contexts can be attributed to the
turn-of-the-century burgeoning scientific revolution that challenged the
existence of religion, met by Spiritualism and Neo-Vedanta not with a rejection of the supernatural but with a softening of the divide between science and religion, matter and spirit.[39] This chapter's juxtaposition
illuminates how the similar epistemological, historical, and political forces

that form these traditions are trumped by radically contrasting cosmologies involving the insistent presence or absence of spirits. Rather than analyzing embodied spirit encounters—or lack thereof—simply in light of social and historical forces, this chapter attends to the ways these sacred encounters become forces in themselves, shaping religious and ethical frameworks in their wake.

The postscript to this book completes our adventures in comparison on a slightly different register by aligning academic and religious processes, allowing the practices of ethnography and ritual to speak to one another. Our point of departure is a rather unnerving incident in which I found myself, as requested by the head priest at the upstate New York temple, reading my entire book manuscript before an audience comprised of the temple goddess and a group of (human) temple regulars.[40] This ritualized reading of ethnography not only blurred genres but reversed customary roles between observer and participant—between those who traditionally analyze and those who perform rituals. The postscript's juxtaposition highlights how ethnography and ritual, conventionally understood to hover above earthbound contingencies as objective and timeless practices, respectively, are more meaningfully viewed as anchored in and enlivened by human subjectivities and risky indeterminacies. By framing and comparing ethnography and ritual as such, made possible by this unanticipated temple event, the postscript invites the reader, once again, to consider the importance of bringing otherwise lofty conceptions and efficacies down to eye level. In so doing we are encouraged to recognize the potential benefits the human condition has to offer ritual participants and scholars alike.[41]

This ritual reading of ethnography and observations emerging from it that humanize and blur academic and religious endeavors also diffuse established oppositions. This theme in which earthbound (religious) expressions and interpretations undermine and/or dispel traditional dichotomies repeats itself throughout this book, enacted differently in each comparative context. In the first chapter, sacred figures supported by a nationalist Irish and Indian Church are built upon and emphasize distinctions between colonized and colonizer; their folk renditions explicitly ignore or defy these same distinctions. Chapter 2 describes how religious orthodoxy in both Hindu and Christian traditions boldly demarcates between body and spirit and between those who can and cannot assume religious privilege, both of which Hindu and Christian "liberation theologies" work to undermine. In chapter 3, Rajneeshee utopian strategies for sanctifying land depend on exaggerated insider/outsider rhetoric reminiscent of settler colonizers, contrasted with diaspora Hindu heterotopias that sanctify land in a more fluid manner, melding old with new, local with foreign sacrality. Finally,

Icelandic Spiritualism and Indian Neo-Vedanta arise in response to turn-of-the-century trends that strictly divorce science from religion and, correspondingly, real from imaginary; practitioners' experiences—validated by their respective spiritual traditions and scientific explanation—in turn confound these classifications.

This volume, held together by a common set of challenges and religious responses to these challenges, incorporating an eclectic bag of tricks gathered since the 1980s, was written over a span of seven years. It was not, at its inception, a premeditated venture. My first chapter is based on a conference paper I delivered in June 2004 at the Galway Conference on Colonialism, whose theme that year was Ireland and India. In November 2006 I participated on a panel on social justice in Hindu traditions at the American Academy of Religion Convention in Washington, DC, from which my second chapter stems. In June 2007 I returned to the Galway conference, the theme this time Settler Colonialism, where I delivered a paper that became chapter 3. By the summer of 2007, it occurred to me that these three papers, all of them comparative, could be dusted off and expanded to form part of a volume.[42] With this in mind, my field research in Iceland during my 2009–10 sabbatical was explicitly aimed, from the start, for inclusion in this book.

As I see it, my strongest personal endorsement for the comparative method is the (initially) unanticipated manner in which this book took shape. I did not set out to write most of its chapters with the agenda of retrieving the lost art of comparison—as important as I consider this to be. Rather, the valuable, ongoing, and often surprising lessons that comparison has taught me about the qualities, contours, and efficacies of religion have naturally drawn me again and again to this dynamic process. In a similar vein, J. Z. Smith likens comparison to the creative process of translation, something he distinguishes from straightforward description. He approvingly describes translation/comparison as an endeavor that "can never be fully adequate, it can never be total. There is always discrepancy. If there is not, then one is not translating but rather speaking the other language" (2004: 31). I agree that comparison is at its best and without apology an interactive adventure that is never complete, perpetually enticing those who engage into further exploration and discovery.[43]

CHAPTER 1

✧∿✧

The Suffering Indian Nun and the
Wandering (Drunken) Irish Priest

Orientalism and Celticism Unplugged

The suffering nun and the wandering priest of India and Ireland, respectively, have much in common. As emblematic Roman Catholic figures, both are engaged in political as well as religious matters; they have similar supporters and foes, stand for similar causes, and both have shifting personas that reflect shifting allegiances.

First and foremost, they are upstanding embodiments of institutional Catholic values in their respective home countries; their suffering and wandering represent Orientalist and Celticist colonial stereotypes that their respective Churches seem to have adopted and inverted. British colonial portrayals of the irrational, nonmodern Indian and the rootless Irish become for an anticolonial Indian and Irish Church, enacted through these figures, a means for demonstrating religious and nationalist efficacies. Further inversions of the suffering nun and the wandering priest (who is now drunken) take place in local lore. Here, we find a pattern in which colonial and anticolonial tussles get derailed and tidy colonial and postcolonial binarisms for which Orientalist and Celticist themes of suffering and wandering typically stand become diffused. Colonial stereotypes passed on and appropriated from one group to another essentially wind up, when they enter the realm of local expression and earthly concern, unplugged from earlier, oppositional self/other distinctions.

With the suffering nun and the wandering priest standing arm in arm, the following comparison illuminates striking cross-cultural patterns. It demonstrates how emblematic religious figures inhabiting distant locales can join the fray of anticolonial political rhetoric and leave it to their local avatars, enlivened not by politics but by everyday human needs and desires, to dismantle the same.

ST. ALPHONSA: HER SOUTH INDIAN CONTEXT AND LIFE OF PAIN

St. Alphonsa lived from 1910 to 1946, spending the last half of her short pain-filled life as a nun in a remote convent in the village of Bharananganam, in the southwest Indian state of Kerala. She was canonized on October 12, 2008, and bears the honor of being the first native-born Indian to be granted the title of Catholic saint (Figure 1.1). Alphonsa belonged to an ancient and esteemed branch of Indian Christianity known as St. Thomas or Syrian Christianity, further split into a variety of Catholic, Protestant, and Orthodox streams. Regardless of denomination, Syrian Christians fairly uniformly take pride in their lofty heritage. While I was conducting

Figure 1.1
Newly refurbished entryway to St. Alphonsa's chapel, constructed in honor of her canonization on October 12, 2008.

fieldwork at Alphonsa's pilgrimage shrine during the mid- to late 1990s, one gentleman was quick to point out to me, for instance, that Kerala was Christianized and brahmanized (that is, civilized) while "most people in Europe were still running around like barbarians." Legend has it that St. Thomas the Apostle boarded a merchant ship and brought Christianity to Kerala in the year 52. Left in his wake was a community of Christianized Brahmans that, several centuries later, was fortified by waves of Syrian Christian merchants who settled in Kerala.[1]

While historian skeptics (mostly non-Indian) question whether Kerala's Christian origins are quite so grand or old, many do date the beginning of the Church, established primarily by Syrian merchants, as far back as the fourth or fifth century. Beginning in the late fifteenth century, Portuguese colonizers forcibly converted these Christians to Roman Catholicism, and half of these converts maintained their allegiance to the pope after Portuguese power dissipated. Today, Roman Catholicism rooted in Kerala's ancient Syrian tradition has a liturgy that differs significantly from that of the other, mainstream Catholic branch in Kerala, known as Latin Catholicism. Roughly equal in number to Syrian Christians, Latin Catholics are largely descended from low-caste fisher-folk converts from Hinduism during Portuguese times. Despite Syrian Catholicism's peripheral relationship to Roman tradition, this economically prosperous sect enjoys a prominent po-sition in Vatican affairs relative to other Indian Catholic communities.

One of the by-products of Syrian Catholic clout at the Vatican is that its members currently in line for canonization in Kerala greatly overwhelm those of Latin Catholics, the ratio being somewhere around twelve to one. St. Alphonsa presents an interesting case not only because she has vastly out-paced her saintly competitors but also because she forged her position even though, unlike all the other Keralite contenders, she did very little to impact Church or society during her lifetime. While other sainthood candidates earned their fame through feats such as founding religious orders, thwarting schisms, or introducing the printing press to the region, Alphonsa is consis-tently portrayed by devotees in Rome and Kerala as an obscure nun who qui-etly and heroically withstood debilitating disease and excruciating pain.

Described by the numerous shrine pamphlets available at her Bharananganam pilgrimage site, translated into a range of Indian and European languages, Alphonsa's troubles began from birth. She was born prematurely after a snake startled her mother into labor, and when Alphonsa was only three months old, her mother died. She spent most of her childhood in the care of an aunt who, by all accounts, meted out the strictest of discipline in order to pre-pare her extraordinarily beautiful niece for the rigors of domesticity. Alphonsa described her "mother" in one of her letters to her priest confessor:

Even for the slightest shortcomings my mother used to chide me severely. I was
not allowed even to justify myself. Having cultivated such dumb endurance it
has become impossible for me now to retort even in jest. My mother never let
me enjoy any freedom whatever. I had to talk always in very low tones. Many
times have I paced to and fro in the kitchen. [...] Mother got angry with me
frequently and it grieved me much. I used to tremble with fear. [...] If I tried to
excuse or justify myself when my mother scolded me, that was considered crimi-
nal on my part. If I held my peace, she would accuse me of stubbornness—"See,
she hasn't a word to say to all this," she would say. If I tried to speak, she would
burst out: "And you, have you the cheek to answer me back?" (Quoted in Chacko
1990: 31)

It seems that from a young age Alphonsa desired, contrary to her aunt's
designs, to become a nun. Once marriage matches were under way and it
seemed nothing could dissuade her aunt, Alphonsa decided to derail the
process by disfiguring herself. She chose to burn her feet in an ash pit that
was smoldering by the side of her house, but, underestimating the depth of
the ash, she ended up with burns that were more severe than intended.
Alphonsa's plan to thwart matrimony was realized, and in 1927 she joined
the Franciscan Clarist Convent in Bharananganam, where she received further education and spent a short stint as a teacher. Eventually, a steady
stream of illnesses forced Alphonsa to spend the majority of her convent
years bedridden. As described in the official shrine pamphlet published on
the occasion of her canonization, "The last twelve years of her life were
years of unrelieved suffering which she bore heroically for the greater glory
of God. She considered herself a sacrificial offering that God was pleased to
consume with the fire of suffering. The more she suffered, the closer it
brought her to God" (*St. Alphonsa* 2008: 4).

Sr. Vengaloor, one of Alphonsa's hagiographers, writes particularly vivid
descriptions of the "waves of hardship [that] started kicking her about"
from the time Alphonsa took her final vows (Vengaloor 2006: 46). Whether
it was hemorrhage, blood that "oozed out of her mouth and nose," a 105-
degree fever that lasted for two months, or mental and emotional torment,
Vengaloor describes Sr. Alphonsa as bearing it all heroically. Although
Alphonsa's letters to her confessor express fleeting fears that her sufferings
would upend her, it seems she always managed to land with her spiritual
feet firmly planted:

I have abandoned myself completely into the hands of Jesus. Let Him do with
me what is pleasing to Him. To suffer hardships for the love of God and to rejoice
in that—I wish to do only this in this world. I have been facing a lot of physical

and mental problems for a long time. Sometimes the pain is beyond my capacity to endure.... My present condition is like that of a worm writhing in the midst of a flame. I even feel hopeless. Immediately I repented and begged forgiveness and regained my peace of mind. My good God does see all my hardships and consoles me. (Quoted in Vengaloor 2006: 48)

While conducting fieldwork in Kerala, I spoke to nuns and family members who knew Alphonsa personally, and many of them expressed the belief that official accounts slightly exaggerated her suffering to highlight her holiness. Family members felt that Alphonsa's life was not, in fact, miserable from the start and that she actually had a happy childhood. Convent sisters remembered Alphonsa as being deeply loved by many, contrary to accounts depicting her as regularly derided and belittled by some of the other nuns. All accounts did corroborate, however, that Alphonsa was largely bedbound and excruciatingly ill during the final years of her life and that she managed, quite heroically, to maintain a prayerful, pleasant continence throughout.

The trait that most impressed eighty-four-year-old Sr. Mercy, a school and later convent friend of Alphonsa's, was her extraordinary self-discipline from an early age. So strong was Alphonsa's determination to act according to rule that Sr. Mercy remembers people warning her that she "would go mad if [she] continued such a life." Sr. Mercy told me that she did not consider Alphonsa to be particularly holy when she was alive, but she nevertheless loved her dearly and respected her for an abiding faith that enabled her to bear her pain so heroically. Sr. Mercy recalled for me an instance when she entered Alphonsa's room after Alphonsa had endured severe bouts of vomiting. Knowing she was in complete misery, Mercy was surprised to find her smiling sweetly. When she asked Alphonsa how she could manage to smile, she replied, "God makes me so happy and helps me to smile through the pain. I don't know, I'm just so happy today." This answer touched Sr. Mercy so deeply that, as she put it, tears began to roll down her cheeks.

Sr. Xavier, in her seventies when I spoke to her, entered the convent a decade after Alphonsa, who by that time was bedridden. She remembers looking up to Sr. Alphonsa and, like many others, would run to her for comfort during difficult times. She remembers drawing spiritual inspiration from her as well:

Alphonsa used to tell me that we should suffer the pains without complaining to others: "Nobody should know about our pains. We should pray to God and seek strength to bear the pain. If we speak about our pain, it would be like a hen laying her eggs and making noise after that. When we hear the hen making noise, we take away the egg. In that way, if we speak about our pain, Satan would come and take away the merit." In listening to her, I thought there was something holy about her.

The steady stream of admirers who visited Alphonsa's room included a good many schoolchildren. Women I spoke with who, when schoolgirls, regularly visited Alphonsa's garden window for conversation—and sometimes sweets—recalled her kindness, playfulness, and extraordinary beauty. They also remember her as one who confidently and accurately prophesized future events and whose prayers ensured that even the dullest among them would pass her exams. Many who recalled Alphonsa's death and immediate aftermath told me that it was these same children who were responsible for starting Alphonsa onto the road to sainthood. While most convent nuns seemed oblivious to the depth of Alphonsa's sanctity, the children proudly proclaimed their faith. Sr. Pius, a schoolgirl at the time of Alphonsa's death, describes the scenario:

> One Sunday morning, after our Sunday school, somebody came to us and said that Alphonsa was seriously ill. We rushed to her, but the Mother [Superior] told us to go away. Disappointed, we turned back to go but, at that moment, we heard someone saying that Alphonsa was dead....Nobody wanted to believe that Alphonsa was dead. They all tried to believe strongly that it was someone else who had died. Her body was later taken to the chapel. On the way, during the procession, people from the shops commented that the Sisters put makeup on Alphonsa for her burial. She was that pretty. She seemed like an angel on her death cot. One of my friends, Marykutty, was able to obtain Alphonsa's mat on which she was lying. She cut off pieces from it and then distributed it among us, telling us that this was something sacred. Children began to proclaim, "Alphonsa is a saint! Alphonsa is a saint!" But the elders, mostly nuns, did not like that.

Once Alphonsa was buried, the children continued to insist on Alphonsa's sanctity, defying adult admonishment and hopping over graveyard fences in the process. As described by Sr. Agnus, then a schoolgirl who lived in town:

> After Alphonsa's death, we children used to go to her tomb in groups with baskets of flowers with us. After Alphonsa's death, the cemetery was a lonely place except when there was a funeral procession....We used to put flowers on her grave and pray, then return home. After one or two days, the watchman of the cemetery told us not to enter the cemetery, and we were denied the ability to go

there. One day, when new kinds of white flowers grew in our garden, my brother and I plucked them, put them into small baskets and spread them on her grave. One of the Sisters complained about this to my father, saying that we should not be picking the beautiful flowers from the garden, but he didn't mind at all.

Sr. Pius's account of daily pilgrimages to Alphonsa's tomb then relates how the groundskeeper eventually had to soften his position for the safety of the children who insisted on visiting her grave site:

We would go in groups because we had to go through dangerous roads where there can be serpents. We used to climb on the cemetery walls and jump onto Alphonsa's grave. After offering the flowers we had brought, we would kneel down before the tomb and pray for our future career and everything. It brought us great mental peace. Once, we were discovered by the caretaker of the cemetery. He scolded us because we were jumping onto the grave. He advised us not to because, when jumping, we might hurt ourselves. So, for the children, he opened the gate to the cemetery. It became a practice to go and meet Alphonsa every day after classes. The children used to take things from the cemetery, considering them to be sacred. But their parents and elders scolded them, telling them to stop bringing the remnants of ghosts.... Eventually, elders started to come with us. Favors began to be received by the people, and thus there was a great rush to the place.

A decade and a half has passed since I first heard these and other vivid childhood memories during my extended fieldwork stint in the mid-1990s; the amused expressions of these elderly nuns remain fresh in my memory. I thus find it striking that shrine pamphlets rarely mention Alphonsa's role in the lives of these children and the part the children played, in return, in Alphonsa's posthumous rise to fame. Written accounts almost uniformly describe Alphonsa as invisible to the world, scorned by her convent companions. Her sanctity was reportedly known to only a few, most notably her priest-confessor, Fr. Romulus, who declared during his funeral sermon for Alphonsa that if people had only known the truth about her, crowds would have flocked to her funeral. Today Alphonsa's death anniversary indeed attracts sizable crowds—as it has for decades—yet very little credit is given to those responsible for getting the ball rolling.[2]

Theologically speaking, this official understanding of Alphonsa as a solitary heroic sufferer makes sense, given the enduring saintly tradition of *imitatio christi*, typically practiced by women, and promoting Christ-like, redemptive sacrifice (Bynum 1991: 131; Weinstein and Bell 1982: 229).[3] Published selections of Alphonsa's own writings often frame her suffering in this way. Reflecting a fondness for metaphors, Alphonsa identifies herself in one instance not just with Christ but with his physical presence in the sacraments:

> When the grains of wheat are ground and crushed, then the wheat flour is obtained that is baked and transformed into the host for the Holy Eucharist. Even so must we be ground and crushed and transformed by suffering like the host. It is when grapes are pressed that we get the juice, the wine; they do not yield wine of themselves. When God by suffering purifies us, we become like good wine. (Quoted in Tharakan 2008: 68)

Alphonsa's *imitatio christi*, a favorite theme for her hagiographers, also finds its way into songs composed in her honor. The following is from a commercial cassette filled with devotional songs dedicated to Alphonsa, composed by priests at the Potta Charismatic center in Kerala. So dominant is the *imitatio christi* theme that it is impossible to tell whether the song's perspective is Alphonsa's or Christ's until the final stanza's reference to a body that remains in a tomb.

> This chalice is full of bitter drink.
> I shall drink it
> According to Thy Holy Will, my Father.
> I shall become the Lord of life to this people.
> I shall struggle upon the cross
> Raised on the peak of Calvary.
> My blood, falling drop by drop,
> Will remit their sins.
> My soul, having been entrusted into Thy hands,
> I shall remain buried in the tomb
> So that they may be arrayed on the right side
> At the second glorious coming on the clouds.[4]
> > Fr. Michael Panachicken
> > "This Chalice"
> > (Ī Kāsa)

The theme of suffering, with or without the related strains of *imitatio christi*, highlighted in official accounts of Alphonsa's life to the near exclusion of other features, continues to bear important weight when we turn our attention from Church tradition to nationalist inversions of Orientalist stereotypes. Colonial depictions of a rational, modern "West" that must come to the rescue of a technologically backward and irrational "East" have long been appropriated by Indians who, reversing the hierarchy, depict a modern, morally decrepit West as redeemable only through encounters with a traditional, spiritually superior East (see Nandy 1983; Said 1993). This reversal, which gave impetus to the Indian Independence movement and still has currency today, maintains the core elements of the colonial equation while turning the structure of authority and privilege onto its head. The East, still considered to represent tradition, simplicity, and spirituality (originally glossed as backwardness, ignorance, and superstition), combats oppressive colonial authority and its promotion of crass materialism and immorality (originally, rationality and modernity).[5] Since Kerala's Syrian Christians are more than familiar with this nationalist formula, Alphonsa as humble, redemptive sufferer—who died in 1946 one year before Indian Independence—offers Syrian Catholicism an ideal emblem of Indian spiritual supremacy.

Signaling this reversal are Sr. Vengaloor's reflections on Alphonsa's message to today's world, where "the life of the modern man who beats the drum of self reliance" has become hollow and empty. Vengaloor warns that "material values and worldly attitudes are corroding us. Many things that cannot be discovered by looking through the microscope of science can be discovered by looking through the third eye of faith" (Vengaloor 2006: 61, 65). Alphonsa's official canonization pamphlet likewise offers that her life of suffering, misunderstood by worldly powers, will ultimately reign victorious: "In the life of St. Alphonsa there shines the mystery of the cross, the cross which was foolishness and a stumbling block not only to the Greeks and the gentiles of apostolic times, but also to worldly men of every age" (*St. Alphonsa*: 2008: 5). Fr. T. N. Siquiera's introduction to Alphonsa's first official hagiography, written two years after her death and one year after Independence, proclaims that Sr. Alphonsa, champion sufferer, "teaches us in this pleasure-intoxicated age that unless a grain of wheat fall to the ground and die, it cannot bear any fruit." He continues:

> Surgery has become almost painless; diseases can be mostly prevented and if they do, could be easily and even pleasantly cured; electricity has neutralized the changes of weather and the season; food and clothing and lodging have become as convenient and pleasant as they can be. And even in India, where our standard of living is still low, the upper and middle classes have made their lives much more comfortable than ever before. What, then, becomes of the law of suffering which is inexorable both in the natural and supernatural plane? (Siquiera 1948: 19)

Given the associations between the Western world and material comforts— and Keralite Christian adaptations of these associations—Alphonsa as antidote to material excess functions to stave off not only the sinful secular world but the West itself.

CELTICISM AND THE WANDERING PRIEST

In Ireland, the figure of the heroic wandering priest, defender and avenger of the indigenous Irish and typically from the remote west of Ireland, enacts a similar reversal of colonial stereotypes. Described by folklorist Lawrence Taylor, local tales of heroic priests, set in the eighteenth through early nineteenth centuries, typically construe him as battling "the evil forces of the Protestant ascendancy in their local incarnations: landlords, agents, bailiffs, Protestant farmers, and the rare Catholic collaborator" (Taylor 1990: 163–64). Offering an inversion of negative colonial Celticist stereotypes of the backward Irish west and its rootless peasantry, the wandering priest from the wild west is, similar to Alphonsa in India, representative of pure and positive Irishness, bulwark against foreign infiltration.

Stories of wandering priests who offer supernatural solutions to Protestant domination are set during the era of Penal Law when the Irish Catholic Church existed in a semi-legal state. Priests in the west of Ireland during this time typically had limited contact with parishioners, since their pastoral work required coverage of several thousand square miles of mountainous terrain, traversed by horseback on poor roads, risking arrest in the process. As a result, regular Mass attendance was impossible, and in many cases, official liturgies were held in the open air. As described by a Protestant traveler in the mid-eighteenth century, an outdoor Mass in northwestern Donegal was conducted in the side of a mountain, where

> a sort of Amphitheatre is formed on the rock; here I saw several hundred people spread all over that plain spot and the priest celebrating the Mass under the rock, on an altar made of loose stones... for in all this country for sixty miles west and south as far as Connaught, they celebrate in the open air, in the fields or on the mountains; the Papists being so few and poor, that they will not be at the expence [*sic*] of a public building. (Pococke 1752 quoted in Taylor 1995: 50–51)

Heroic wandering priest stories, told in abundance during the late nineteenth and early twentieth centuries and accessed through archives, are related by storytellers in the present day as well. As described by Taylor, these tales set in earlier Penal Law times contain certain enduring themes etched in popular memory. Plots tend to include the priest's supernatural powers as working on behalf of the poor and misfortunate, performing wonders such as leading salmon into the bay or delivering Protestants from Purgatory in order to teach them a lesson. Although a rootless, churchless wanderer, the priest typically incorporates the paraphernalia of the official Church, often donning a priestly stole and reading from a holy book while performing his feats (Taylor 1985: 709).

The heroic priest also works in collaboration with the sacred landscape of the Irish west, particularly with sacred wells that strike back at the enemy and, with the help of the heroic priest, set straight those who belittle or doubt their power. In these cases, the enemy—the outsider or Protestant known as the Gall—either obstructs pilgrimage practices that take place at the well or attempts to contaminate or disprove the well's efficacy. When, for example, a disrespectful Gall puts his or her foot in the sacred water, he is punished on discovering it cannot be removed. A heroic priest arrives on the scene to save and "unbind" the helpless perpetrator from the well and, sometimes, to convert the newly freed (Taylor 1995: 63).

Stories of the heroic priest of the penal days consistently use the language of binary opposition between Catholic and Protestant, insider and outsider, Gael and Gall. Noting the stubbornness of these binaries, Taylor observes, "Three centuries of living together have not made one people—at least not in that discourse, not in that genre of story. The stark opposition of Gael versus Gall is in fact the one used in every such story in the archives, wherever the plot involves such characters" (Taylor 1995: 56).

These tales relating clear opposition to the outsider Gall is underlined by the heroic priest's quintessential Irishness—his western location and his wandering—exalted qualities otherwise degraded by the British. The west of Ireland has long been considered by the British to be "beyond the pale" of positive colonial influence, believed to be home to the most stubbornly uncivilized and superstitious of Irish peasantry, yet stereotypes of the Irish as irredeemable wanderers did not emerge until the mid- to late nineteenth century. Although the penal-day priest of the Irish west, living during the eighteenth and early nineteenth century, indeed roamed the wilds on horseback and had no church building to root him to a particular place, the colonial depiction of the Irish as rootless vagabonds did not emerge until later, provoked by the waves of famine-stricken immigrants who came to Britain to find work during the latter half of the nineteenth century, populating slums that became Irish ghettos.

The late nineteenth century furthermore produced social Darwinian theories that cemented understandings of essential "Britishness" and "Irishness" that became racialized and held in stark, permanent opposition. The Irish peasant, configured as a repulsive, threatening, ape-like creature, contrasted with the orderly British "elect," was placed at the bottom end of an evolutionary scale that exalted modernity over tradition. It was during this period that "Irishness" was marked most specifically and consistently as wandering and migratory, understood to be the result of biological forces that were beyond the power of enlightened English administrators to control or fix (Mac Laughlin 1998: 53–55).

In addition to social Darwinism, racist conceptions of the Irish were also related to "a whole range of Victorian attitudes to culture and progress which linked these to orderliness, cleanliness, industry, temperance, and deference to authority.... [The Irish] were considered gregarious social vagabonds and as such they were the bane of a settled modernity" (Mac Laughlin 1998: 56). Whereas the "Irishry" living in Ireland was considered irrational for misgoverning itself as Catholic and as smallholders, the Irish who immigrated to Britain were associated with disorder and drunkenness, as a pestilence to be stamped out. They were rigidly set apart from the settled communities because of their nomadic migratory ways and their "foreign" Catholic practices, all of which threatened settled Anglo-Saxon society (Mac Laughlin 1998: 60).

Tales of the heroic priest who wandered the west of Ireland, defending his flock from Protestant outsiders, flourished during a period when Irish Revival literature adopted and inverted colonial stereotypes to forge a romantic nationalism. This late-nineteenth- and early-twentieth-century Irish movement (promoting nationalist constructions similar to those emerging around the same time in India) extolled the qualities of "Irishness"—most explicitly the wandering western peasantry—that previously had been derided by the British. Revivalists considered the peasants of the rural west, whose class and geography placed them farthest from British influence, to be preservers of true Irish identity. As such, they represented "a rejection of the pernicious infiltration from the east of fallen, English values." The pure Catholic—or at least the non-Protestant—native Irish of the wild west became the symbolic means for refuting and fending against the "gross naturalism" and "scientific barbarism" of England that had long infiltrated Ireland's eastern shores (Richards 1998: 100–101). The Revivalist valorization of wandering itself, built upon British disdain for the wandering Irish, draws also from an earlier nostalgia in late Victorian England for "preindustrial" vagrancy. This English nostalgia in many ways represented "a patriotic declaration of love for the quintessential British countryside" that was also connected to a British fascination with and romanticization of the gypsy. This gypsy craze gave rise to Victorian British walking clubs, caravanning, and "gypsying" that reflected an anthropological fascination for the rare and disappearing race (Burke 2009: 84).

The Revivalist valorization of wandering in Ireland, specifically national-ist in tone, substituted—for a short period—romanticization of the British foreigner-gypsy with a quintessentially Irish wandering type, the "tinker" (Burke 2009: 59). As described by José Lanters, 1902 was "the year of the tinker's wedding" for Irish playwrights, as three prominent Revivalists, William Butler Yeats, Douglas Hyde, and John Millington Synge, had either finished or begun writing plays that featured itinerant "tinkers" and their weddings. These glorified wanderers, typically inhabiting the wild Irish west, represented the premodern, prebourgeois freedom of the open road. They stood for concentrated, authentic "Irishness," indigenous exotics that were everything decidedly not British (Lanters 2008: 41–58; Burke 2009: 79). Their nonmodern wandering lifestyle, freeing them from outside con-tamination, made them preservers of ancient traditions, postfamine recla-mations of all that colonizers considered negative, an "embodiment of all that was antithetical to contemporary civilization" (Burke 2009: 84).[6] Not only did Revivalist representations of tinkers reconstitute the British valo-rization of the wandering gypsy; they also refined the category of the "tinker" itself, previously considered merely one of the many varieties of Irish poor (Burke 2009: 81). Roughly a decade later, while Revivalists still extolled the virtues of wandering and wanderers, their focus on tinker so-ciety was mostly redirected and aimed at individual tramps and vagrants who were more easily romanticized and dignified than were the Travellers, about whom Irish society maintained—and continues to maintain—a cer-tain amount of anxiety (Lanters 2008: 59).

A more religiously explicit Revivalist antidote to the encroachment of unwanted foreign influences emerges in the later work of Yeats. As an Anglo-Irish Protestant who became disillusioned with Christianity early in his career, Yeats looked to find authentic Irishness in the retrieval of pre-Christian, pagan traditions that he understood to be practiced still by Irish peasants in remote regions of western Ireland, far from British influences. As described by John Rickard,

> Central to Yeats's conception of Irishness, of Celticity, then was the conviction
> that the Irish were the most "ancient" of races and Ireland by extension the most
> ancient of places in Europe ... a place where ancient Indo-European connections
> were intact, a repository of pre-Christian, pre-modern beliefs that could be
> useful in what he hoped would be a reaction against the materialism of the 19th
> century. (Rickard 1997: 99)

But by 1933 Yeats feared that even the western peasantry, guardians of the old traditions and ancient gods, could not withstand the forces of modernism, bringing essential Celtic traditions to the brink of extinction. Resigned to the idea that even the Irish west was not far enough outside of Europe's reach, Yeats turned to Indian religious philosophies and to a romanticized Orientalism. Similar to Indian nationalists, Yeats defined India and Indians as essentially spiritual and a counterforce to Western influences.[7] Yeats's belief in an Indian solution to a particularly Irish problem was based on a theory, widely circulated in his day, that Irish country folk were originally from Asia and had lived there since the Battle of the Boyne. For Yeats, ancient Indian philosophies offered an important foundation for an essential Irishness that was untainted by what he understood to be the ills of modern society, which had, by then, seeped into Ireland's entirety.[8]

Yeats's spiritualized conception of an India that was ripe with potential to return Ireland to its original state, secure from Western influences, echoes Indian constructions of Alphonsa as emblematic of Indian spirituality and defender against Western encroachment. Yeats's anticolonial language, reflecting overlapping Indian and Irish nationalist rhetoric, was furthermore fortified by his interest in Theosophy at that time. The Theosophical Society, comprised largely of European and North American adherents, was founded on the idea that a superior, spiritualized India could save the West from its nonspiritual, modernized self. As chapter 4 elaborates, those who were concerned with the evils of Western influences during the late 1800s and early 1900s—whether European, American, or Indian, Theosophist or anticolonialist—often boiled these evils down to the problem of "science," a term that largely connoted rationalism, empiricism, materialism, and modern urban culture. Yeats's loathing for what he referred to as "science" lay at the heart of his objections to modern culture; while colonized Ireland seemed to have capitulated, Yeats's idealized India, although also colonized, managed to avoid contamination. For Yeats, the corruption of modern society was not due solely to the evils of science and technology but had to do with the loss of an essential spirituality still thriving in India. As he put it, "Science separated from philosophy is the opium of the suburbs" (quoted in Rickard 1997: 104).[9]

Roughly a century has passed since the heydays of the Irish literary revival and the Theosophical Society, movements that helped form and were informed by Independence struggles in their respective countries. It has been over a half century since Fr. Siquiera wrote extolling Alphonsa's virtues as a powerful sufferer who provides a healing balm for the technical advances that cause an overly comfortable world to go awry. The various literary, political, and religious movements that have championed the moral and spiritual high ground of authentic Irish and Indian society, aided by the figures of the suffering nun and the heroic wandering priest, may have waned in intensity, but their rhetoric lives on. This is witnessed in the more recent writings of Alphonsa's hagiographers, such as Sr. Vengaloor, who proposes that more can be learned through the third eye of spirituality than through the microscope of science. It also lives on in contemporary recountings of heroic Irish priest tales that maintain themes of good/evil, Gael/Gall, west/east, and that, although set in a bygone Penal-day era, continue to resonate today. This lingering disdain for outside influences was poetically described by one of Lawrence Taylor's neighbors as the two of them strolled along the seashore in southwest Donegal. A stiff breeze blew in on them from the ocean, prompting the elderly gentleman to remark, "That's a west wind.... There's rain on that wind and it's a good clean wind, not like an east wind. The east wind's a dirty wind—it brought us flu from the eastern world" (Taylor 1995: 42).

COMPLICATED ALLEGIANCES

For the Irish in postfamine Ireland, the seat of power that increasingly rivaled British rule was the Church whose administrative center was in Dublin, on the eastern side of the island, and whose seminary for training priests was in neighboring Maynooth. By the middle of the nineteenth century, the Church's rhetoric of persecution, reflected in stories of churchless priests who ran from the law and performed Mass in the wilds, alternated with the rhetoric of empire. Folk stories that emphasized the heroic priest's displacement and persecution were increasingly in competition with tales featured in the Catholic popular press depicting nonwandering, churchbound heroic priests and loyal tenants as "doing freedom's battle" against the evils of English landlords. The theme of empire, as described by Taylor, not only had to do with the ability of the hierarchy to "provide an alternative state to British Ireland, they could also claim to head an alternative world empire. If Australia was a British colony, then Catholic Australia was increasingly an Irish dominion" (1990: 169). These two seemingly contradictory approaches worked in tandem: the theme of persecution allowed for the kind of powerful resistance that emerges from the periphery and, building on this, the theme of empire represented the Catholic Church as an alternative center of world power (Taylor 1995: 137).

Catholic representations of Alphonsa and the wandering Irish priest, both emblems of indigenous worth and repellents against unwanted foreign influences, seem to be fairly straightforward reversals of colonial constructs. Their anticolonial positions are fortified by the ways the Catholic Church in both India and Ireland have staked their claim as alternative centers of authority, the recentering process legitimized by nationalist rhetoric that promotes an essential spiritual superiority and a moral high ground that they understand to have gained through centuries of colonial oppression (Taylor 1995: 137–38). For both Alphonsa and the heroic priest, the power they—and their respective churches—garner is similar to the spiritual strength awarded to the physically disciplined ascetic, the power of the persecuted.

But dip beneath the surface and seemingly clear allegiances become muddied. Most basically, the Catholic Church in both Ireland and Kerala holds ambiguous positions as champions of local interests against foreign powers, since each branch, in its own way, draws legitimacy and strength from these same foreign forces. The Catholic Church in Kerala, drawing much of its religious authenticity from its ability to stave off Western influences, must nonetheless look westward to Rome—and in some cases to the United States—for institutional authority. I found this ambivalence to emerge in numerous ways within Syrian Catholicism, particularly in connection to its tradition of saint devotion.[10] In Ireland, the Catholic Church's self-promotion as an alternative empire was made possible largely thanks to the changing tide of support from British power structures. The aim to promote middle-class civility, a concern shared by British administrators and the Catholic hierarchy, also ran counter to the perceived role of the Irish Church as the defender of the poor peasant.[11]

The idea that exemplary modes of human holiness are not, for Kerala Christians, simply a one-way, east-to-west flow is most starkly visible on the walls and niches of Catholic churches throughout the state, populated by statues of European-looking saints. This challenge to Syrian Christian claims to be spiritual exemplar for European and American society, visibly posed by these European-looking saints, was further substantiated during my conversations with elderly nuns who knew and revered Alphonsa when she lived, bedridden, in the convent. The majority of the women I spoke with, all of whom considered Alphonsa to have lived an extraordinarily holy life, did not give a first thought to her being a saint. Nearly all of them explained their position by saying that saints, as they understood them at the time of Alphonsa's death, were exclusively European. Sr. Marguerita, an eighty-three-year-old nun who was particularly close to Alphonsa when she was alive, described to me and a small group of elderly sisters the scene surrounding Alphonsa's death: "There was great faith in her sanctity. People had gathered around her to touch some of their belongings to Alphonsa's body. I brought some of my own items with me and touched them to her. But did I consider her to be a saint? No, they were all European." The incongruity between Sr. Marguerita's actions and her final comment prompted the group of us listening to burst out laughing. The actions of those around Alphonsa's body, conferring sacred power onto material items through contact with the deceased—in essence making sacred relics—were expressions of faith in her sanctity. Yet despite their faith, due to Alphonsa's non-European status none considered her to actually be a saint. Perhaps if the children, also convinced of Alphonsa's intercessory powers, were equally constrained by cultural conceptions of sainthood, devotion to Alphonsa would never have gotten off the ground at all.[12]

Similarly, the position of the Irish Church during the Revival period, understood as supporting nationalist concerns and staving off colonial oppression and influences on behalf of the Irish masses, is not so clear-cut. Clergy who served during the days of Penal Law, on which the stories of heroic wandering priests are based, may have indeed been outlaws who conducted wilderness Masses for their flock under constant threat of persecution. But by the beginning of the nineteenth century, colonial anti-Catholic laws were relaxed, and with Catholic emancipation in 1829, the British increasingly found the Irish Catholic hierarchy to be willing partners in their campaign to tame the "wild Irish." Members of the Church hierarchy, still in principle opposed to Protestant rule and positioned as representatives of indigenous Irish interests, epitomized by a romanticized peasantry, nonetheless engaged in a civilizing mission aimed at reining in stereotypically Irish aspects of popular practice (Inglis 1987: 139–56; Taylor 1990: 168–69).

This civilizing mission grew out of a series of Church reforms instituted during a time when the Catholic Church in Ireland grew more wealthy and powerful. Backed by the power and money of Irish bishops, a seminary was established in 1795 in Maynooth, fifteen miles outside Dublin, to create a new class of educated priests who could now afford to impose a "devotional revolution" of sorts. Reformist clergy began to demand that people attend Mass and attempted to deflect them from popular practices which did not require priestly sacramental interventions and during which improper and raucous activities tended to take place (Taylor 1985: 9–10). Reformist energies were focused on curtailing excesses such as game playing and bawdy singing, common at wakes and patron saint celebrations, yet the primary preoccupation seems to have been to banish the most stereotypical of Irish behaviors—that is, drunkenness—at these events (Connolly 1982: 66, 161–62; Taylor 1995: 53, 116).[13] Some historians note, in hindsight, that the reformist bishops and priests newly trained in Irish seminaries, in their fervor to control if not obliterate certain types of caricatured Irish behavior, particularly in the west, made them seem more Protestant than the Protestants themselves (Taylor 1995: 53).[14]

It makes sense on a number of levels that an emblematic suffering nun and wandering priest emerge as important participants within their respective south Indian and Irish Church landscapes. As enlivened, inverted colonial stereotypes, they animate potent images and ideas in order to challenge a larger system of authority from whence these images and ideas come. Yet it also makes sense that the tidy us/them binarisms created and expressed through Orientalist and Celticist ideas and images—enforced and reinforced by both secular and religious authority structures—fall apart in the real world of complicated histories and concerns. This ambivalence within the Irish and Indian Church does not necessarily signal a problem with misplaced loyalties; the "problem," if anything, is with the perception that allegiances and their adherents could ever be uncomplicated or undivided. Official religious depictions of Sr. Alphonsa and the powerful wandering priest are victims of, if not complicit in, this misperception, yet the conversation does not end here. By shifting the discussion further in the direction of local piety, we find that these figures—or perhaps more accurately their close relations—have more to say about the matter.

ALPHONSA OF THE PILGRIMAGE SITE

Alphonsa is memorialized for suffering heroically not only by official Church depictions but also by her devotees. When shrine pilgrims describe her life, pain is persistently central and significant to her holiness. Pilgrim's descriptions, although less detailed, thus diverge little from official shrine pamphlets in this way. Official commentaries expand on this theme by elevating Alphonsa's suffering—the highest of virtues in this day of material comfort and scientific skepticism—as something to be emulated. As exemplar of a morally superior India vis-à-vis the hedonistic West, the standard of behavior set by Alphonsa is one to which shrine materials explicitly encourage devotees to aspire. Further driving home this point is a pair of six-foot-tall tablets installed at the pilgrimage site just before Alphonsa's 2008 canonization. Etched in iron and set on decorative cement slabs are selected quotes gleaned from Alphonsa's letters to her confessor, largely familiar to those who have read the shrine pamphlets. Revolving around the theme of self-sacrifice, humility, and faith, these quotes feature sayings such as "The only thing I desire here on earth is this: to endure all trials and troubles for the sake of love and rejoice in them. Not for me are any of the worldly pleasures, I am convinced," or "Jesus loves us by granting crosses. To those He loves, He sends more crosses and sorrows. As for me, suffering is delightful; a day without a chance to suffer I feel empty." Prominently displayed to the left of Alphonsa's hilltop shrine, behind a trough of sand filled with candles prayerfully lit by visitors, these iron tablets seem poised to inspire those entering and exiting the chapel containing Alphonsa's marble tomb.

Despite hagiographical inspiration and displayed reminders of Alphonsa's philosophy of redemptive suffering, the vast majority of pilgrims who come to Alphonsa's shrine, although largely aware of her life of unrelenting pain and, to a lesser extent, her philosophies, translate this pain in nearly the opposite direction. Rather than a model for withstanding life's difficulties, Alphonsa is, for them, a sacred conduit for miraculous powers—powers meant to eradicate the very hardships that the Church advocates for holy living. In such instances, Alphonsa's suffering is not a redemptive end in itself, but a powerful means for healing physical and psychological ills and transforming the material deficiencies of those with faith. Local, devotional interpretations of powerful suffering, seemingly unconcerned with—and in some ways contrary to—antitechnological, antimaterialist Orientalist inversions promoted by the institutional Church, thus derail colonial and postcolonial associations.

The fact that pilgrims come to the Alphonsa's shrine nearly exclusively to ask or give thanks for favors granted—rather than to seek inspiration to suffer heroically or lead nonmaterialistic lives—was somewhat of a disappointment to Sr. Josephina, my research companion. I learned this after I had been visiting Bharananganam nearly every day for several months, interviewing pilgrims, with Sr. Josephina's assistance, about their experiences and understandings of Alphonsa and her pilgrimage shrine. One day, when she and I had decided to split up and talk to different sets of pilgrims, I was finishing an exchange with a small group of young women when I spotted Sr. Josephina in my peripheral vision, hurrying toward me with a middle-aged man in tow. When they arrived, she excitedly announced that she had found someone with the "correct" response to our question. She then asked the man to speak for himself, and the gentleman reiterated to me that he was visiting Bharananganam in order to learn more about Alphonsa's saintly life to gain inspiration for his own life. It was indeed the first time I had heard this perspective from a pilgrim, but because Sr. Josephina always listened intently and responded warmly to pilgrims' repeated accounts of or hopes for miracles, I hadn't realized that this was the answer she had been waiting for. This was also the first time it occurred to me that nearly all the pilgrims flocking to Sr. Alphonsa's shrine were, according to official sights, slightly missing the mark.

Months earlier, the very first pilgrim I spoke with in Bharananganam, a middle-aged woman named Mrs. Varuguese, keen on relating her extensive history of miraculous encounters with Alphonsa, set the stage for subsequent exchanges. Mrs. Varuguese began by describing her daughter's trials with serious and seemingly untreatable asthma, which had prompted someone to suggest they visit Sr. Alphonsa's shrine. Mrs. Varuguese's husband was in the military, which meant that their family lived in far-flung regions of India for years at a time, thus their visit to Bharananganam had to wait. According to Mrs. Varuguese, when they finally made the trip, the girl's asthma immediately and inexplicably subsided. Several years later, Mrs. Varuguese suffered an intestinal blockage and was told by the doctors that her only hope for survival was surgery. Since she had recently undergone several other surgeries, she refused treatment in spite of the doctors' warnings. Instead, she and her family turned to Alphonsa in prayer and, to the doctors' shock and consternation, she was cured. The purpose of Mrs. Varuguese's visit to the shrine on the day I met her was to pray for success in her daughter's exams. She was looking forward to spending peaceful hours near Alphonsa's tomb in the chapel on the hill (Figure 1.2). As she put it, "Coming here is like sitting in my mother's lap."

In the months after my conversation with Mrs. Varuguese, Sr. Josephina and I heard many similar—although usually less involved—stories of cures and comfort attributed to Alphonsa. Pilgrims repeatedly described how they, like Mrs. Varuguese, had traveled to the shrine with requests for Alphonsa's aid and/or with prayers of thanksgiving for favors received. Their concerns involved a spectrum of issues affecting physical, psychological, domestic, occupational, material, and educational well-being. Although these testimonials may not have supplied, for Sr. Josephina, the "correct" answer, neither were they completely incorrect. Church authorities rely on Alphonsa's capacity to confer blessings to prove to the public at large that her suffering is indeed redemptive; medical corroboration of favors granted has successfully paved the road to her canonization.

Inching yet further from institutional prescription are the recollections of elderly nuns who recounted for me their experiences, as children, of Alphonsa's miraculous powers when she was alive. The following account, related to me by Sr. Gracia, seems conventionally acceptable in that Alphonsa's power of prayer—and therefore God—was responsible for conferring blessings. But, as worded by Sr. Gracia, some of the credit is, less conventionally, given to Alphonsa herself. Although similar accounts of Alphonsa's miraculous abilities freely circulate among those who knew her, they go largely unmentioned in shrine literature. As interpreted by Sr. Gracia, her encounters with Alphonsa did not simply instill awe in her miraculous abilities, but provided lessons about the importance of squelching one's pride so that miraculous power can take hold.

Figure 1.2
Pilgrims gather to pray around Alphonsa's marble tomb, January 2009.

When I was studying in ninth standard, I was bright in maths but my friend was never that good at maths. During one of the intervals, my friend told me that there was a sister in the convent who was considered very holy. "Let's go and meet her," she said. But I did not agree to it. I said that I scored high marks because I studied. My friend took no notice of me, and she alone went to visit Alphonsa. She told her, "I am not that good in maths and I am sure that I will fail in my exams." When the results came, I failed, but my friend passed. I asked my friend if she had asked Alphonsa to pray for me as well, but she reminded me that I said that my studying was what got me my marks, and that I didn't ask her to pray. I felt very sad, because I was the best student in maths. I failed by one mark. From that I understood that Alphonsa helped my friend to succeed, but because of my overconfidence and pride, I failed my exam. From that day onwards, I prayed to Alphonsa before going to my exams. It was a common occurrence that anyone who didn't go to Alphonsa would surely fail in their exam. Everybody who prayed to Alphonsa would surely succeed in the exam. That was a miracle. If I'd have passed my maths, I'd surely never remember now.

As described by Sr. Gracia, it is not simply human need but the humility to acknowledge these needs that prompted the children to approach Alphonsa. The belief that Alphonsa worked wonders on their behalf while she was alive convinced the children to continue asking for favors after her death, eventually converting the disbelieving prideful adults, producing yet more wonders, and causing a larger cult to materialize.

While conducting research in Kerala, I remember being struck by the fact that, amid a dozen other fledgling saint campaigns involving famously prominent men and women, the cause of an obscure bedridden woman would have, by far, the greatest groundswell of popular support. When I visited the pilgrimage shrine dedicated to Fr. Chavara, the other Kerala native beatified in 1986 by Pope John Paul II alongside Sr. Alphonsa, I found his shrine museum packed with the knickknacks and personal belongings of an extraordinary man, one who managed to found a religious order, establish the printing press in Kerala, and stave off Church schism. The impressive shrine grounds were, at the same time, virtually empty of pilgrims. I chatted for a while with the nuns who worked at the museum, and decided, after some time, to raise the perhaps sticky issue of Sr. Alphonsa's popularity. One of the nuns suggested that perhaps it was Alphonsa's suffering that attracted devotees, since suffering, after all, was far easier to emulate than Chavara's many accomplishments. I agreed with her, at the time, that Alphonsa's life demonstrates how sanctity could be achieved by virtually anyone—as long as they graciously accept life's tribulations as gifts from God. But, as I came to understand after spending more time in Bharananganam, although her devotees indeed valued her suffering, for them it was a powerful means for relieving their fears and deprivations. Chavara was no doubt a powerful man worthy of honor, and, in a different way, so was Alphonsa. But when considering the desires of pilgrims—health, wealth, and happiness—Alphonsa's power from the periphery contains the potency they need.

THE DRUNKEN WANDERING PRIEST OF LOCAL LORE

Offering an analogous disengagement from official prescription is the figure of the miracle-making wandering priest of western Ireland who is drunk. Powerful priests with a propensity to drink appear in local narratives but are not contained by them; actual priests with reputations for miraculous powers—and for drinking—have been sought out for their healing powers, particularly for curing, as well. Although stories of drunken priests with magical powers are not as pervasive today as they once were, they are still in circulation in southwest Donegal, particularly among the elderly (Taylor 1990: 165; 1995). Similar to his sober counterpart, tales of the powerful drunken priest depict him as unmoored from his ecclesial settings, not found in a church but rather walking in nature or among his people in their homes, shops, or in pubs.

Unlike his counterpart, the drunken wandering priest does not suffer displacement due to British Penal Law restrictions; rather, he is banished by his own reformist-minded Church superiors due to his propensity to drink. Also unlike his wandering counterpart, the drunken priest infrequently encounters Protestants, and when he does, they are almost never the enemy. Foes of the drunken priest tend to be unwitting members of his own flock, guilty only of depriving him of drink or money. According to local lore, the disenfranchised, drunken priest has powers to cure and to curse unavailable to more conventionally powerful clergy and, in contrast to the wandering heroic priest, the drunken priest has powers that are not propped up by Church paraphernalia—such as the stole and the book—but arise from the man himself. The following story was collected in the early twentieth century by folklorist Ó'hEochaidh in southwest Donegal:

There was a priest here not long ago, and with all respect to his cloth, he had a taste for a wee drop. He was up in the village one day, and he with a drop taken. Well, he went into a pub and asked the boy that was there behind the counter for a drink. The boy said that he wouldn't give him one, that he had had enough as it was. "Well," said the priest, "if I come in to you at this time tomorrow and ask you to give me a drink you'll get it for me and welcome the sight of it!" He went out the door then and said not another word.

That was fine, the boy went to bed that night, and on the next morning when he arose he was so blind he couldn't dress himself. Well, he knew that it was the priest who had brought that upon him with the words he had spoken the evening before. He sent a messenger for the priest, who came to him in his own time.

"What's kept you in your bed there?" the priest said when he went into the room. "O Priest," he said. "Whatever happened to me since I went to bed last night I am blind and can't put on my clothes." The priest only put his two fingers on the boy's eyes in a short while he had his sight back as good as ever before. "Now," said the priest as he was leaving, "when I come again and ask something of you that I want you'll know not to refuse me!" (Ó'hEochaidh 1945: 43–44, translated by and quoted in Taylor 1990: 163)

Taylor describes this story as typical of the many drunken priest tales scattered throughout the more than seventy volumes of folklore collected by Ó'hEochaidh. The priest is often recalled by name and identified as living sometime during the late nineteenth through the early twentieth century. Other examples include a drunken priest whose host refuses him a drink and, neglecting to mention the bottle he has hidden away, tells him that has no more left in the house. The priest angrily demands that the man go to the hiding place to retrieve the bottle, and later the man loses five sons to consumption. Another story features a shopgirl who refuses to loan the priest money for drink and wakes up the next morning with a beard (Taylor 1990: 171). Along with curses, the drunken priest often performs miraculous cures. Although managed without the aid of ecclesial accoutrements, other sacred props, typically associated with the landscape, come into play such as holy wells, sacred salt, or dirt from the priest's shoe. Since the same priest is often responsible for both curses and cures, he is not portrayed as strictly good or evil; his powers are simply strong and capricious (Taylor 1990: 171–72).

Although powerful drunkenness does not have the same religious or nationalist resonance that priestly wanderings and convent suffering do, the fact that drunkenness has been an insistent Celticist theme—a focus of disdain by the British and central impetus for reform by the Irish Church—is not without significance. Similar to local interpretations of Alphonsa as antidote to the suffering that the Church endorses, the tradition of the powerful drunken priest could be understood as subtle resistance against the impositions of a reformist Church and its sobriety-centered "civilizing" mission, which was particularly strong in northwestern Ireland (see Taylor 1995: 149). Also notable are the ways this drunken miracle-working figure is unhinged from the colonial and anticolonial oppositions of self/other, insider/outsider. Local stories of the drunken priest, unlike those of his heroic counterpart, do not describe him as battling undesirable outside influences; rather, he battles incredulity in his midst. The drunken priest cures Protestants and Catholics alike who come to him for aid and curses indiscriminately those who do not comply with his demands—often for money and drink (Taylor 1995: 150–52).

ALLEGIANCES DISMANTLED

Stories of Alphonsa's power to bestow blessings, even when presented through official channels, lack the religious binarisms found in heroic priest stories. As such, they never discriminate between religious insiders and outsiders: Hindu, Christian, or Muslim. One of the two miracles submitted to clinch her canonization was the healing of a Muslim boy's clubbed feet, an event well circulated among her devotees—clergy and convent Sisters included. Given that India's religious insiders, particularly in Kerala, have been religiously diverse for centuries, in contrast with Ireland's fairly homogenous Catholic population, this makes sense. Amid this lack of religious distinction, nationalist Self/Other binarisms unreservedly hold forth within Alphonsa's official depictions.

Local accounts of Alphonsa's sacred power, on the other hand, similar to the drunken priest's, convey both blessings and curses that disregard both religious and nationalist distinction, emphasizing the importance of individual faith in the suffering nun. For example, one of several curse stories I heard from Bharananganam locals features a Hindu man who disparaged Alphonsa's newly constructed shrine, only to find himself and his entire family with a severe case of diarrhea the next morning. Once the family visited the shrine and prayed for forgiveness, they were cured and converted—not from Hinduism to Christianity, but from impudence to respect, from disbelief to faith in Alphonsa's powers. Local tales featuring Alphonsa's propensity to curse as well as bless, similar to the powers of the drunken priest, are, of course, completely absent from official shrine publications and upsets another dimension of official religious understandings, in which saintly power is expected to be exclusively benign. Local emphasis on Alphonsa's earthly favors, deflecting her role as emblematic sufferer, likewise helps to diffuse her earlier position as antidote to ubiquitous foreign influences.[15]

What then of the qualities of suffering and drunkenness themselves? How do we understand their potency in the context of local piety where they no longer adhere to earlier associations? Familiar us/them, domestic/foreign dichotomies are derailed, strict divisions between good and evil are dismantled, Celticist and Orientalist stereotypes once secure in their established political and religious contexts seem adrift of meaning. Their continued usefulness can be understood in part by taking into account indigenous pre- or early Christian understandings of supernatural powers associated with suffering and drinking. Asceticism and bodily discipline, commonly believed to offer mundane as well as soteriological benefits within Christian traditions, are central to various Hindu practices, as well. *Tapas*, an inner heat and power resulting from physically demanding asceticism, is often connected with severe bodily discipline undertaken by gods, demons, and humans alike. Powers associated with *tapas* are often unwieldy, used for good or evil ends, depending on the adept who has acquired them.[16] As for drunkenness, a link between drinking and supernatural powers harkens back to the Irish figure of the court poet—or *file*—whose drunkenness inspires words with the capacity to bless as well as curse (Taylor 1995: 162). Wandering likewise resonates with older Irish traditions of revered medieval saints, many of whom were poor mendicant monks who roamed the countryside. Like drunken priests, they had powers to cure associated not with the trappings of the official Church but with the Irish landscape and particularly with holy wells. They also, according to folk tradition, possessed tempers that occasionally flared and inflicted harm (Taylor 1990: 181).

According to countless conversations with pilgrims at Alphonsa's shrine, people naturally equated suffering with miraculous power. They took for granted that a life of pain honed by discipline and prayer could be channeled into miraculous abilities both during a person's life and beyond the grave. By contrast, when Taylor asked informants why they thought priests who drank possessed supernatural powers, many did not have a ready answer. Those who did felt that it was the drunken priest's disengagement from Church structures that made his powers stronger and that outside institutional control they were potentially unwieldy (Taylor 1990: 179–80). The fact that drunken priests were perceived as dramatically separated from Catholic authority structures is historically grounded in a trend at the end of the eighteenth century in which reformist Catholic bishops, working to stem devotional excesses and drinking among the parishioners, also aimed to stop what they felt was excessive drinking among the older, nonreformist priests (Taylor 1995: 116). Their persistent drunkenness becomes a sign of priestly subordination by those who, according to local lore, have been cast off from their parish assignment, sometimes silenced, and reduced to wandering by Church authorities.

It also stands to popular reason that the further a holy figure rises in the ranks of officialdom, the further diminished is his or her miraculous charisma. Fr. Chavara, for all his impressive worldly and ecclesial achievements, cannot begin to compete with Alphonsa in his capacity and reputation for miraculous power. It is precisely in these instances of worldly compromise and weakness—in the drunkenness and westerly wanderings of the priest and the obscurity and suffering of Sr. Alphonsa—that these figures gain their unearthly power, understood locally as sacred. This sacred power from the periphery is well described in Taylor's illustration of Ireland's impoverished monks, whose removal from ecclesial structures allowed them to wander the wilds and come "in closer contact with God and the angels, with whom they had rather continuous communication" (Taylor 1995: 42).

While local portrayals of Alphonsa and the drunken priest appropriate and reverse colonial stereotypes of Indian suffering and Irish drinking, respectively, and support popular logic that confers supernatural powers to the periphery, their ability to dissemble Orientalist and Celticist frameworks is, as I see it, their most significant feat. While these localized figures do indeed invert power equations in familiar ways, their revolutions turn on a different axis, such that old associations lose their grip and new ones find traction. The Catholic hierarchies who promoted Alphonsa and the wandering priest as antidotes to colonial constructions imposed expectations of their own; local renditions of the powerful suffering nun and drunken priest in turn repeal these impositions. Absent from these local reversals, most importantly, are the central us/them dichotomies that typically glue such systems together. The localized suffering nun and drunken priest who curse as well as bless, although deflective of clerical expectation, are nonetheless a priest and a nun—representatives of the Church. Rather than pitting laity against hierarchy, these figures simply seem to read the Church and its powers on their own terms. They emerge as hybrids who, unlike their official counterparts, candidly reflect inevitably mixed loyalties and associations.

Breaking the cycle of colonial/postcolonial paradigms is no minor accomplishment. Native populations offer a foil against which colonial virtues are built; while the imperial "race" is established as the norm, the Other is reduced to a distortion in need of correction and assistance. This same promotion of the Self contrasted with a deficient Other also lies at the heart of decolonialization. The liberation of the postcolonial Self from the new Other, the colonial oppressor, leads to "a new ideology of the Self, a new nationalism, this time with a new nation as the norm, and the old colonial power as the distortion" (Bachorz 2001: 8). This process in which one nationalism is simply replaced by another postcolonial nationalism, invariably producing "an imitative, repressive entity" (Graham 89), has prompted postcolonial theorists to contemplate strategies for groups somehow to extricate themselves from a seemingly inevitable and oppressive cycle.[17]

By referring to the local suffering Indian nun and the drunken Irish priest as candid hybrids or as representatives of Orientalism and Celticism unplugged, I do not mean to suggest that they have finally "solved" the us/them oppositions promoted by their official counterparts. Instead, it simply seems that through them the axis of concern shifts in ways that allow for the complication of such dichotomies. Distinctions between us and them based on national or religious affiliation and authority are undoubtedly far from meaningless for those who engage the realm of local piety, yet the assumption of value, of good and bad, that typically inhere in these distinctions dissipate when issues of sickness and health, destitution and plenty, are at stake. The axis of concern for local devotees of Alphonsa and the drunken priest, that of healing and well-being, has nothing to do, so we learn from pilgrimage accounts and local legends, with constituting the Self in contrast to an evil or immoral human Other. The menacing, oppressive Other against which devotees hope to mend and construct the Self is, instead, everyday conditions of calamity and despair.

Postcolonial theorists preoccupied with dismantling once and for all the entrenched colonial and nationalist binaries of Self/Other propose a range of solutions. While some may uphold the importance of positive colonial stereotypes for forging nationalist identity, others argue that postcolonial identity can free itself from its colonial roots only by realizing a space where self and other, colonized and colonizer, are enmeshed and indistinguishable.[18] By maintaining Orientalist and Celticist structures yet disregarding their foundational value, the local figures of the suffering nun and drunken priest suggest something in between. This process, as I understand it, is similar to what Theodor Adorno recommends. Contrasted with Homi Bhabha's proposed metaphysical "Third Space," which confounds us/them dichotomies, Adorno argues that differences cannot and should not realistically be dismantled, while the values seemingly inherent in them can and should. Adorno proposes that totalitarian structures that distinguish the normal from the abnormal can be replaced by "reconciliation" systems in which participants understand the Other as a potential norm or normal. Reconciliation does not deny or try to solve difference, but accepts difference as necessary.[19]

As idealistic as I make Adorno sound, the concerns represented by localized suffering Alphonsa and the drunken priest suggest one way in which Adorno's process of "reconciliation" might realistically take place. Instances in which difference is maintained yet de-electrified, acknowledged when we take into account these folk figures, are not grandly imposed from above by politicians, religious leaders, or theorists; rather, much more practically, they arise from our imperfect earthbound condition. Far from offering a permanent solution to forging unfettered postcolonial identities, the suffering nun and drunken priest of local lore point us, at the very least, in a hopeful direction.

CHAPTER 2

❧

Arguing Equal Access
to an Earthly Sacred

Christian and Hindu Theologies of Liberation

Before turning my attention to the study of South Asian religions I was a student of theology at the Graduate Theological Union in Berkeley. This was in the late 1980s, when liberation theology was all the rage at progressive seminaries. For those readers who are unfamiliar with them, liberation theologies emerge out of the experiences of the marginalized, from sectors of the society typically denigrated and dismissed due to such factors as economics, ethnicity, gender, and sexual preference. By nature, liberation thought—labeled Latin American, black, feminist, and gay theology, among others—is critical of traditional theologies that uphold conventional economic, racial, gendered, and social privilege. Departing in many ways from established Christian convention, liberation theologians, as described by José Miguez Bonino, claim "their right to 'mis-read' their teachers" and to "find their own insertion into the theological tradition, to offer their own interpretation of the theological task" (1975: 62).

This chapter offers descriptions of several Christian liberation theologies and juxtaposes them with Hindu instances in which religious orthodoxy is consciously and similarly "misread" and critiqued. Departing from the first chapter's portrayal of folk figures who arise from everyday material realities and challenges—representing, in their own ways, "misreadings" of institutional prescriptions—here we find deliberate realignments of convention undertaken by theologians and religious leaders, likewise in response to everyday realities and inequities.

As to be expected, the following Hindu-Christian comparison features types of discrimination and sacred tradition that differ significantly across religious divides. The critiques under consideration—in substance as well as execution—nevertheless cohere in a variety of ways. Most fundamentally, they are both suspicious of traditional religious frameworks that diminish the sanctity of the material world—of earthly, bodily existence. Related to this, both understand their respective inequities and discriminations to arise from systems that keep the sacred largely out of everyday arm's reach, reserved for positions of privilege and for exclusive, transcendent realms. The Hindu and Christian orthodoxies under critique are not only found to be socially problematic; based on critics' deliberate (mis)readings of scripture and tradition, they are regarded as theologically misleading as well. Through comparison we find that, when inspired by concerns for human rights and equal access to the sacred, Hindu and Christian reformers, although using different vehicles and navigational maps, fuel their critique in similar ways and arrive at similar understandings of divinity as earthbound and intimately tied to human affairs.

The sacred immanence promoted by Hindu and Christian proponents of "liberation theology" includes the messy world of human imperfection with which both sets of critics must contend. A conundrum unavoidably arising for those inspired to build earthly equality and social justice is that their efforts will, in essence, never fully be realized. Freely admitting to this difficult state of affairs and in significant ways propelled by the endless struggle it signifies they manage to find practical and theological reasons to faithfully persevere.

The Christian theologies detailed below, founded on those I encountered decades ago in Berkeley, reemerged as flashbacks when I set out to learn about a Hindu temple in Rush, New York. As I began doing field research in early summer 1998, I was struck almost immediately by the acres of common ground shared by this temple's social vision and that of Christian liberation theologians, particularly of Latin Americans and feminists. In spite of this—and mostly because I felt I had other work to do—I kept these observations to myself, conducting a dialogue of sorts between these two overlapping worldviews in my head. It was not until I had been visiting and writing about the temple for nearly eight years that I finally aired this dialogue, offering it to Aiya, the Sri Lankan head guru/priest, a self-proclaimed maverick and guiding force behind the temple.[1] This chapter involves a culmination of both my private reflections over the years and the more recent, enthusiastic conversations on the topic of liberation theology that Aiya and I shared in January and June 2006.[2]

Something I failed to mention in the previous chapter's discussion of St. Alphonsa was that I actually had planned on experiencing this theological confluence when I first set out to do field research in Kerala in 1994. I had, for a variety of reasons, imagined that my theological background would come in handy while studying Indian Christian saint devotion, but quickly learned that this was not to be. I discovered that liberation theology was largely unknown or unacknowledged by Christians with whom I worked, who largely belonged to the ancient Syrian or St. Thomas tradition in Kerala.[3] Furthermore, I found that Syrian Christian religious authorities, rather than focusing on social activism and uplift, as liberation theologians do, tended instead—as chapter 1 describes in detail—to emphasize and uphold individual suffering as religiously meritorious.

I should admit that I was at the time, and still am, enamored of the principles of liberation theology, so much so that this disconnect between my theological expectations and Kerala Christian religious realities, particularly during my first month in south India, left me rather disappointed. It was during this period that I found myself heading to the bus stop one morning, on my way to Bharananganam and Sr. Alphonsa's pilgrimage site, falling into step with a priest who lived in the Syrian Catholic seminary up the hill from our home. I did not know the priest well but, not one to keep my thoughts to myself, decided to describe to him this disconnect. I told him how I was finding, in shrine pamphlets and during daily conversations about the life and lasting power of Sr. Alphonsa, an emphasis on and glorification of her suffering. I explained—naively and perhaps insensitively, I now realize—how my seminary training back home emphasized religion's potential to effective critique and correct unjust social structures that cause suffering. I mentioned how difficult it was to reconcile these two religious approaches, one whose primary aim is to banish sinful structures that lead to suffering and the other that glorifies individual suffering as a means for acquiring holiness.

Rather than instructing me on the nuances of the prevailing theology or, at very least, acknowledging my confusion, the priest sharply responded, "How do you expect to understand suffering? You are a Westerner!" After shaking his head for a moment he added, "You Westerners try to build Utopia." He then changed the subject as we continued walking apace, leaving me feeling nonetheless left in the dust.

Putting aside for the moment the illusiveness of Utopia—which perhaps deserves the priest's disdain—I propose that Westerners and lefty Christians are not the only ones, by any stretch, who try to build it here on earth. Four years after this roadside exchange, I found my liberation theology background returning to roost not in a Christian but in a Hindu setting, at a goddess temple led by a Sri Lankan Tamil priest/guru with whom I have enjoyed exploring the natural affinities shared by these two systems. Yet I must add one caveat. Preventing me from waxing too idealistic is the fact that liberation theologies—and no less Aiya's socially informed religious convictions—are not meant to be left in the abstract. They necessarily involve a self-informing cycle of theory and practice requiring constant reflection, fine-tuning, and, invariably, frustration amid attempted implementation. My conversations with Aiya have reminded me that reality-infused idealism is bound to be difficult. Yet, tempered by faith and hope, the hard work of implementing idealism is, in the end, well worth and even redemptive of its inevitable failures.

TURNING THE WORLDLY ORDER ON ITS HEAD

Aiya's defiance of Hindu convention largely takes place in a one-story barn in the town of Rush that in 1998 was converted into a Hindu temple and dedicated to the goddess Rajarajeshwari. Rush temple participants dedicate themselves to practices associated with an otherwise secret Shrividya tradition, one of the last bastions of male brahmanical privilege within Hinduism today. By encouraging all those interested—women, non-Brahmans, and non–South Asians—in learning the lengthy and intricate *homam* fire offerings and *puja* rituals in accordance with this exclusive tradition, the Rush temple openly defies caste and gender convention, while at the same time it celebrates ritual orthopraxy in abundance.

If we stand back and view the Rush temple in light of larger Hindu frameworks, we find that Aiya's critique of orthodox exclusivity is not exactly new or even original. Of particular note is the bhakti movement's powerful defiance of caste and gender restrictions that swept south India from the seventh through the ninth centuries, spreading to the north by the twelfth century. This movement, which in many ways successfully turned orthodoxy on its head, lives on today, although significantly muted and dispersed, throughout the Hindu traditions.[4] Aiya's theological argument for breaking with religious convention is straightforward and similar to rationales proposed by the bhakti movement: the Rush temple Goddess in her eternal benevolence would never reserve her considerable blessings for a select few. Those truly devoted to her deserve full access—ritually and otherwise—regardless of superficial designations of caste or gender. Aiya asserts, and liberation theologians and bhakti practitioners would agree, that religious standards set by flawed humanity are quite unlike, if not at odds with, divine standards. Those marginalized by society and/or religious institutions are not only loved by God or the Goddess; they are, in many cases, preferred. As Aiya sees it, the Rush temple righteously reflects the Goddess's true egalitarian nature and, on occasion, her socially subversive preferences.

Aiya validates his perspective in a variety of ways, as we shall see, but draws his greatest human inspiration from his own guru, known affectionately as Guruji, a Brahman from Andhra Pradesh, south India. Aiya first met Guruji when both men lived in Zambia; Aiya was working there as an architect, and Guruji taught nuclear physics at a Zambian university. Aiya recalls one of their first exchanges that took place at a gathering where Guruji and a small group of students were discussing religion and philosophy. Guruji was speaking about the ways certain mantras were taught only to men, off limits to women, a fact that had long bothered Aiya. Not able to contain himself, Aiya chimed in that these practices made no sense, since women were largely responsible for the existence and intelligence of their children. Women brought men into the world, raised them, and formed them as human beings. At this, Guruji stood up, walked over to Aiya, and hugged him, saying, "I'm so glad to know somebody who thinks like me." Later, when Guruji initiated Aiya into the Shrividya tradition, he instructed him, against convention, to teach the practice to everyone regardless of gender or caste.

Aiya's concern for social justice is not therefore a recent development, nor is it limited to gender inequities. When he was in his late teens in Sri Lanka, before his conversion experience at the age of twenty, he was an avid Marxist and atheist.[5] Although his explicitly Marxist leanings have since faded into obscurity along with his atheism, Aiya's concern for social justice and egalitarianism lives on and continues to propel his commitment to keeping temple practices open and available to all, particularly to those whose caste and gender would otherwise prevent their access. This is similar to Latin American liberation theologians, who argue that theology must be built from the ground up and with a primary concern for the experiences of the marginalized. While liberation theology also leaves behind Marxist atheism (critics accuse them otherwise), their forms of analysis have been, particularly in the early decades of the movement, avowedly Marxist in their concern for injustices that arise from economic disparity. As described by Bonino, Marxist methodology emerges in Latin American liberation theologians' integration of "praxis and theory and in their insistence on the rationality, conflict, and radicality of the political realm. It can also be seen in the recognition of class struggle" (1975: 71).

The work cut out for Aiya and liberation theologians of all kinds is not simply a religious critique of societal inequities, but a critique of what they understand to be corrupt religious structures that have fueled and supported these inequities. Similar to Latin American liberation theologians, Aiya enlivens his dedication to social justice with faith in a religious tradition that he believes contains, at its core, prophetic, egalitarian impulses. As he sees it, the Rush temple in upstate New York is therefore not breaking with tradition—as it certainly appears to some—but, rather, returning tradition to its original egalitarian form. At the end of the one-year anniversary celebration for the temple, Aiya made this point to the group gathered, in the context of the previous evening's rituals, which had culminated in a grand, raucous procession around the temple grounds:

> This is the secret behind the temple. You will notice that all the *pujas* are being done by men, women, children, old people, young people—there are no exceptions. If you were here last night for the *sappara tiruvila* [festival procession] you would have noticed how everybody enjoyed themselves. There is no difference between us. And that is the way it was in the old days. Unfortunately it has changed. We must change it back—otherwise we will not deserve the little bit of knowledge that has been given to us. Change it back we will, or die trying!

In *The True Church and the Poor*, Jon Sobrino begins his introduction with a similar yet more cautiously worded appeal, calling for the Church's return to a more authentic and egalitarian state:

> The realities and problems I deal with in these pages are, beyond all else, Christian realities and Christian problems. Faith in God, the building of the kingdom of God, the practice of justice, the option for the poor, the holiness of the new being—these are the very substance of Christianity.... These things are basic for the Church if it is to be truly the Church of Jesus.... I am not offering an ecclesiology that is a systematic reflection on all that the Church is and ought to be. My intention is rather to shed light on some basic problems faced by a Church that desires to be faithful to its Christian nature and to recover the essence of Christianity in a creative way at this time in history. (1984: 1)

The strategies Aiya and his liberation theologian counterparts use to reclaim what they believe to be authentic, prophetic truths of their respective traditions are in many ways similar. One of the most common is the employment of scriptural evidence and exegesis. In some cases, they bring to light scriptural passages that are largely, and conveniently, ignored by established orthodoxy. In others, they interpret well-known passages of scripture in ways that invert conventional religious understandings.

This latter strategy is employed by Latin American liberation theologians when, for instance, they highlight the oft-cited beatitude phrase "Blessed are you who are poor, for the kingdom of God is yours" (Luke 6:20). Conventional theology tends to decipher this passage in a spiritualized fashion, commending the poor as blessed and therefore deserving of God's heavenly Kingdom. Liberation theologians read this passage in the context of Luke's larger message of social uplift. Noting the use of the present tense, they understand the poor as blessed not because of their poverty and future reward in heaven but because of their present struggle for justice, a struggle synonymous with the realization of the earthly kingdom of God. While traditional theology views this passage as upholding the earthly status quo and otherworldly spiritual uplift, liberation theologians read it as a prescription for religiously generated societal transformation that does not privilege the spiritual over the earthly planes but melds the two. Leonardo Boff deduces from such scriptural passages that "the kingdom of God, contrary to what many Christians think, does not signify something that is purely spiritual or outside this world. It is the totality of this material world, spiritual and human, that is now introduced onto God's order" (1986: 56).

Liberation theology conceives of Jesus as present in the struggle to bring about the earthly Kingdom, augmenting and refocusing his traditional capacity as heavenly savior. Prophesying Jesus's role as social agitator is his mother, Mary, an unlikely spokeswoman for social revolution given her traditional portrayal as pristine, virginal Queen of Heaven. The traditional portrayal of Mary as pure and submissive tends to focus on a moment in scripture when she hears from the angel that she will give birth to a savior, to which she responds, "Be it done to me according to your word." This phrase, typically interpreted as acquiescence befitting a woman idealized for her meek compliance, is nonetheless a response to the angel's annunciation that proclaims her greatness: "The Lord is with you.... You are full of grace...have found favor in God...will bear the Son most high...whose Kingdom will have no end," provoking Mary's in-kind reply, "All generations shall call me blessed" (Luke 1:26–38).

Of greater importance to Latin American and feminist theologians than these allusions to Mary's greatness is the larger frame of Luke's Magnificat. Here, in sharp contrast to conventional First World portrayals of a compliant figure, we find Mary's words of revolution. Once Mary learns of the magnificence of the child she is to bear, she proclaims God's righteousness with language that is certain and strong: "He has shown might with his arm, dispersed the arrogant of mind and heart. He has thrown down the rulers from their thrones but lifted up the lowly. The hungry he has filled with good things; the rich he has sent away empty" (Luke 1:51–53). As interpreted by Leonardo Boff, Mary's words refer not only to the dawning of a new reality that turns the present one on its head, brought by the birth of her son, but also to an upended world, reflected in the fact that she, of all people, is chosen to bear him. This passage shows, according to Boff, how God's idea of greatness and that of humanity are clearly at odds if not in opposition: "The glory of God is made manifest in humility, revealed in insignificance, made concrete in the marginal" (1979: 126).

Aiya's rationale for upending the status quo at the Rush temple includes a similar reenvisioning of traditional scriptural interpretation. One of his favorite religious texts to read against the grain is the *Purusha Suktam.* Here we find a description of the "Cosmic Man," or, as Aiya prefers it, the "Universal Being," who emanates the four castes in descending order: Brahmans from his mouth, Kshatriyas from his arms, Vaishyas from his thighs, and Shudras from his feet. Refuting the conventional view that this verse supports caste hierarchy by placing Brahmans at the top and Shudras at the bottom, Aiya flips this reading—and the Universal Being—on its head. He described to me his seemingly Tantric-inspired interpretation, one that allows for earth-imbued divinity that gives the otherwise lowly Shudra a place of prominence:

> The first thing, when a person is walking, in touch with *terra firma*, in touch with the earth, the only point of contact, twenty-four hours in the day, between the created earth and the person, is the feet. And the soles of the feet, because they are in touch with Mother Earth, are considered to be absolutely pure, absolutely blessed, absolutely loving, absolutely compassionate. So the emphasis is not on the head or on the hands or on the thighs but on the feet. Always.

Aiya also noted that the feet are an exalted body part inasmuch as they are the place through which grace flows from the deity or the master (most specifically, I learned, from between the big toe and the second toe). Touching the feet of one's elders is a common means for showing respect in South Asian cultures, and touching the feet of a holy person or a priest after performing a temple ritual offers the added benefit of receiving divine blessings.

Aiya also questions the assumed exaltation of the head, or the mind, since it is often one of the biggest stumbling blocks to spiritual progress. He based this on the fact that the Shrividya tradition requires devotees to supplement their elaborate ritual practices with regular meditation that, ideally, allows for encounters with divinity residing within. Crucial to effective meditation is the very difficult task of switching off one's sensations as well as thoughts. Given the value placed on the meditational state—and given that the intellect often presents the greatest obstacle to effective meditation—Aiya went on to argue that the body's head is not as "high" as it superficially seems,

> so I think that the *rishis* were intelligent enough when they described the *Purusha*, the Universal Being, that they also knew that the furthest away from the foot is the head. And this alludes to the fact that when you become intellectually exposed, intellectually enlightened—*intellectually* enlightened—you get further and further away from the divine reality. . . . So I think that the *rishis*, the seers, knew that with knowledge would also come arrogance. With knowledge would also come the possibility and the greater chance of abuse, abuse of power. With knowledge comes power, and that power can be abused. And we have seen that, right?

Although Aiya's unconventional approach to running his temple is fully supported and largely inspired and instigated by his like-minded guru, his reading of the *Purusha Suktam* was not handed down to him by his guru or by a larger tradition. Rather, as Aiya describes it, these and other interpretations emerge from his own reflections and meditational experiences. He recalls previously being "bothered" by seemingly exploitative passages in scripture, particularly in the ancient Vedic literature, and thus as new interpretations strike him as correct if not divinely inspired, he gladly draws on them in his efforts to challenge the status quo.

Aiya concluded our discussion of the *Purusha Suktam* by furthermore arguing that the Universal Being, commonly translated into English as the Cosmic Man and understood to connote maleness by many native speakers of South Asian languages, should more accurately represent gender-neutral humanity.

> It's not to be interpreted as part of a *man*—it's not a man—it's humanity. And just because [the Sanskrit] does not say "man slash woman," it doesn't mean that we have to say, "It doesn't say here 'woman.'" Although I have heard that—from priests I have heard—they would say, "You're allowing women to do *puja*? See what the *Purusha Suktam* says!" And I used to tell them, "Hey look, it does not say it is this. When they say "*naara*"—*naara* means human being. They don't say "*nara*" [to connote] masculine. OK, maybe they don't say "*naranari*"—*nara* is man, *nari* is woman. But you can't expect the *rishis* to be politically correct (laughing) and say "*naranari*."

Aiya's insistence on gender neutrality in this context is a matter of theological import based on linguistic accuracy. At the same time, his insistence goes beyond simply accuracy. When Aiya calls attention to the text's use of the word *naara*—not *nara*—he does so because of the social implications, because of the potential difference one letter could make in the religious lives of half of humanity.

IN MEMORY OF HER: ENVISIONING INVISIBLE WOMEN

Aiya's commitment to providing women access to ritual leadership roles at the Rush temple is central to his work as a guru. He rationalizes this particular break from convention in a variety of ways, often calling on scripture and tradition as he does so. One of the sacred texts Aiya most commonly draws on is the twelfth-century Tamil *Periya Puranam*, which relates and extols the life stories of sixty-three extraordinary Shiva devotees, known as Nayanmar saints, three of whom are women. Rather than simply drawing inspiration from the lives of these three officially recognized women, Aiya often highlights extraordinary women not ascribed saintly rank nor even, in many cases, a name.

In listening to the stories of anonymous Hindu holy women as Aiya tells and frames them, I have often been reminded of Christian feminist Elisabeth Schüssler Fiorenza's classic work, *In Memory of Her*. The book title recalls the nameless woman in Mark's Gospel who anoints Jesus's head with oil, after which Jesus proclaims to his disciples, "And truly I say to you, wherever the Gospel is preached in the whole world, what she has done will be told in memory of her" (Mark 14:9). In spite of Jesus's grand pronouncement, however, this nameless woman is largely forgotten by tradition. At best, she is conflated with sinning women of later Gospels who anoint Jesus's feet.[6]

Schüssler Fiorenza argues that while the anointing of feet was a commonplace gesture in first-century Palestinian Jewish society, not worth reclaiming as notable, it is likely that these Gospel accounts, written after Mark's, are redactions of the original story of the woman who—quite notably—anoints Jesus's head. Prophets in the Hebrew scriptures designate Jewish kings by anointing their heads; the act of anointing Jesus's head thus prophetically identifies him the Anointed One, the Messiah. Since it is a woman who performs this prophetic act, it becomes, as Schüssler Fiorenza describes it, "a politically dangerous story" (1983: xiv). As such, subsequent redactions and interpretations function to divert our attention from her; the remaining evidence of social transgression in Mark's Gospel is left largely ignored. Schüssler Fiorenza notes how the biases of scriptural selection and transmission ultimately mislead our sense of history: "Early Christian traditions have manufactured the historical marginality of women, but they are not a reflection of the historical reality of women's leadership and participation in the early Christian movement" (1983: 52).

Aiya likewise asserts that many women in the *Periya Puranam* remain nameless and forgotten not because they are insignificant but, to the contrary, because they are exceptional. They are dismissed precisely because their actions challenge gender norms of the day, or, as Schüssler Fiorenza put it, because their stories are "politically dangerous." Aiya's efforts to draw attention to the nameless and commonly overlooked women in these ancient Tamil stories are, like those of feminist theologians, his way of retrieving the priestly legacy he feels is due to women and, just as importantly, due to the tradition as a whole.

One of Aiya's favorite nameless women appears in the hagiographical account of the ninth-century Nayanmar saint, Kungiliya Kalayar. She makes her appearance in the middle of the male saint's legend, in a big Shiva temple two towns away from his hometown. The *Periya Puranam* describes her as entering the temple after bathing, a wet cloth tied below her armpits, carrying a flower garland for the Shiva lingam—a spherical representation of Lord Shiva—in both hands. Upon approaching the lingam, her cloth begins to slip. To protect her modesty and to keep the cloth from falling, she flaps both elbows to her sides and, from this position, struggles to reach and ring the garland around the lingam. Miraculously, the Shiva lingam accommodates her by leaning in her direction and accepting the garland. Then it stubbornly stays that way. When the king, assisted by his soldiers and royal elephant, is unable to straighten out the lingam, Kungiliya Kalayar hears of his plight. He saves the day by traveling to the temple and, using the garland of flowers around his neck, effortlessly pulls the lingam upright.

During our discussion of the nameless woman whom Shiva miraculously accommodates with his forward lean, Aiya reasoned, "Now, if that had been a man, maybe if he had a weight on his head and he could not lean over and Shiva had accepted the garland... [Aiya pauses and then claps his hands together] he would have been made into a saint. Now this woman has almost disappeared." Underlining the disconcerting extent of this woman's obscurity, Aiya proceeded to describe an encounter the previous year in New Zealand:

What happened was, I was relating this story and there was a theologian there who had studied the scripture—properly. In fact his life is ruled by the

Periya Puranam. He said, "I had never heard of this woman!" And I said, "Oh my God!" And then he said, "I have read Aramukanavala's writing on this." Aramukanavala, for your information, was a great scholar of Tamil literature and Shaivism from Sri Lanka. But he was a bachelor. And he also had the same leanings toward the fairer sex, like Manu [the author of the Hindu law book *The Laws of Manu*].[7]

Sounding like the people's version of Elisabeth Schüssler Fiorenza, Aiya finished his commentary by bemoaning the way Aramukanavala and other influential MCPs (male chauvinist pigs) have so frequently and irresponsibly contorted tradition: "Yes, so he was an MCP, too. So he has quietly left this out. This scene, he has left it out. So you know, he only picks up the story when the Shiva lingam had kind of slanted, leaned, and then he straightened it out. He does not tell you how it was..."

As Aiya trails off, I interject, "...how it got that way." Nodding, Aiya continues, "So he quietly eliminated her. Now, if that were a man, they would have made a huge deal about it....And people think that this is the gospel for them! You know that is why, I think, when somebody writes something that is going to be on record for all of eternity, you don't play favorites."

In an earlier discussion I heard Aiya elaborate on another aspect of this woman's story: the simple yet startling fact that she is inside the temple sanctum, typically off limits to all except the temple priest. Tradition tends to overlook this detail, but for Aiya, it provides important evidence of women's priestly access in earlier centuries and further validation for the practices he advocates at Rush (Figure 2.1):

> Now, the sideline to this story is this lady, the very fact that she went to the Shiva lingam—the Shiva lingam that is always, in a Shiva temple, in the sanctum. Okay? And she was allowed to garland it. To garland you have to go really close. That means women had access. [...] I always make sure that I tell people this. She had access there and somewhere along the line these fellows changed it. Now, they might give the explanation, "Oh, *that* Shiva lingam was not inside the sanctum. It was outside." Bull![8]

Another of Aiya's favorite nameless and forgotten women of the *Periya Puranam* is the sister of one of the most famous of Nayanmar saints, Thirunavukkarasar. Her obscurity has baffled Aiya since he was young.[9] He feels it was not fair that, despite her tremendous devotion and subsequent spiritual gifts, she was not somehow given a place of honor by tradition.

Figure 2.1
Rush temple member performs priestly duty of offering milk *abhishekam* to the Shiva lingam while others wait their turn.

According to legend this woman, whose parents are deceased and whose betrothed is killed in battle, despairs that she no longer has reason to live. Her brother, Thirunavukkarasar, asks her to live for his sake and she agrees. Thirunavukkarasar subsequently converts to Jainism, enters a Jain monastery, and quickly rises in the ranks to become an esteemed teacher. His sister, an ardent devotee of Shiva, prays every night that her brother will return to the fold. As Aiya described it,

> she was very upset that he was a fallen-off Shaivite. And so she pleads with Shiva, "You have to protect my brother from eternal darkness." And Shiva appears to her and says, "Don't worry. I will visit him with a disease that can only be cured by sacred ash." And from the description, from the story, the disease appears to be Crohn's. He appears to have had excruciating pain, and the Jains tried all their powerful chants and medicines and—nothing doing. Then on the sixth day, when he is near death, he remembers his sister. Out of desperation, he sends his attendant to see his sister with a message that says, "I need to see you because I think I am dying," and he asks her to come. The sister tells the attendant, "I will not set foot into a place where Shiva has not given his blessing. I refuse to see my brother unless you bring him here." So the attendant

travels back and somehow manages to take him to her. And he comes and he falls at her feet, at his sister's feet.

At this point, Thirunavukkarasar's sister makes a paste out of holy ash and, while chanting Shiva's name, applies this to her brother's stomach. The pain immediately subsides and Thirunavukkarasar revives. When his sister informs him that he fell sick because he had abandoned their god, he begins to sing extemporaneous hymns to Shiva, begging his forgiveness. Thus begins the career of one of the most poetic and prolific Nayanmar saints. Aiya ended his story with the following reflection on the forgotten woman:

> What I'm saying in all of this is that he's recognized as one of the four greatest. His sister, the one who is responsible for bringing him back into the tradition, is not given a place. You have to realize the times when this was written. That's how orthodox they were. This lady's name was omitted. And at that time I think she was also considered a widow. You see. So social convention is there.

Aiya surmised that the dearth of recognition for this woman's extraordinary faith and favor with Shiva, responsible for saving her brother's life, returning him to the fold, and in the process giving the Shaiva tradition one of its greatest saints, is not simply because she is a woman. She is moreover a widow and thus inauspicious in the eyes of convention. Further highlighting the skewed gender dynamics of the tradition, Thirunavukkarasar is largely responsible for designating who is (and is not) listed on the Nayanmar saint roster. The fact that he would exclude the source of his own salvation is, as Aiya sees it, further evidence of how cultural bias can override better judgment. Months later, when Aiya and I returned to this subject, he had just seen the movie *The Da Vinci Code*. Reflecting on the interreligious and cross-cultural theme of the devout woman unfairly snubbed by convention, he concluded that because Thirunavukkarasar's sister was an inauspicious widow "she was not—just like Mary Magdalene, just like that—she was not acceptable to the male-dominated, hierarchical society."

HOLY YET FLAWED HUMANITY

Aiya's disappointment in Thirunavukkarasar does not seem to undercut his appreciation for him as a great saint. He accepts that holy people are bound to be flawed inasmuch as they are products of flawed society. He thus takes

for granted the fact that scripture and tradition are transmitted and interpreted by human beings who invariably lug behind them the baggage of
bias. As such, Aiya's task—as well as liberation theologians'—is often to
extricate the prophetic message from the sometimes less-than-prophetic
messenger. As described by feminist theologian Rosemary Radford Ruether,
the process of weeding out problematic passages in the Bible is a matter of
identifying core scriptural ideals having to do with, for example, compassion and forgiveness and disregarding those segments that—due to societal and human limitation—contradict these core ideals. As Ruether sees
it, this is not just important practice for feminists but ensures the integrity
of the tradition itself:

> It is blasphemous to use the image and name of the Holy to justify patriarchal
> domination and law. Feminist readings of the Bible can discern a norm within
> Biblical faith by which the Biblical texts themselves can be criticized. To the
> extent to which Biblical texts reflect this normative principle, they are regarded
> as authoritative. On this basis many aspects of the Bible are to be frankly set
> aside and rejected. (1983: 23)

A religious figure whom feminist theologians find particularly vexing,
known for his mixed messages about women's roles in the early Church,
and whose writings in scripture they partially reject, is Paul, a man esteemed for his role in the spread of early Christianity. On one hand, segments of Paul's epistles affirm Jesus's radical stance toward women, lauding
the significant roles they played as leaders and traveling missionaries in
early Christian communities. In the final passages of his letter to the
Romans, Paul most specifically references the value of his female coworkers
in Christian mission. In Romans 16:1–16, Paul greets and commends by
name a number of leaders in the Christian community, about one-third of
whom are women. Phoebe, whom he refers to as a deacon, seems particularly important, as is Junia—also referred to as Julia—whom he admires
as "prominent among the apostles" (16:7).[10] In his letter to the Galatians,
Paul furthermore proclaims that gender distinctions—along with ethnic
and social distinctions—are obliterated in the light of Christian faith:
"There is neither Jew nor Greek, there is neither slave nor free person, there
is not male and female; for you are all one in Christ Jesus" (Galatians
3:28).

More consistent with the mores of the first-century society in which
Paul lived are some of the most restrictive passages found in the New
Testament in regard to women, also attributed to him. This stance is em-
blemized by his admonishment in 1 Corinthians that women not speak

while in church: "As in all the churches of the holy ones, women should keep silent in the churches, for they are not allowed to speak, but should be subordinate, as even the law says. But if they want to learn anything, they should ask their husbands at home. For it is improper for a woman to speak in the church" (1 Corinthians 14:33–35). Due to the dramatically uneven views about women's leadership attributed to Paul, many scholars, based on close attention to the structure of the original Greek, surmise that there were, in fact, at least two evangelists who wrote in his name. Some of the antiwoman passages in Paul's epistles seem to have been added later to align scripture more closely with societal norms.

Before exonerating Paul entirely from the trappings of patriarchy—and thus conferring onto him the impossible perspective of a twenty-first-century feminist—it appears that some of the more troubling passages attributed to him were written in a style similar to those that are radically redeeming. In light of this observation, scholarly theories proposing that more than one "Paul" exists and that misogynist passages were added later become more difficult to support. Although it appears possible to separate some of the good news from the bad, some of the original Paul from later additions, it appears he nonetheless worked within the confines of his human and societal limitations. As scripture scholar Amy-Jill Levine puts it, "Feminist studies appears to be moving toward a consensus that recognizes Paul as a product of his own time; he is androcentric and patriarchal and he does value the spirit over the flesh, but he also supports women's leadership, agrees that in baptismal ecstasy divisions of ethnos (Jew and Greek), status (slave and free), and gender/sex (woman and man) collapse" (2004: 1).

One of the most highly esteemed Hindu religious leaders of all time, who is known, like Paul, for his extensive travel and far-reaching religious influence, is the ninth-century Adi Shankaracharya. Aiya not only considers Shankara to be one of the most influential figures and reformers in the history of Hinduism; he also considers his teachings to be of critical importance to his own Shrividya path. Despite the adulation Aiya gives to Shankara, he remains realistic about his limitations, similar to feminist theologians' realism about Paul's. As Aiya sees it, Shankara was not immune from cultural blind spots and, in some cases, dramatic inconsistencies.

Aiya illustrated this point to me by first relating the story of how Shankara had promised his widowed mother that he, her only child, would, perform her last rites. This promise defies convention, since, as a renunciate monk from a very young age, Shankara was supposed to have cut all family ties. Shankara's mother died when he was still a boy, so as he prepared for her cremation, he asked his fellow villagers to help him gather firewood and carry her body. Steeped in orthodoxy, unwilling to help him break with tradition, his neighbors would have no part in assisting him. Shankara apparently persevered: after gathering enough wood to make a funeral pyre, he cut his mother into three pieces and carried her dismembered body to the fire himself, piece by piece.

After finishing this story, Aiya went on to point out how Shankara, despite his willingness to buck tradition for the sake of his mother, did not always bring his reformist tendencies to their logical culmination. Those monks who today walk in Shankara's footsteps, understood to live out his legacy, are furthermore the epitome of restrictive orthodoxy. As Aiya sees it, things could have turned out differently if only Shankara's teachings had been more consistent with his actions:

> Now Shankara—whose own mother was a widow, right?—he went there and cremated her. And this is the guy after whom all the *matams* [monastery ashrams] are named. He was the one who created the *matams*. If the monks at a *matam* even look at a widow, they won't eat for a whole day! To prevent this [prevailing view that widows are inauspicious and therefore polluting] he at least should've laid down the law. So, we don't know what social conventions are there.

Further exemplifying how Shankara's reputation for holiness does not immunize him from human fault is a traditional tale in which he was rightfully brought down to size for his caste consciousness. This theme in which the lofty are laid low is a common thread in Hindu storylines and a favorite of Aiya's. In many cases the person who teaches arrogance a lesson appears to be socially marginalized—someone who, envisioned by the *Purusha Suktam*, resides farthest from the head yet who, in fact, is divinity in disguise:

> And Shankara himself was challenged in Kashi—in Banaras. He's taken a ritual bath in the Ganges and now he's all pristine, pure, and everything. He's walked into the Shiva temple, the main temple in Kasi. And as he goes, a *Chandala* appears in front of him. A *Chandala* means somebody of really low birth. With four dogs. And Shankara tells him, "Move! Move!" And that person retorts, "Which portion of me are you asking to move—the body that will perish or the light inside of me that will never perish? Which are you asking to move?" And Shankara was supposed to have looked up and seen a vision of Shiva, of Vishvanathan. He was supposed to have seen him. What I am saying is that even Shankara was not immune to this.

Another tale Aiya is fond of telling provides two related lessons. One is that the holy haughty will be brought down to size and the other is that we should never—without risk of dire consequences—underestimate the importance of women, human or divine. Aiya related this story in January 2006, egged on by Priya, one of Aiya's young students who had joined our conversation and for whom this tale is a favorite:

> There is supposed to have been a great seer, a *rishi*. He did not want the association of a feminine force in his worship. So the story is that he went to Kailash, the abode of Shiva. And Shiva and Shakti [Shiva's wife] are seated there. He wants to go around Shiva [clockwise, as a way of honoring him] but he does not want to go around the feminine. So he goes around and he's thinking, "How the hell do I avoid her?" And he takes the form of a fly and tries to fly between them. And the all-knowing Mother closes the distance [Aiya shows with his hands a deliberate closing in then, smash!] and the guy is caught! [Priya and I laugh.] And the first screech he lets out is "Amma!" ["Mother," a common epithet for the goddess] You know, when you call out to Her, She will always take care of you.

Aiya finished by extracting the moral, in the form of a warning, inscribed in the story: "The moral is that, even at that level of spiritual concentration, you may be lost in your own delusions. You're still deluded." In other words, no matter how fabulously enlightened and revered a person might be— even if his mastery of spiritual discipline enables him to take the shape of an insect—the delusions of societal expectation, bias, and ego still have the capacity to ensnare and derail. No one is immune.

PROBLEMS WITH UTOPIA

Now we return to the problem of Utopia, raised at the beginning of this chapter by the Keralite priest who was suspicious—and perhaps rightly so—of my plucky idealism. The problem as I unpack it, reiterating the views of Aiya and liberation theologians, can be broken into two parts. The first has to do with the impracticality of Utopia, with the sheer impossibility of a truly egalitarian society. As demonstrated by St. Paul and Shankara, the lure of elitism and exclusivity ensnares even the best of humanity. The second part of the problem has to do with the desirability of Utopia in the first place: we are well within our rights to ask whether Utopia is—quite frankly—a destination worth pursuing.

In June 2006, my interview session with Aiya that started on a Monday morning and extended over several days began with a mini-lecture, by me, on the basic tenets of liberation theology as I have learned it. Aiya listened patiently, punctuating my explanation with vigorous nods of his head and occasional comments. When I finished, I told him how I repeatedly had been struck, over the past eight years, by the ways his flattening of gender and caste distinctions at the Rush temple—and his rationale for doing so—reflected a similar religious outlook. He agreed with me wholeheartedly, assuring me that my observations struck a chord in him as well. As is typical of so many of our conversations, Aiya then proceeded to complicate my tidy picture. Although he felt that the temple community indeed had managed to derail gender and caste restrictions, he identified other types of elitism—having to do with class, age, family ties, and ritual knowledge—that seemed inevitably to creep into the picture. He furthermore was concerned that some temple members who would have otherwise been marginalized by convention had begun to establish their own sense of entitlement to ritual leadership. As he put it,

> I see that there is a general question among people around here. "Why him and not me?" And when you ask that question, "Why him or why her and not me?," in your mind you're implying that you're more qualified than he is, that you deserve this [esteemed temple role] more than the other person. And that is because of your so-called knowledge, your so-called position in society, your so-called status in the temple. Because it can work the other way, too. Let's say I nurture somebody from an underprivileged class, somebody who is not very well accepted by the white collar and the professional people. And that person will begin to take on an air of importance. That then is also there. And then they become oppressors.

Aiya and I agreed that this trend is not new or surprising given the human propensity to build hierarchies. Efforts toward egalitarianism seem, in any context, to be never-ending. Aiya continued this train of thought by observing, "These are all problems that are there in any institution, whether you are in an ashram or in a temple. It's there. Even if it's a privately owned company." Reflecting on this unanticipated turn in our conversation, I remarked, with a note of sadness, "What you're saying sounds to me that all the idealism that you've brought to this temple, all the breaking of convention, it's not over." Aiya immediately responded, "It's not over. It's a lifelong battle."

Thinking back to liberation theology, I then recalled to Aiya that, not coincidentally, one of the biggest challenges faced by liberation theologians is that of keeping elitism at bay. Or, more accurately, one of the most common critiques leveled at liberation theology is the recognition that elitism is an inevitable human tendency, a lifelong battle—which raises certain conundrums: What happens when the poor, purportedly preferred by God, are no longer poor? If marginalized groups are given privilege by a tradition that turns conventional society on its head, what prevents them from taking advantage of this privilege?[11] In the end, the human condition seems to dictate that although the players may change, the structures of inequity, despite our best efforts, tend to remain. This is something about which Aiya, based on his own experiences—and despite his irrepressible optimism—has no illusions.

But let us say we could conjure up a hypothetical Utopia. Would this even be a desirable state? The following Wednesday, Aiya and I sat near the *homam* fire pit eating lunch; several devotees joined our discussion, while others sat in the wings, listening. Aiya raised and addressed the problem of Utopia as follows: "Just imagine if all the people who are in this temple—we all have some degree of expectation in our mind—let us say that all those expectations are met." Clearly enjoying the direction the topic was taking, Aiya called out to an elderly woman (a retired teacher known as Teacher) and asked her to join us. As he explained that he was answering a "philosophical question," she smiled and sat down next to me with her full plate of food. Aiya continued, "... all those expectations are met, 100 percent, all the time. That means that any Tom, Dick, and Harry that walks into the temple is going to have all his expectations met. Let us say that there is some massive miraculous power here that is granting every EDT..."

I interrupted to ask what EDT is, to which Aiya responded, "Every Damn Thing." All of us listening burst out laughing. At this point a woman named Beena arrived at the temple and performed a *namaskaram* greeting to Aiya and received his blessing. Aiya then continued, incorporating Beena, known for her devotion to Shiva, into his explanation:

> So let's say that everything is that easy. And now this lady walks in and she comes with the expectation that she has to take care of Shiva—that she has to get an answer in return—because she loves the guy so much. So as soon as that expectation is met, two things will happen. One is that there will be utter chaos. Right? Simply because there is some miraculous power here that will grant everything, people will start to flock to this place like they flock to the Black Madonna. Trains and planes and hotels, the roads and everything will be traffic-jammed, not to speak of our toilets and septic tanks, everything will be overwhelmed. [Aiya says this with laughter in his voice; the listeners laugh along in the background.] The people in the kitchen will be completely overwhelmed; you can't do anything.

Aiya paused and looked at me for confirmation. I nodded and punctu-
ated my nod with, "Right." Aiya continued: "Right. Two: if every need is
being met, pretty soon this place will be totally *bor*-ing. Because there are
no challenges inside. There is no fire!" Confirming what I understood to be
his point, I interjected, "So although you're trying to build Utopia, it has to
be in the knowledge that it will never be built because you don't really want
it." Aiya underscored this statement by saying it is not only undesirable,
but actually impossible: "There is no Utopia. It is a theoretical place." Aiya
and I agreed that the challenges of building—not reaching—Utopia are
what fuel and enliven the temple and inspire individuals toward greater
enlightened states. At another point in the conversation, again using the
metaphor of fire, Aiya mentioned that a utopian state "very quickly will
become redundant. And then, what will happen is that the rituals become
empty. Because there's no fire to push you forward."

In the language of liberation theology, a utopian vision enflamed by
faith is crucial to what would otherwise be simply a material, sociologically
geared project. Faith in Utopia pushes the horizons of science and material
analysis to new levels, "demanding the creation of new instruments and
hypotheses" (Bonino 1975: 71). Yet at the same time, while the vision of a
final Utopia inspires liberation theologies, an arrival at Utopia is admittedly impossible. It is the struggle and hope for justice unattained that
fuels and propels the Kingdom of God on earth. As Latin American theologian Jon Sobrino admits, faith and justice are "by their nature...utopian
notions that can never be completely made real within history" (1984: 66).
Rather than abandoning as futile the struggle for unmitigated justice,
Sobrino prescribes a dialectical approach that both acknowledges and rejects the inevitable presence of disbelief and injustice—human qualities
that are just as stubbornly enduring as utopian faith and justice are elusive.
By nonetheless entering into the fray while realistically acknowledging the
inherent tensions and challenges therein, this realism helps the process
"escape from certain impasses that are created by purely theoretical approaches" that view liberation in purely positive, utopian terms of faith
and justice (1984: 66–67).

As Aiya describes it, these eternal challenges to utopian goals are necessary in that they stoke the "fire" that pushes us forward. Though he might get
frustrated by flawed human behavior, he would be unrealistic to wish it away,
and furthermore, his struggle for divinely inspired justice would fall flat if—
hypothetically speaking—such behavior ceased to exist. In Sobrino's more
recent work, *Where Is God?: Earthquake, Barbarity, Terrorism, and Hope*, he
deepens this indebtedness to human imperfection—and even to catastrophe—by viewing Utopia from the underside. Making use of Christian catego-

ries, Sobrino understands it as more potently present in the cross than in the resurrection. At the cross, lived through the daily lives of the poor, Sobrino finds a seemingly implausible yet resurgent hope amid catastrophe that, for him, constitutes Utopia. Sobrino is quick to add that he does not intend to promote a utopian masochism or cult of sacrifice, but wants to call attention to the life-giving and humanizing potential found in struggles against all odds: "We have to struggle with all our power against barbarity, and in truth that doesn't happen very often. But I would insist that we must cultivate the signs of life, no matter how small." In the end, this utopian humanization and hope in the face of catastrophe, difficult to achieve but not impossible, is transformative. It "means struggling against evil, with a willingness not only to overcome it, but to redeem it" (Sobrino 2006: 151).

In spite of the many similarities that this chapter draws between the Utopias-eternally-in-process proposed by Aiya and various liberation theologians, I would not want to give the impression that they are in any way indistinguishable. The communities involved obviously face distinct challenges, and the theologies used to support their efforts, embedded in their respective scriptures, are also in many ways radically different. Another disparity worth mentioning involves the institutional or ecclesial structures with which both groups must contend. Both Aiya and liberation theologians work to counter inequities and exclusivities that are either ignored or exacerbated by their respective religious orthodoxies. As a result, they must answer to religious authorities that, to different degrees, push back against their implicit—and sometimes explicit—critique.

In Aiya's case, the force of Hindu orthodoxy is mitigated by the fact that his temple is in North America and not South Asia. I have found over the years that Aiya is fully aware that many individuals, typically religiously conservative south Indians or Sri Lankans, consider the public performance of temple rituals by women and non-Brahmans to be blasphemous. Although some of these individuals are temple priests who wield a certain religious clout, the fact that their authority is not centralized allows the Rush temple basically to carry on amid the critique. Those who speak ill of Aiya largely stay clear of the Rush temple, and this is fine with him. The temple continues to grow in popularity each year, particularly among the youth who have lost interest in the more conventional temples typically patronized by their parents.

For liberation theologians, particularly for Catholic theologians in Latin America, orthodox critique is centralized, wields a much larger stick, and can be impossible to ignore. Vatican criticisms of Latin American liberation theology, leveled most specifically at the Marxist roots of the tradition, began in earnest in 1982, led by the newly appointed chairman of the

Congregation for the Doctrine of the Faith, Cardinal Ratzinger. One of Ratzinger's first and most highly publicized investigations was of Leonardo Boff's book *Church, Charism, and Power,* in which Boff criticized the absolute power held by the Church hierarchy and called for a return to the "fraternal and collegial" structure found in early Christianity. Boff described the ways in which the current hierarchical configuration amounted to "pathology" and its abuse of power over the powerless amounted to a violation of human rights (1981: 163, 133; see also Sigmund 1990: 155). Ratzinger's investigation of Boff's work culminated in a 1984 letter written on behalf of the Congregation that accused Boff of using language that is "polemic, defamatory, and pamphleteering, absolutely inappropriate for a theologian." Ratzinger criticized Boff for championing principles of a "certain neo-Marxist inspiration" that advocated a "certain revolutionary utopia which is foreign to the church" (quoted in Sigmund 1990: 158). Boff defended his position, insisting that his book conformed not only to scriptural authority but also to Church orthodoxy. The matter was settled by the Congregation in April 1985 when it mandated an institutional silence on Boff that lasted for eleven months. In 1992, after continued pressure from the Vatican, Boff was forced to resign his vocation in order to continue his work with the poor. He remains active as a liberation theologian but as a third-order lay Franciscan rather than as an ordained priest.[12]

The simultaneous critique and support of tradition, epitomized most dramatically by Catholic liberation theologians who work on behalf of yet must defend themselves against tradition is, again, part of what gives "fire" to the liberation movement. As Paolo Freire explains, these two poles cannot be separated; they represent a "mutually dependent denunciation and annunciation" (1971: 119). Understandable though it might be to abandon a religious tradition that denies a person rights due to gender, caste, or economic status, liberation theologians draw on what they believe to be truths that run steadier and deeper than the tradition's injustices— truths that stand as the lived tradition's most compelling critique. They insist on building, contrary to Cardinal Ratzinger's statement, a revolutionary Utopia they feel is not foreign but fundamental to the Church. Catholic theologian Rosemary Radford Ruether writes,

> Only by finding an alternative historical community and tradition more deeply rooted than those that have become corrupted can one feel sure that in criticizing the dominant tradition one is not just subjectively criticizing the dominant tradition but is, rather, touching a deeper bedrock of authentic Being upon which to ground the self. One cannot wield the lever of criticism without a place to stand. (1983: 19)

Not only do liberation theologians strive for the utopian unachievable for the sake of their tradition; their faith in their communities and traditions—the rock on which they stand—is what enables them to do so.[13] Aiya's confidence that Rush temple practices rightly return to earlier uncorrupted forms of his tradition—and that egalitarian temple reenactments are pleasing to the Goddess herself—likewise provides the foundation on which he and temple practitioners stand in order to defy orthodoxy's caste and gender exclusivity.

During my final conversation with Aiya in June 2006 I wound down our formal interview by recounting to him my story, told at the start of this chapter, of the Keralite priest who disdainfully accused me of trying to build Utopia. I wanted to know how Aiya, the comeback king, would have responded if he had been in my shoes. Once I finished the story I asked him, "If you had been walking with this man and had told him about this temple, or if a narrow-minded Brahman had said to you, 'You're just trying to build Utopia' in a dismissive way and then changed the subject, how would you have responded?" At the ready before I even completed the question, Aiya shot back, "I would have told him, 'Isn't that what you're trying to do too?!'" Taken aback by his answer—and wishing I had been so quick with such a response—I leaned toward Aiya with a grin on my face and said, "Oooh. That's really good. That's very good." Aiya continued,

> I would have asked him, "Yes. Yes, I'm trying to build Utopia—it's the same thing that you're trying to do, isn't it? You're trying to tell people, 'You do this, you do this, you do this, you suffer.' You're doing the same thing. Except I'm doing it by encompassing a larger section of the community." So, y'know, I would've come back at him and asked him, "Aren't you doing the same thing?" Of course we're all trying to build Utopia! Who's not? Everybody is. That's what we're trying to do. In our individual lives we're trying to make things better. Everybody is trying to do that. And when you try to take a whole community with you, people have a problem.

Fair enough. Most of us try to build Utopia for ourselves in one way or another, and religious systems are particularly responsible for encouraging this tendency. The difference between the Keralite priest's perspective and those of Aiya and liberation theologians is that, as Aiya observes, the former promotes personal—and, I would add, exclusively spiritualized—redemption, while the latter aims toward collective redemption established on earth. This leap from the private to the political, from the abstract to the concrete, is something with which some people, as Aiya put it, "have a problem." Accordingly, liberation theologian José Miguez Bonino notes how traditional Christianity's promotion of an exclusively otherworldly Utopia focusing on individual salvation creates a context in which

> temporal, collective life has no lasting significance except as it may help or hinder the individual to achieve and/or to express the religious and moral values which belong to the Christian life.... The [spiritualized] Christian and Marxist Utopias have, therefore, quite opposite historical consequences. The latter galvanizes for action, the former leads to accommodation to present conditions; the latter lends value and meaning to history, the former empties history of meaning and value. (1975: 133)

Liberation theologians argue that foundational to the Christian message is a call to enter history, to bring about social redemption and justice on earth. Central to this Christian impulse are strains of faith and hope, vital to the task, and largely absent from a purely Marxist approach.

The religious stock Aiya and liberation theologians place in earthly justice is directly proportionate to their disinterest in or suspicion of suffering and asceticism as religious ends in themselves. They clearly distance themselves from otherworldly Utopias, promoted in no small measure by both Hindu and Christian traditions, that separate and privilege the spiritual over the material realm. The Shrividya Tantric tradition practiced at the Rush temple celebrates a Goddess furthermore understood to pervade the earthly, bodily plane as much as the cosmic plane. She is not viewed as a divine creator who guides the earthly sphere from afar but is envisioned as immanently present on earth, throughout all creation. Ideally, then, the earth and all its creatures (particularly those of the female persuasion) are to be revered as tangible manifestations of the divine. In contrast with Hindu ascetic traditions that prescribe spiritual advancement through the denigration and denial of the body, Tantric traditions understand the body as a necessary vessel for experiencing and accessing divine power and enlightenment.[14] In the largely male-oriented Hindu ascetic traditions, victory over sensory desires is often epitomized by victory over sexual impulses, casting women in a negative light as representing not only sexual entrapment but also materiality itself and all that separates the male adept from his goal. It should be noted, however, that despite Tantrism's ideological challenges to hierarchical dualisms, and despite the tradition's positive evaluation of materiality and femininity, its practices throughout the centuries have tended, ironically, to support not just caste orthodoxy but also male privilege.[15] In such cases, women have been used as instruments for male enlightenment and less so as agents of enlightenment in their own right.[16]

Similar to Tantrism, liberation theologies, suspicious of systems that promote a heavenly Utopia achieved at the expense of earthly well-being, promote theologies that understand spirit and matter to be interconnected and interdependent. This nondualist approach has led a number of Latin American and feminist liberation theologians to contribute to the more recently developed field of environmental theology. Radford Ruether's *Gaia and God: An Ecofeminist Theology of Earth Healing* connects the exploitation of humanity with that of the environment and appeals to increased efforts for "a healed relationship between men and women, between classes and nations and between humans and the earth. Such healing is possible only through recognition and transformation of the way in which Western culture, enshrined in part in Christianity, has justified such domination" (1992: 1). True to the core theme of denunciation and annunciation within liberation theology, Ruether argues for Christianity's capacity not just to harm but to heal this multifaceted web of domination through a deeper understanding of divine immanence. In *Ecology and Liberation*, Leonardo Boff proposes a very Tantric-sounding panentheism that likewise supports the idea that care for the earth is our sacred duty: "Not everything is God, but God is everything. . . . God flows through all things; God is present in everything and makes all reality a temple. . . . The world is not only a bridge to God. It is also a place where God is honored and worshipped and the place where we meet God" (1995: 49, 51).[17]

Allow me to recall once more my exchange with the Keralite priest and Aiya's proposed comeback that he too was trying to build Utopia—a comment meant to deflect the priest's insinuation that only fools chase after Utopia. I would like to suggest that, although it was probably not intended in this way, the priest's insinuation could infer something noble as well. Aiya and liberation theologians freely acknowledge that earthly utopian justice is an unachievable—and perhaps an undesirable—impossibility, yet they endlessly engage in building it for the sake of their communities. I suppose this is the epitome of foolishness. From religious perspectives that understand the sacred as earthly and immanent, however, such foolish hope in the face of hopelessness, buoyed by faith in earthly divine presence and compassion, can be admirable. Viewed through Rush temple practices and liberation theologies, it is not only that divinity is rightfully accessed by and made present through all beings—male and female, high and low caste, rich and poor, human and nonhuman—but that in fact the most concentrated moments and forms of sacred access can be found amid frustration, in the lower reaches of earthly reality. In such instances, it is not the depths themselves that make these moments and forms sacred, but foolish hope that overrides despair, reckless optimism that overcomes doubt, and blind faith that disregards all odds. It is not the realization of Utopia that wins the day, revolutionizing and redeeming flawed existence, but a divinely inspired, earthbound foolishness that continues to believe in and strive toward the impossible.

CHAPTER 3

ঙ৯

Making and Staking Sacred Terrain

Rajneeshee and Diasporic Hindu Settlers
and Unsettlers

ontinuing with the sticky issue of Utopia but on a different—literally physical—plane, this chapter focuses on earthly terrain as a means for accessing the sacred and compares how two newly arrived communities from India sanctify and settle on North American landscape. Departing from previous chapters' comparisons of overlapping and shared themes, the following is mostly a study in contrasts. Featured first is the nonconformist community headed by Bhagwan Rajneesh, which transferred its headquarters from bustling Pune to the arid mountains of eastern Oregon in 1981. I juxtapose this with Hindu diaspora communities that have been establishing sacred territory in North America since the early 1970s, no small feat given that Hindu divinity is so often tied to topographical features that, until recently, have been exclusively associated with the South Asian subcontinent. The process of establishing religious roots on North American soil has been important and challenging to both diasporic Hindu and Rajneeshee communities, yet I argue that their strikingly different approaches—identified here as heterotopian and utopian, respectively—have largely determined how one community continues to make and stake sacred land against considerable odds, while the other no longer does.

I add further resonance to the following comparison by incorporating settler colonizers into the conversation. We find that Rajneeshee and Hindu diaspora strategies for claiming sacred land are and are not reminiscent of

North American settlers before them who, under considerable duress, worked the land, renamed and reestablished territory for themselves, and did so with significant consequences to prior inhabitants.[1] The inclusion of settlers into this discussion of sanctifying land also coincides with recent work by historians of religion who recognize religious sites as frontier spaces—not as static plots with secure boundaries but as zones of intercultural contact packed with conflicting meanings and stakes. As such these spatial frontiers are often "model sites of struggle over nationality, economic empowerment, and basic civil and human rights to freedom of religion and self-determination" (Chidester and Linenthal 1995: 3, 25). Each attempt at sanctifying terrain reveals a process that is ultimately "a political act, whether that positioning involved, in its own terms, selection, orientation, limitation, or conquest" (Van Der Leeuw 1992: 210).[2]

By juxtaposing two communities' efforts to establish sacred space in contemporary North America—viewed in light of settlers before them—this chapter compares possible responses to the challenges of intercultural exchange and of conflicting territorial stakes encountered at the frontier. We consider how Hindu diaspora settlements have managed to meet this challenge by accommodating and incorporating a variety of cultural layers embedded in New World sacred terrain. Features of this "heterotopian" strategy are brought into sharper relief when examined beside the Rajneeshee experiment, which promoted an abstracted Utopia that ultimately required a flattening of heterotopian realities. We discover, then, how these divergent approaches to establishing sacred land mark the difference between largely benign versus colonizing settlements and, in the context of late-twentieth-century North America, between those bound for success or failure. A component of intercultural contact that emerges regardless of settler context are "native" resistances embedded in the contemporary landscape. This tendency represents, as I understand it, a longstanding and forgetful reaction to newcomers, armed and at the ready with its own religiously laden, utopian, and decidedly nonlayered conceptions of sacred space and sacred nation.

THE STORY OF RAJNEESHPURAM[3]

Bhagwan Rajneesh, born as Rajneesh Chandra Mohan in 1931 in Jabalpur, received a master's in philosophy in 1957, taught for nine years at the University of Jabalpur, and traveled for ten years throughout India, lecturing and debating in a provocative, controversial style that was to become his trademark. After resigning his lectureship in 1970 he settled in Bombay, where he held regular evening discourses on a variety of spiritual topics and began to initiate disciples. By late 1971, although his public discourses were still delivered in Hindi at the time, he began attracting a small group of Western disciples who agreed to work on the ashram grounds and follow his teachings. As his community grew and Rajneesh suffered from allergies, the ashram moved to Pune, where, beginning in 1975, he preached increasingly in English and began integrating therapy groups into ashram life. By the late 1970s, as word caught on about this charismatic and innovative guru, an estimated 30,000 visitors from all over the world attended ashram activities each year, with more than 6,000 sannyasin initiates staying onsite at any given time.[4]

At the Pune "Buddhafield," as Rajneesh called it, he conducted, with ever-changing methods, "a gigantic experiment" with Jainism, Hinduism, Islam, Christianity, Taoism, and Tantra, all aimed at discovering human potential. Arguing that authentic religion was a way of being that cannot be taught, he critiqued traditional religious paths that appealed to the intellect and to faith. Rajneesh proposed that his alternative, authentic way of being would ultimately create a "New Man" who could live in the world without attachment to ego, religion, worldly politics, or traditional ideas of relationships that were, each in their own way, dominated by externally imposed rules, expectations, and stereotypes.

Rajneesh professed a belief in the sanctity of India's terrain—a view that is consistent with Hindu orthodoxy and thus, for him, was rather uncharacteristic. As such, he was determined never to emigrate despite his growing dislike for the country (Fitzgerald 1986a: 87). Yet, on May 31, 1981, due to failing health as well as apparent pressure due to investigations of unpaid taxes on his Pune ashram, he left for the United States.[5] Sheela, a devotee who had recently begun managing his affairs, had prepared the way by purchasing a plot of land in eastern Oregon that was to become the new Buddhafield for Rajneesh and his followers. This 64,000-acre piece of land, known to locals as the Big Muddy and eventually renamed Rancho Rajneesh, had been badly managed, was severely overgrazed by sheep, and had been lying in disuse for years. Only about 400 acres were suitable for dryland farming, and about 300 acres could support irrigated crops. After only two years in residence, Rajneeshee sannyasins had dramatically transformed the land, cultivating about 2,700 acres, planting crops, vineyards, orchards, herb gardens, and fodder for livestock. Birds and animals that had fled the area began to return.

The sophisticated planning that went into the development of Rancho Rajneesh included strategies for water conservation, self-sufficiency, and environmentally sound practices. Sannyasins planted thousands of trees to stop erosion, dug wells for drinking water, reshaped creek beds, and built 140 check dams to slow water flow. Gurdjieff Dam created the forty-five-acre Krishnamurti Lake, which held 350 million gallons of water that could be piped underground to nearby fields. Crop irrigation was self-sufficient, open pits provided natural sewage treatment plants, and 75 percent of all waste was recycled at an onsite recycling plant. Ranch workers experimented with crop rotation to minimize the use of chemical fertilizers and alternated rows of vegetables and flowers to reduce the need for pesticides. In addition to growing produce consumed by residents, a poultry and dairy farm produced all the necessary milk and eggs. The sizable city itself that eventually grew onsite was constructed on over 2,000 acres of land deemed completely infertile.[6] By the end of the first year, after spending $20 to $30 million on the ranch, the Rajneeshees had established Rancho Rajneesh as the one of the largest, most developed, and richest commune experiments in the United States. By the summer of 1985, it accommodated 2,500 permanent residents and as many as 2,000 additional long-term visitors at any given time.

Besides the physical transformations, Rancho Rajneesh terrain was further altered by place-names that reflected Rajneeshee religious eclecticism. In addition to Krishnamurti Lake and Gurdjieff Dam, streets were given names such as Zarathustra Drive; the eating hall was christened the Magdalena; orchards were known as Jesus Grove, Buddha Grove, and Walt Whitman Grove; and bus and air transport were coined Buddhafield Transport and Air Rajneesh.[7]

The nearly miraculous makeover of Big Muddy into Rancho Rajneesh naturally required superhuman dedication from Rajneesh sannyasins. During a 1983 tour for a visiting journalist from the *New Yorker*, a tour guide named Veena explained while motioning to devotees working in the fields: "Work is our worship. We sannyasins work twelve to sixteen hours a day. But it doesn't seem like work. It's our meditation. And Bhagwan taught us that work is play" (Fitzgerald 1986a: 52). The Pune ashram also encouraged this approach to work; when done with awareness and grounded in love it was understood to be a celebration and a means for attuning oneself to "the dance of human energy" (Thompson and Heelas 1986: 47). While tasks in Pune mostly involved cleaning, cooking, accounting, and gardening, expectations in Oregon were far more extensive and urgent. The lengthy workday began with breakfast at the Magdalena between six and seven in the morning and ended at seven in the evening, with lunch and afternoon tea breaks in between. Sunday, the only day off, was reserved for meetings. Helping to mitigate these heavy demands was a kitchen staff that prepared all meals and cleaning crews who washed and ironed clothes and cleaned sannyasins' A-frame and trailer homes. Amenities such as toothpaste, soap, and other toiletries were provided by the ranch as well (Fitzgerald 1996a: 60).

Sannyasins living at Rancho Rajneesh were largely college-educated. A good number had left successful professional careers, many of which were in the mental health industry. Their willingness to undertake heavy manual labor for long hours throughout the week is testimony to Rajneesh's powerful appeal. Yet by June 1981, before leaving for the United States, Rajneesh took a vow of silence. Unlike in India, where he had captivated audiences with his provocative philosophies and wit, he made no public speaking appearances in Oregon until the final months of his stay. The appeal of the movement in Oregon is thus more difficult to convey, seemingly having to do with a contagious joy felt by those who lived on the ranch, and Rajneesh's teachings, which linked sannyasins to a guru tradition and to the Self-Growth Movement fashionable at the time. Rajneesh's worldview also seemed particularly appealing to the financially and professionally successful, people he felt were best suited for the Buddhafield, since, as he saw it, their material needs met, they could surrender more effectively to his teachings.[8]

The lasting symbol associated with Rajneesh, recalled decades later by many non-ashram members for whom details from the 1980s commune are but a vague memory, are his Rolls Royces. Rajneesh began acquiring his fleet while in Pune, a collection that culminated in ninety-three vehicles by 1985. This conspicuous display was in many ways consistent with Rajneesh's views, as he held no particular disdain for wealth and unabashedly supported capitalism as a mature economic system.[9] The Rolls Royce, symbol of opulence, success, and, more specifically, of colonial Britain, set the stage for a guru who built an empire of sorts with cheap labor and of settler sannyasins who acted in some instances, as we will see, more like invaders of local terrain than the benign settler agriculturalists they also were, who brought the land back to life.[10]

RAJNEESHEES AND SETTLER COLONIZATION

Twenty miles from Rancho Rajneesh, with a 1981 population of forty mostly retired residents, is the town of Antelope.[11] When Rajneesh sannyasins began arriving in eastern Oregon, spokeswoman Sheela assured their Antelopian neighbors that their transplanted community was simply planning to create a lovely farm with about forty residents living onsite. Sheela's projected scenario came to pass—and then some, as Rajneeshees not only farmed the small patch of existing fertile land but improved it dramatically. Forty residents did come to stay at the ranch, but the number of occupants steadily grew into the thousands. This latter detail was, in the eyes of Antelope residents, the first on a long list of deceptions and betrayals doled out by their new neighbors. It is possible that population explosion alone may not have posed a problem; according to some reports many locals were fairly open-minded about the newly arrived unconventional community (Gordon 1987: 121–22). Neighborly conflict began in earnest due to territorial rather than population expansion and to Rajneeshee designs on real estate beyond the borders of Rancho Rajneesh. In some instances, those who stood in the way of these designs met with serious consequences.

Escalating Tensions

Initial intercommunity antagonisms can be traced back to October 1981, three months after the first sannyasins arrived. The community had acquired property in Antelope where they planned to build a printing plant and office complex big enough to accommodate a hundred workers. Since Oregon land-use laws forbade them to build a structure this size on Rancho Rajneesh, which was zoned only for agricultural use, sannyasins looked to Antelope for a solution. Due to a water shortage and the amount needed to maintain a hundred-worker printing plant, the city council denied them the required building permits for Antelope as well. What followed was a series of special elections, challenges by local interest groups, and, by June 1982, the accumulation of about a dozen lawsuits between the Rajneesh community and the Antelope city council.

By November 1982 sannyasins who had settled in Antelope succeeded in outvoting city council members and creating their own Antelope city council comprised entirely of Rajneeshees. The printing plant was never built, but in the ensuing months, as described by a *New Yorker* reporter, the hostilities between Rancho Rajneesh and original Antelope residents escalated such that "driving between them was like commuting across Belfast" (Fitzgerald 1986a: 53). Most of the original residents of Antelope left town by 1983, the exodus hinging on a number of factors. Rajneeshee spokespeople attributed local hostility and flight to bigotry and religious intolerance, which no doubt played a part. Yet Rajneeshees were likewise hostile, publicly branding townspeople as "rednecks" and "ignorant old people." They took to photographing locals, videotaping town meetings, and taking down license plate numbers of cars that breached town borders—behavior

that for many amounted to harassment. While attempting mutually agree-
able settlements involving land use and schooling, Rajneeshees repeatedly
broke promises to the people of Antelope (Fitzgerald 1986a: 54, 83–84).[12]
Perhaps most damaging of all, the new Rajneeshee city council levied taxes
of $1,200 a year for city improvements that locals did not endorse (Gordon
1987: 123).

Likely unforeseen by either side at the start, this series of events culminated in dynamics not unlike settler colonialism. Different from traditional
colonial models, in which invading foreign minorities govern an indigenous
majority according to the dictates of a distant metropolis, the settler context is one in which the native, not the colonist, is superfluous. The settler
approach to indigenous populations thus involves "a logic of elimination"
in which settlers wish "less to govern indigenous peoples or to enlist them
in their economic ventures than to seize their land and push them beyond
an ever-expanding frontier of settlement" (Elkins and Pederson 2005: 2;
see also Kazanjian 2003: 143–44). Although the settler-native dynamic is
less dependent on native society than on land, the two cannot be separated
as land is a precondition for social organization. Territorial displacement of
native inhabitants is therefore fraught, as well, with spiritual, cultural, and
symbolic displacement (Wolfe 1999: 1–3; Johnston and Lawson 2005:
363).

Claiming and Naming Land

In their introduction to an edited volume on settler colonialism, Elkins and
Pederson write that settler colonization, premised on the elimination of
native societies, sets up a dynamic in which "settlers sought to construct
communities bounded by ties of ethnicity and faith in what they persistently defined as virgin or empty land" (2005: 2). This strategy of claiming
ties to empty land applies most directly to Australian settlers who, using
the doctrine of *terra nullius* (contested only as recently as the 1990s), established rights of ownership to land designated "property." In such instances
land becomes property when cultivated, irrigated, built on, and enclosed—
in other words, "improved" from its natural state as a more efficient pro-
vider of human needs. Property becomes private, belonging to those
responsible for it, in order that they enjoy the fruits of their labor. Land
improvement, as such, was often the driving rationale for settlers (Wolfe
1999: 26–27). Empty lands, filled with people, crops, and herds, were also
filled with stories, place-names, and histories that further legitimated
settlement.

The distinction between benign settlement and invasion, described as the difference between the acquisition of empty versus occupied land, becomes murky, since "empty" and "occupied" are not clear-cut designations (Johnston and Lawson 2005: 362, 364). Since the Big Muddy had been lying dormant for years before the Rajneesh community arrived, the benign term "settlement" seems most accurate given the vast improvements worked upon the land. And the Rajneeshee sense of settler entitlement over this land expressed through the naming of its features hardly seems invasive. The spread of the Rajneeshee renaming process into Antelope, however, is another matter.[13]

The act of conferring names is central to colonization most simply because it appropriates, defines, and captures a place in language. It furthermore opens new realities of place that extend beyond words and representation and becomes "in a sense part of the mysterious process of creation" (Ashcroft, Griffiths, and Tiffin 1995b: 391–92). This process of ownership and indeed creation through naming is not necessarily tied to colonization and power, however, exemplified by the naming of places in the Scottish Highlands where previously uninhabited landscapes become "memoryscapes of events, experiences and associations that tend to become integral elements of the places where they occur and indeed cannot be separated from them" (Jedrej and Nuttall 1996: 124). This benign "writing of human activity and personal and collective experience on the landscape" is reflected, albeit with a much shallower history, in the naming of streets, groves, waterways, and buildings in Rancho Rajneesh.

Such "memoryscapes" become colonizing when naming supplants an earlier name, its meaning and ultimately the connection between people and place become lost, the identity, authority, and even the existence of the original bestower is subverted. Yet the significance of a name may become apparent only after it disappears—particularly if the newly imposed name reflects the power relations involved (Jedrej and Nuttall 1996: 125). In 1984, after sannyasins took over the Antelope city council and many original residents had moved away, the council voted to change the names of the Antelope streets. Originally named for ranchers, Indian fighters, and timber barons, the streets were now given names of saints and sages significant to the Rajneesh community. Main Street became Mevlana Bhagwan Street, College Street became Mansoor, and other streets were given names such as Kabir Road and Gurdjieff-Bennett Drive. Some townspeople who continued to attend city council meetings voiced their concerns. An elderly woman present when the name-change vote took place exclaimed, "No one around here knows these people. What's the matter with the old names?" She was apparently—and aptly for the context—gaveled into silence

(Gordon 1987: 124). By the end of 1984, Rajneeshees had changed the name of Antelope itself to Rajneesh.[14]

Rationales, Contradictions, Implosions

James Gordon, an ex–community member who witnessed this episode at the city council meeting, was shocked to see people he had previously known to be gentle and even-tempered acting so severely. When he told his friends that their behavior seemed to him counterproductive, the rationale offered was that sannyasins were simply holding up a "'mirror' for the local people, forcing them to see the aggression that they ordinarily conceal with politeness and politics" (Gordon 1987: 125). Sannyasins, according to this rationale, refused to play the hypocritical game of conciliation and coopera-tion, which, as Gordon perceives it, casts "the sannyasins in the role of therapist, or indeed Master, with the locals as patients or disciples. It is an encounter group, but they have never signed up" (1987: 125). A *New Yorker* reporter witnessed a similarly aggressive scene on Rancho Rajneesh prop-erty in which a cluster of Rajneeshees surrounded a visiting lawyer and land-use planner who were inspecting ranch buildings. At close range they chanted slogans and yelled, "Get the hell out of here, we don't like you!" and apparently aimed anti-Semitic remarks at one of the men. When the circle of Rajneeshees eventually closed in and yelled so loudly that the inspectors could not work, the two men left. When the reporter later asked a sannya-sin about the incident, he denied that there had been any negative harass-ment, claiming that they had just been singing and joking. He added, "To us, such things aren't serious—it's all play. Greenfield's asleep—he's off on his own ego trip. People were just letting him know what they thought of him. Whoever comes in contact with us has to wake up a bit. It's like an encounter group" (Fitzgerald 1986b: 92).

Settler colonizers used similar altruistic rationales to explain their mistreatment of natives. Patrick Wolfe notes, for instance, that during the second phase of settler colonialism in North America, settlers moved in-digenous populations onto missions and reservations as a means to protect and preserve them. The natives were indeed believed to be a dying race; evolutionist ideas pointed to their inevitable demise. This purportedly phil-anthropic discourse of protection and preservation contrasts strongly with the homicidal rhetoric of the first phase of settler colonization (Wolfe 1999: 29). Portuguese campaigns in Angola and Mozambique that lasted from the late 1940s to the mid-1970s rationalized their continued settler projects by arguing that, based on the Brazilian experience, Portuguese were intuitive colonizers who had a special way of civilizing people, melding races rather than dominating or displacing them. This of course masked the way the natives were in reality dehumanized, exploited for labor purposes, and only "civilized" when in contact with whites (Penvenne 2005: 80–81, 90).[15]

An instance when the rhetoric of philanthropy most strikingly contradicted the expansionist aims of the Rajneesh community involved something known as the Share-a-Home Project implemented by Sheela in August 1984. The plan was to bus homeless persons from cities across the United States—from Los Angeles, Houston, Miami, Chicago, and New York—to the ranch. The new recruits would be offered free room and board and allowed to work or leave as they pleased. Sheela described the project as an experiment in communal living, proclaiming, "We have such an abundance here and we want to share it" (Fitzgerald 1986b: 99–100). From September 2 to October 12, sannyasins gathered between 3,700 and 4,200 homeless men from forty-one cities across the country and bused them to the ranch. Most immediately, Sheela's description of abundance fell flat, given that the new arrivals amounted to three times the number that the ranch could accommodate. A significant proportion of newcomers were violent or disturbed, fights erupted, and many were asked to leave. By late October 1984, more than half the Share-a-Home arrivals had left. Although they were initially guaranteed return tickets to their place of origin, so many wanted to leave that the overwhelmed sannyasins simply dropped them off in groups in nearby towns. Enraged townspeople held demonstrations against the Rajneeshees, while the Salvation Army reportedly spent roughly $100,000 to feed the imports and provide them with return tickets to their cities of origin.

The greatest disjunction between the expressed humanitarian purpose of the venture and an alternative reality can be found—and were well founded—in suspicions that the new ranch members had arrived just in time to elect a Rancho-friendly candidate onto the Wasco County Court. With the correct swing of votes, land-use issues would be resolved such that Rajneeshpuram, the almost-incorporated city within Rancho Rajneesh, could remain a viable city, allowing onsite construction to continue. Those imported from the nation's streets happened to all be over eighteen with no felony records, thus all were eligible to vote in the November county election. Only twenty days of residency were required to qualify a person to vote, and the last bus arrived twenty days before the election. In the end, however, Rancho Rajneesh still did not have nearly the number of voters needed to sway the election, and the Share-a-Home Project, from the perspective of Rajneeshee county politics, was a failure.

Consistent with Sheela's altruistic rationale, about two hundred of the Share-a-Home recruits indeed stayed on the ranch, seemingly thriving, enjoying the work, benefiting from Rajneesh's message to take responsibility, and basking in the sannyasins' overall kindness and supportiveness. As one transplant from the streets of San Diego explained, the ranch provided an environment that was, for him, revitalizing: "There aren't any drugs here, and I've been doped up for a dozen years. But I don't care. I'm getting high on life" (Karlen 1984: 35). By the summer of 1985, 100 to 150 Share-a-Home participants remained (Gordon 1987: 138–46; Fitzgerald 1986b: 98–102).

Viewed from the perspective of settler colonialism, the Rajneeshee retrieval of street people could be compared with the practice of importing outsiders—typically African slaves or convicts—to help settlers work the land (Wolfe 1999: 27; Shafir 2005: 44; Elkins and Pederson 2005: 10). Yet unlike conventional settlers, Rajneeshees had little need for free labor, since it was so readily available from within the community itself. Reflecting settler patterns, however, are the ways that the Share-a-Home Project was tied to plans for expanded land ownership and use, despite rhetoric to the contrary. As a result, the project not only stirred further suspicion in the local community, but also ratcheted up fears throughout Wasco County that the Rajneeshee Community would stop at nothing to carry out their expansionist designs. As *New Yorker* journalist Frances Fitzgerald observed, these designs seemed completely divorced from reality: "That the Rajneeshee leaders had somehow imagined that the county and the state would let them get away with rigging the election showed just how far they had retreated into their world of illusion" (1986b: 102).

As the Share-a-Home Project wound down, emotions escalated and threats against the Rajneesh community became commonplace. In central and eastern Oregon, one could buy T-shirts with the slogan "Better Dead Than Red," referring to the red clothing worn by the sannyasins. Another placed one of Rajneesh's Rolls Royces in the center of a gunsight. Leaflets widely circulated throughout the Northwest, appearing as though published by the Department of Fish and Wildlife, that revealed dark hunting humor, announcing the closure of "the 1984–1985 Big Game season [for] deer, elk, antelope, bear, cougar and squirrels...[but] an open season on the central eastern Rajneesh, known locally as the Red Rats or Red Vermin." In response to increased threats leveled at the sannyasin community, Sheela declared to a reporter from the *LA Times*, "If the state harms any one of my people, I will have fifteen of their heads"—a statement sounding, to many, like a declaration of war (L. Carter 1990: 203; Gordon 1987: 143).

It appears, in retrospect, that many sannyasins felt rather in the middle of a battle raging between eastern Oregon citizens and Sheela's leadership entourage and became increasingly uncomfortable with Sheela's strident public persona and with decisions she made that affected those outside as well as inside Rancho Rajneesh. The fact that the Rajneesh community was under threat by an increasingly hostile public did not make matters easier. This fraught middle place, representing the "radical ambivalence of colonialism's middle ground," is typical of settler colonizers (Slemon 1995: 107). Postcolonial theorists who identify colonialism as involving both resistance to and complicity with the imperial enterprise find that the settler experience best exemplifies this in-between place. The fact that settler colonizers are subjected to restraints on their freedom and are both colonized and colonizing complicates simplistic understandings that the imperial center wields absolute control over a colonial margin—that no one at the imperial center is marginalized, while everyone in the colony is. New World states were born of a dual defeat—of the indigenous population and (at least a weakening) of the imperial metropoles that held settlers in dependence.[16]

Pressure from the Rajneesh "metrapole," most visibly represented by Sheela and the few sannyasins who worked closely with her, came in various guises, reflecting deep contradictions and ironies. One of the most paradoxical constraints, present from the group's inception and articulated by Rajneesh himself while he was still delivering lectures, had to do with an ethos of freedom made possible by rule-bound structures. On one hand, Rajneesh advocated a life unfettered by societal rules and expectations—the freedom of Buddhahood was all that mattered. Yet in order to be free, his followers were urged to surrender their egos; through surrender they could more easily accept the many rules of conduct, hygiene, and work imposed on them. Compared to the Pune ashram, freedom at Rancho Rajneesh required surrender to a more elaborate list of everyday stipulations having to do with fire prevention, safety, cleanliness, and dress. The implementation of Rajneesh's vision via Sheela indeed transformed Rancho Rajneesh into a large-scale organization with ever-increasing rules, regulations, and rituals, and ever-decreasing liberty. The teaching that freedom could be gained through obedience may have shifted sannyasins toward unquestioning submission, yet this is a paradox not unfamiliar to religious, particularly monastic, systems. When one's life and work are fixed by external rules, freedom for inner exploration is gained; the process of surrender coincides with the dropping of the ego. It is perhaps for this reason that, as rules tightened, people tended to accept them (Thompson and Heelas 1986: 111–18; Fitzgerald 1986a: 88).

In retrospect, one of the most difficult impositions for Oregon sannyasins was the formation of an official Rajneeshee "religion." This occurred even though Rajneesh himself, while he was still publicly speaking in Pune, repeatedly and stridently critiqued organized religion. In typical style, he once proclaimed, "It will not be possible to make a dogma out of my words....Every institution is bound to be dead....I am destroying your ideologies, creeds, cults, dogmas, and I am not replacing them with anything else" (Fitzgerald 1986a: 91). Yet in December 1981 Sheela announced that "a new religion has been born called Rajneeshism. A Sannyasin can be called a Rajneeshee" (Gordon 1987: 24). With Rajneeshism came religious rules and rituals such as specified Sanskrit prayers to be chanted in unison at the beginning and end of each workday, performed while kneeling and facing the guru's house. In July 1983 a booklet entitled "Rajneeshism" was published, explaining the beliefs and practices of the religion, including descriptions of the four religious holidays to be observed annually and ceremonies to be performed on the occasions of birth, death, marriage, and caring for the sick. It designated three categories of minister and the number of years of training required to attain each rank.

The rationale for the creation of Rajneeshism in the face of Rajneesh's clear disdain for organized religion was based on the belief that a religion would inevitably arise from the movement and that it was better to help this process along when the Master was still alive and could provide guidance. Although a good number of sannyasins seemed to accept the new plan, many long-term followers expressed their disappointment. One man admitted that the practice seemed to him contradictory, since Rajneesh's central teachings, he felt, were about "blowing preconceptions. The idea of religion is disturbing to me. Those of us who came from religious backgrounds were disillusioned with religion and found freedom in a situation defined only by being with a religious master" (Fitzgerald 1986a: 91).

In response to escalating threats and harassment from outsiders, gears at Rancho Rajneesh switched on other fronts, as well. Expansionist aims began powering down as the community became increasingly insular. Rajneeshee leadership called for the formation of a police force, dubbed the Peace Force, to be stationed at the ranch.[17] As tensions mounted, the Peace Force extended its duties into the renamed city of Rajneesh, where, from the perspective of the locals, activities such as shining spotlights on homes and filming townspeople and their visitors for no apparent reason constituted harassment (Gordon 1987: 126; Fitzgerald 1986a: 65). By late 1983, proclamations purportedly originating from Rajneesh and delivered to sannyasins by Sheela became apocalyptic, anticipating nuclear annihilation and floods from which only Rajneeshee members would be spared. In early 1984 the AIDS scare provoked the formation of new rules restricting sexual practices and the prediction that the disease would cause mass destruction of which commune members would be the sole survivors (Gordon 1987: 131; Fitzgerald 1986b: 96). In October 1984 Rajneesh broke his silence, apparently hoping to stem the tide of negative press, and agreed to give televised interviews. When he began addressing his sannyasins publicly again in June 1985, this sense of embattlement nonetheless continued, visibly witnessed by the four sannyasins with Uzis that flanked him, along with additional guards positioned for further protection in the rafters (Fitzgerald 1986b: 104–6).

Gordon describes the eastern Oregon community in its final days:

> If the ranch and other communes were the womb of the new man, the Nietzschean Superman on whom the future of humanity depended, if Rajneesh was his midwife, then any and all measures to insure his and their survival and well-being were justified. The atmosphere of self-protectiveness and secrecy thickened each month. The demands for physical and ideological purity became even more intense. In time, the ranch became an armed camp with a siege mentality. (Gordon 1987: 132)

This separatist supremacy, decidedly divergent from the earlier expansionist designs more typical of settler colonizers, nonetheless maintained the us-them mentality intrinsic to the ways European settlers constructed— and united—themselves in opposition to aboriginal societies. Many sannyasins interviewed after things fell apart agreed that this divisive mentality was ultimately the downfall of the Oregon movement. As one woman put it, echoed by several others, "I hated this us-them syndrome that Sheela created. I never felt that all outsiders were hostile, and I felt that we were just driving people away" (Fitzgerald 1986b: 121; see also 122–25).

In September 1985 Sheela departed for Germany accompanied by a small group of devotees. Rajneesh blamed her for bad public behavior, for poisoning him and others, and for promulgating indoctrination, guns, and power in his name. He proclaimed the religion of Rajneeshism to be dead, instructing sannyasins to ritually burn the six thousand remaining copies of the Rajneeshism book and to stop wearing colored clothing. Antelope was given back its name, and houses in town were sold back to their former residents (Gordon 1987: 187; Thompson and Heelas 1986: 28–30). After Sheela's departure, Rajneesh admitted that Rajneeshpuram had become "a concentration camp" under her guidance. Egos ruled, power was grasped, hierarchies formed, and the positions with which people identified had become their prisons. All this and the paranoia and acquisition of guns were, according to Rajneesh, the result of egos reasserting themselves (Thompson and Heelas 1986: 114).

The question of blame loomed large as Rancho Rajneesh disassembled itself. Most blamed Sheela, others blamed the broader leadership including Rajneesh, and others saw the movement's demise in a more complicated light. I reserve my terrain-based analysis for later, concluding for now with the heartfelt explanation offered by the editor of the *Rajneesh Times* in the November 11, 1985, edition: "What we did here was basically impossible. We scraped together millions of dollars, slogged through the seasons of mud and dust, and worked so many hours that the days began to dissolve into one another. However, Bhagwan was not responsible for what we did. He had insisted endlessly that we are born alone, we live alone, and we die alone. WE are responsible for everything." Those not guilty of harassment and bad behavior, "who didn't do anything wrong," were "guilty of being too innocent. We watched and sometimes cooperated while Ma Anand Sheela and her fascist gang ran roughshod over our friends, us, and anyone else who got in their way." He concludes that there was, nevertheless, "real nourishment, love and ecstasy at Rajneeshpuram. Otherwise, no-one would have come and no-one would have stayed. Things which might have taken us lifetimes to get round to we experienced at supersonic speeds. Bhagwan is gone, but He is still in our hearts. I love Him more than ever, but less desperately" (quoted in Thompson and Heelas 1986: 130).

DIASPORIC HINDU SETTLEMENTS

In the midst of Rajneeshee settling and unsettling, mainstream diaspora Indian communities have been making their mark across the North American continent—sanctifying land, establishing wide-ranging pilgrimage networks, conferring South Asian names on rivers and mountains, and building impressive temple edifices. While these communities have met with significant resistance along the way, they also have received overriding societal support that seems to gather momentum as the decades roll by. Unlike the Rajneesh settlement, diasporic Hinduism appears to be in the process of establishing itself permanently into the very landscape of North America.

As Rajneesh himself remarked before embarking on his Oregonian adventures, Indian terrain is held to be sacred by many Hindus. Topographical features are often equated with divinity such that rivers are commonly liquid incarnations of goddesses—most famously, the River Ganges is considered to be the goddess Ganga. Mountains are often the abode or embodiment of divinity—the Himalayan Mt. Kailash is, most significantly, considered the embodiment of Lord Shiva. Countless other South Asian natural landmarks, known as *shakti pithas*, or "seats of the goddess," are scattered throughout the subcontinent and Sri Lanka. The sanctity of the entire Indian landmass itself is reflected in the (currently dwindling) concern among ultraorthodox Brahmans that travel to foreign shores will jeopardize one's high caste standing.[18]

Given this traditional conception of sacred land, the prospect of establishing Hindu sites of worship outside India presents a challenge. Diaspora communities have responded repeatedly to this challenge by enlivening and sanctifying New World temple terrain with Old World associations and superimpositions. For example, the Pittsburgh temple nestled in the Penn Hills, modeled after the south Indian Venkateswara temple in the Tiru Venkatam hills, celebrates the sanctity of the local landscape. It becomes, according to the Pittsburgh temple's visitors' pamphlet, "a piece of Tiru Venkatam in America." The pamphlet notes furthermore that the surrounding Pittsburgh area is sacred because of the presence of a *sangam*, or convergence of three rivers. The meeting of the nearby Allegheny and Monongahela and a subterranean river is reminiscent of India's sacred convergence of the Ganga, the Yamuna, and the underground Sarasvati (Narayanan 1992: 162).[19]

The most common superimposition of Old World sanctity onto New World terrain by Hindu diaspora communities is indeed the Indianization of rivers, most commonly as the Ganges, or Ganga, the banks of which are often referred to as Banaras, or Kashi, India's holiest city. For decades, water from the Ganga has been brought from India and ritually poured into, thus purifying, North American rivers, although many of these rivers are now becoming sacred in their own right. At the Rush temple outside Rochester, New York, devotees have renamed the nearby Railway Creek "Ganga," and on its banks, dubbed "Kashi," devotees honor the deity Shiva and perform regular rituals to his spherical representation or lingam (Figure 3.1).[20] Other examples of temples that reside near an American Ganga are those in Flint, Michigan, and Sebastian, Florida. In rural Pennsylvania the Vraj temple dedicated to Krishna resides next to a stream renamed the Yamuna (Eck 2001: 121–27).

The relabeling of land is another strategy used by diaspora communities, occurring ritually during the Sanskrit *sankalpam*, recited at the beginning of temple rituals, sanctifying the location, time, and intention of the rite. As traditionally recited, the *sankalpam* marks the ritual's location in relation to South Asian geography. The priest establishes a sacred connection to the earth by invoking Mt. Meru (also known as Kailash), set in the

Figure 3.1
Shrine dedicated to Shiva at the Rush Kashi, situated along the banks of the Ganga, also
known as Railway Creek.

Himalayas, and the land south of Meru, referring to the landmasses of
India and Sri Lanka. He then invokes a list of sacred rivers on the Indian
subcontinent that further identify and sanctify the land on which the
ritual is performed (Eck 2001: 127). When chanted in North America, the
sankalpam's wording rarely changes, seemingly situating the ritual on a
far-off subcontinent. This disconnect between ritually locating the event
on Indian terrain and its actual performance outside India appears to
imply diaspora resistance to the nonsacred New World or perhaps represents a kind of naming, claiming, and benediction of *terra nullius*, or empty
terrain, religiously speaking. Yet, as the following attests, matters are not
that simple.

Another means by which diaspora communities sanctify non-Indian terrain through Hindu resonances has to do with explicitly Hindu supernatural signs. It seems many temples in the United States (and nearly all in
India) are founded on encounters with divinity in natural formations such
as mountains or caves or in visions or dreams that instruct the recipient to
build a place of worship in a particular location. Vasudha Narayanan notes
that this process is particularly common in North American temples dedicated to Shiva. The LOTUS Temple in Yogaville, Virginia, destined to be

built overlooking a mountain redubbed Kailash, in honor of Shiva, arose in response to a vision received by its founder, Swami Satchidananda. The Iraivan/Kadavul temple in Kauai was built after Gurudeva, the temple's founder, received three visions of Shiva, who appeared to him seated and walking in the meadows near the Wailua River where the temple was later built (Narayanan 1992: 155–56; Eck 2001: 121).[21] Aiya, founder of the Rush temple, likewise reports that soon after purchasing the temple property he had meditational experiences in which the goddess asked him to install a trident, a symbol linked to Bhairava, a protector form of Shiva. The goddess specified that the trident be placed near a tree outside the temple's northeast corner—a logical location, since Bhairava traditionally holds forth in northeast regions of temples. After installing the trident, Aiya circumambulated the tree as ritually prescribed and noted an old yet unmistakably trident-shaped scar etched on its trunk. This mark confirmed for him that the property, although newly purchased, had long awaited the temple's religious associations and powers.[22]

In addition to sanctifying terrain through associations with Indian deities and landscapes, diasporic Hindu communities commonly acknowledge and, on occasion, appropriate indigenous layers of sanctity as well. Gurudeva, whose threefold vision of Shiva led him to build a temple on Kauai, acknowledges the contribution of Hawaiian sacred power to the site. The temple website quotes him as proclaiming that his visions "led me and my followers to the lovely Garden Island of Kauai, held the most sacred of all by the Hawaiian peoples long, long ago." This sanctified land rests alongside, as he described it, the "sacred Wailua River."[23]

An example of a partial appropriation of local sanctity emerges at the Wahiawa site, where Hindus recognize a Hawaiian healing stone known as Keanianileihuaokalani to also be a spherical representation of Shiva or a Shiva lingam. Although the stone's early history is murky, it seems that during the 1920s and 1930s the site drew a good many Hawaiian pilgrims in search of healing. After World War II the stone fell into disuse. It was rediscovered in 1988 by a group of Hindus whose Hawaiian friends brought them to see the six-foot-tall stone. The Hindu visitors recognized its resemblance to the Shiva lingam and, according to local literature, once Hindu priests performed rituals to the stone they recognized that "the place was indeed special, sacred, and holy" (quoted in Narayanan 1992: 156). After the Office of Hawaiian Affairs granted its approval, the lingam received regular official worship from members of the Hindu community. Over time, the congregating crowds grew and in 1996, the run-down cement walls that surrounded the stone were refurbished with white marble.

In 2005, a group of Hawaiians interested in preserving and reviving traditional healing practices expressed concerns that the marble shelter built by the Hindu community prevented their healing stone from getting necessary nourishment from the rain. After initial suspicions that the sacred stone was being mistreated, a small contingent of concerned Hawaiians attended a Hindu ritual to see for themselves. Once convinced that the stone was being treated respectfully, productive dialogue began between Hawaiian traditionalists and local Hindus. Dr. S. Ramanathan, past president of LOTUS, the society that has organized Hindu worship at the site since 1988, expressed to reporters what he felt was a general lack of conflicted interest and an overall Hindu openness to Hawaiian perspectives. Stating that Hindus believed the stone to be a Hawaiian god, but that, for Hindus, it is also Shiva, he added, "We don't own that place; we don't claim it. We are just one of the worshippers" (Viotti 2005; see also Adamski 2005; UPI 2005).[24]

Another example of a North American Hindu sacred site that coincides with and is bolstered by a Native American system stems from Aiya's reported visions at a prior place of worship in upstate New York. During a period when his temple practices were conducted in his one-and-a-half-car garage in a Rochester suburb, Aiya regularly received visions of a Native American woman who simply stood in silence and smiled at him. After repeated sightings, Aiya decided to enquire with the curator and local authority on Native American traditions at a Rochester museum. He described for him her clothing and, at his request, sketched her beadwork. From this they ascertained that the woman was an Iroquois medicine woman. When I asked Aiya how he interpreted these apparitions, he said he felt she was buried in the land beneath his house and appeared to him because she was pleased with their form of worship. He, in return, seemed encouraged by her endorsement.

Similar to the Hindu community in Hawaii who discovered the power of the healing stone after performing rituals to it, Aiya feels that temple rituals have given further vitality to the Rush property that was clearly, in his view, already sacred. During a conversation we had in January 2007, he mentioned that the temple land is layered with sacred resonances. He noted that its creeks and banks have been named after holy sites in India, and the discovery of the trident affirmed that the property was divinely primed for the temple's arrival. As he sees it, this sanctified land becomes all the more sacred through the performance of temple rituals: "Now, all these can be rolled into one thing because when you perform the rituals, the belief is that the place becomes even more vital. Because it has certain [sacred] locations already in the property, those places especially become even more vibrantly spiritual with the infusion of mantric powers."[25]

Another layer of sanctity embedded in Rush temple property involves the natural contours of the land itself according to ancient *vastu* prescription. As Aiya described it,

> *vastu* has to do with the land that slopes to the northeast. And in the northeast is a stream—Railway Creek, it's called. It runs from north to south. And two miles from the property it circles and joins up with the river that flows from south to the north. And the river is in the correct location—it's on the west side of the property near the northern border. So when this river joins that one and as the river flows up north, if you put an axis at the center of the temple you'll find that the temple is rotating with the water. There is a rotation of the water around the temple in a clockwise direction. That's called *varuna pradiksha*. And that's considered to be extremely auspicious. So that is one of the reasons why this property was chosen.

Varuna pradiksha indeed makes the site ideal for worship, yet unlike the renaming of rivers and supernaturally branded trees, the land's natural contours have nothing to do with South Asian topography or divinity. As such, Aiya was careful to point out that the *varuna pradiksha* would enhance any religious practices performed on it: "No matter if it is Hindu or whether it is Christian or whether it is Buddhist, it doesn't matter." Emphasizing the intrinsic sanctity of land itself, consistent with his Tantric tradition that imbues the physical world with the sacred, Aiya added, "Every piece of land is sacred. Land is what we depend on for our water, for our food. And if we pollute it and we spoil it, we will be in trouble." He brought home the point by referencing the apple trees that temple members continue to nurture even though they have no need of such a large harvest:

> We don't want to see them cut down and thrown out. And even other trees that are here, that we might not use in our lifetime, perhaps in a thousand or one hundred years from now somebody might decide to take that tree and use it for something. But I don't believe we have a right to destroy something that has been here long before we came—just because it's convenient.

A slowly growing practice among diaspora temples, also in seeming acknowledgment of the intrinsic sanctity of the North American landscape, is the departure from the traditionally worded *sankalpam*, one that inserts nearby topographical features to locate and sanctify the ritual. Rather than superimposing features from the Indian subcontinent, the Rush *sankalpam* first invokes, in Sanskrit, the North American continent, situating it north of Mt. Meru. The town of Rush is specified next, located near the holy river Genessee. Finally the sanctum of the Rush temple is invoked as the site where the ritual is to be performed. Aiya has been chanting a local *sankalpan* from the time he started leading rituals in the United States in the early 1980s; he takes pride in the fact that it seems he was, with the encouragement of his guru, one of the first in the United States to do so.

A final layer of sanctity that the Rush temple gleans from its North American environs is entirely unhinged from Hindu landmarks, divinities, practices, ancient prescriptions, or prayers. It has to do with the fact that the upstate New York region in which Rush is situated was the geographical hub of the Second Great Awakening, an early- to mid-nineteenth-century phenomenon in which egalitarian and experimental religious groups flourished, often led by charismatic preachers without seminary training, some of whom were women. I once noted for Aiya the striking ideological similarities between his unconventional temple—inviting all, regardless of gender, caste, or ethnicity, to perform temple rituals—and the fiery religious movements that gave the region its nickname, "The Burned-Over District." Tickled by the ideological and historical convergences, he nodded and announced, "See? History is repeating itself!"

HIDING HETEROTOPIAS

The Rajneesh and Hindu diaspora communities are religious settlements, one fleeting and the other established, that create and imbue terrain with sacred meaning and power in somewhat similar ways. Both communities confidently made their mark on the North American landscape based on a sense of spiritual entitlement to new terrain. The differences between them, reflected in the ways they engage with neighboring communities, is founded on disparate terrain-embedded ideologies—one that is utopian, forcing abstracted uniformity on unwilling landscapes, and the other heterotopian, admitting to realities consisting of multilayered, multi-inhabited locales.

A number of theorists have noted the importance of space and spatial ideologies as a contemporary means of establishing and expressing ideals and identities. Fredric Jameson's "Utopianism after the End of Utopia" describes a shift from temporality to spatialization that, as he sees it, reflects movement from the modern to the postmodern era and signals the end of revolutionary ideologies promoting a singular Utopia. Jameson observes that since the 1960s we have seen "the development of a whole range of

properly spatial utopias in which the transformation of social arrangements and political institutions is projected onto the vision of place and
landscape, including the human body" (1991: 159–60). Cultural geogra-
pher Gareth Griffiths asserts that grand abstractions like nation and nationalism appear to be giving way to older and less easily subverted
grassroots conceptions of cultural identity based on immediate, material
formations. The ability to assert agency and political power in postcolonial
space, hinging on the recovery of a sense of the immediate and the material, furthermore involves a reconnection with older spiritual categories:
"Paradoxically, renewal of the sense of the sacred is tied into a recovery of
the importance of physical land—in a cultural geography that mixes the
categories of the material and the spiritual" (Griffiths 2001: 445).

Foucault, responsible for the term "heterotopia," likewise suggests that
"the anxiety of our era" is fundamentally concerned with space, no longer
with time, and that existing spatial oppositions such as private/public,
family/social, and leisure/work "are still nurtured by the hidden presence
of the sacred" (1986: 23).[26] Foucault asserts that Utopias are sites with no
real place; they propose a society that is perfected or turned upside down
but is fundamentally unreal. Heterotopias, on the other hand, "are formed
in the very founding of society.... They are something like countersites, a
kind of effectively acted utopia in which the real sites, all the other real
sites that can be found within culture, are simultaneously represented,
contested, and inverted" (1986: 24). Ralph Pordzik similarly describes heterotopias as multidimensional spatial Utopias that "are not mimetic texts
embedded in a flow of congruously and purposefully related events directed
towards a logical conclusion, but create themselves a fabric of spatial relations between various discourses, narratives, and points of view sustained
by an endless process of differentiation." Pordzik identifies heterotopian
spaces as quintessentially postmodern, arising from a postcolonial condition that defies the "strictly hierarchical closed-system model that usually
informs our notion of the static uniformity of utopian or dystopian
societies" (2001: 5).

For scholars of religion, Foucault's heterotopia supports the view that
sacred sites inevitably bear layers of significance that, more often than not,
represent incongruity. As posited by Philip Sheldrake, the investigation of
place "progressively reveals new meanings in a kind of conversation between topography, memory, and the presence of a particular people at a
given moment" (2001: 17). Following Foucault, Sheldrake invokes heterotopia to describe a single space that juxtaposes several "spaces" that are
normally incompatible and have "the capacity to question, transgress, and
undermine the alleged coherence of self-contained systems," whereas

Utopia is an imaginary space built on human dreams and hopes (2001: 100–101).[27] Chidester and Linenthal likewise recall heterotopia in their classification of ways communities have claimed land as sacred. Those that manage to avoid domination over prior inhabitants, particularly through the strategy of hybridization, mix and fuse orientations, produce new places, reclaim old ones, and suggest the possibility of altering the terms of the system itself. Hybridization produces heterotopias that are actual sites involving spatial relations; by contrast, uniform Utopia is no place (Chidester and Linenthal 1995: 19).[28]

Strategies for claiming land that lead to domination are, as Chidester and Linenthal describe them, appropriation and exclusion. Since no appropriation is ever complete and no exclusion final, struggles for domination over sacred space tend to be ongoing. Some of the most dramatic examples of continuing struggles over sacred terrain emerge from European settlers' disregard for relationships with landscapes that offered prior inhabitants vital proximity to and identification with the sacred. Subsequent desacralization and desecration of land reflected settlers' inability to recognize alternative orientations to the landscape.[29] Combined with grand rhetoric that expounded demographic revival, geopolitical expansion, national recovery, or racial consolidation, this settler approach, dislodging sacred significance from the landscape, was nothing if not utopian (Elkins and Pedderson 2005: 22).

As to be expected, we find significant exceptions to the above-described proposition that postcolonial societies tend to favor materially invested, variegated heterotopias rather than abstracted monolithic Utopias—suggesting, perhaps, colonial attitudes in a postcolonial world. Bron Taylor describes what he refers to as an ongoing American religious nationalism that envisions America as a utopian space, one that provides a model and a means for achieving God's purpose on earth. Taylor suggests that this religious nationalism is naturally hostile to competing worldviews that either deny the premise that America constitutes a sacred entity or locate America's sanctity in the landscape itself rather than in the U.S. nation-state. Taylor's "archetypal example" of conflict over American postsettler sacred space is the controversy over the building of a giant telescope on Mt. Graham in Arizona. The presence of the telescope, promoted by the University of Arizona and the Vatican, desecrates a mountain that is sacred and foundational to Apache identity. Demonstrating this ideological divide was a Vatican spokesman's misguided attempt to breach it by insisting that the telescope would enhance the mountain's sanctity, since space is where divine mysteries are revealed. As Taylor notes, the spokesman's understanding of God's accessibility outside the biosphere clearly runs counter to the Apache notion of sacred landscape (Taylor 1995: 99, 119, 124–25).

Returning to this chapter's comparison of settler communities, it is clear that Hindu diaspora temples have established claims to sacred land in ways that tend to avoid domination. Their approach, incorporating particular landscapes and topographical features both far and near, past and present, allows sacred terrain to contain multiple meanings and histories, reflecting heterotopian rather than utopian orientations. Like settler colonizers, diasporic Hindu communities navigate between the universalizing Indian "metrapole" and New World particularities when they superimpose rivers like the Ganga or mountains such as Kailash, resonating with pan-Indian sacrality, on diaspora terrain. This pattern of foreign superimposition becomes less remarkable, however, when we note how the same process of sacred duplication is also enacted endlessly throughout the Indian subcontinent.[30] Furthermore, when diaspora temples enfold local religious meanings—Christian, native, and generically spiritual—into their pan-Indian earthly associations, they bypass the monolithic abstracted approach typical of colonialization. This propensity to layer meaning, weaving universal Hindu themes into local ones, both Hindu and American, unhinges universalizing tendencies associated with domination.

It also appears, somewhat ironically, that this localizing heterotopian process of sanctifying earth does not minimize the sacred relevance and power of superimposed pan-Hindu features but, by ensuring the success of Hindu diaspora settlements on a faraway continent, these features enable the continuing significance and power of pan-Indian sacrality as well. This point that localization and hybridization—and resultant heterotopias— help diaspora temples preserve links to pan-Indian religiosity, boosting rather than diminishing their relevance, is strengthened when one compares them with the Rajneesh's failed Oregon experiment.

At the outset, the Rajneeshee community may not have seemed particularly destined for its decline into settler invasion, as their religious vision was entirely heterodox, an eclectic mix of psychological and sexual therapies integrated into a range of religious philosophies and practices. Rajneesh's disagreement with absolutism seems in fact to have been one of the few teachings he sustained throughout his career. The process of renaming the Big Muddy and conferring labels of religious significance upon Rancho Rajneesh's orchard groves, bodies of water, and buildings was not altogether different from the renaming and naming of rivers and mountains by mainstream Hindu diaspora communities. Although the souring of the Rajneesh movement is most commonly, and perhaps rightly, attributed to Sheela's increasing megalomania and paranoia, I submit a more structurally engaged explanation, placing responsibility on a utopian vision that, over time and facing significant odds, allowed little or no room for competing discourses of any kind—spatial, ideological, embodied, or otherwise.

Most obviously and spatially speaking, the Rajneeshee renaming of cities, streets, and businesses outside Rancho Rajneesh reflected a strategy of exclusion and eventual negation of prior connections to the land. In comparison with more conventional temple communities, which typically recognize that the bestowal of religiously meaningful names on rivers and mountains does not replace earlier names but adds layers of significance to them, Rajneeshee renaming involved an erasure that reflected a need not just for bolstering sacred access and identity but for conquest. Amid this naming and renaming, Rajneeshee constructions of the sacred reflect what Bron Taylor described as American nationalist utopian space—as a prized entity with no actual physical coordinates. The Rajneeshee "Buddhafield," described by devotees as an enlivening and healing energy field, was initially envisioned as a universalized, abstracted "space" rather than a concrete, potentially localized "place." Although the Rajneeshee community intended for Rancho Rajneesh to geographically contain this abstraction, to provide a real place for cultivating an idealized humanity and identity, the ranch's inability to accommodate coinciding alternative spatial realities resulted in its eventual devolution into utopian, impossible "no space."[31]

While Rajneeshee spiritual philosophies may have accommodated and melded Asian and alternative European and American approaches, proponents of this heterodox mix deliberately—and sometimes violently—strove to block ideological influences encountered in adjacent eastern Oregon communities. Sanitized and abstracted, the Buddhafield aimed to protect itself from local infiltration. Fortifying this shield against local influences—and supporting the audacity required for harassing locals, culminating in Sheela's alleged attempt to carry out a mass salmonella poisoning before a county election—were, it seems, clear-cut us/them distinctions. Like settler colonizers before them, Rajneeshees constructed their identity in opposition to the natives—and vice versa (Wolfe 1999: 179). They understood their state of spiritual enlightenment to be the inverse of their ignorant redneck neighbors who threatened to violate their Utopia.

Postcolonial hindsight allows us to view how imperial absolutes are mere illusions propped up with significant, often violent, effort. In other words, utopian claims invariably hide heterotopian realities. An instance when actual Rajneeshee heterotopia—an amalgam of clashing, contradictory discourses—presented itself in full discordant view was during a physical face-off in 1983 along a stretch of road in the town of Madras (purportedly named after the textile, not the Indian city, and pronounced MA-dras). The event centered on Rajneesh's daily drives in one of his Rolls Royces, escorted by a jeep carrying armed disciples. This procession proceeded in exactly the same way every afternoon, departing Rajneesh's living quarters at two o'clock sharp, meandering along devotee-lined ranch roads to offer sannyasins their daily *darshan* of their guru, and continuing onto open highway and into the town of Madras seventy miles away. The final destination was always a local Madras supermarket, where a young woman accompanying Rajneesh would go into the store and buy him a soda. Then the convoy would head home the same way it came.

Reverend Mardo Jimenez of the Conservative Baptist Church in Madras, after viewing the procession from his office window for over a year, decided to take action and stage a demonstration. His protests were small at first, with Jimenez alone, standing on a car, a Bible raised in one hand and a large American flag in the other. Numerous parishioners, townspeople, and truckers eventually joined him on his side of the road, holding banners reading, "INS Save Madras" and "Jesus Is Lord," shouting epithets such as "Bhagwan Out of Madras!" and "Repent Your Sins!" and "America Will Be Free!" (Fitzgerald 1986a: 46). To counter, sannyasins started arriving in busses ahead of their guru and, forming a semicircle across the street from the protesters, sang Christmas carols to drown out the din. Before the police broke up the daily demonstrations, the Rajneeshee contingent had swelled to four busloads.

This roadside standoff is not only a stark demonstration of clashing and conflicting ideologies but is also shot through with internal contradictions and ironies that further invigorate the picture. At the center of the collision is an Indian guru who prescribes communal living and hard work for no pay for his white devotees. A vocal critic of imperialism, he drives the ultimate opulent symbol of the British empire. The sannyasins, in an effort to drown out Christian antagonism, choose Christian carols to do so. The Reverend Jimenez, staking his privileged claim to local if not national (to wit, his flag-waving) territory, protesting the invasion of outsiders, is Honduran by birth and gained American citizenship just the year before. All this, in the city of Madras, Oregon. Consistent with Ralph Pordzic's description of het-erotopias in literature, this scene, when viewed with physical and temporal distance, "thwarts all efforts . . . to create a coherent illusion of history, mean-ing and representation in the text. In the de-totalizing and de-temporalizing space it creates, dissent and discontinuity dictate the course of action" (2001: 5).

Perhaps the ultimate irony, not visible to the bystander but steering the event itself, is that Rajneesh, while he was still giving speeches, predicted that us/them ideologies used by imperialists throughout history would eventually destroy the world. Yet the utopian cure his Oregonian movement proposed for keeping that world at bay involved precisely the same, ultimately destructive, dichotomies.

It is instructive to note that settler dichotomies had little to do with Rajneesh's core teachings and lasting legacies but, rather, seem to have been tied to and died along with the Oregon experiment itself, which ended rather suddenly in 1985. The finale, beginning with Sheela's arrest for attempted murder through mass poisoning, ended with Rajneesh's brief imprisonment for immigration fraud and eventual return to Pune, India, in 1986.[32] In India, Rajneesh continued his role as religious leader until his death in 1990. In 1989 he changed his name to Osho, and, as Osho, his influence continues to live on through dozens of books published in his name and in workshops that impart his eclectic philosophies and meditation practices—all of which are increasingly, enthusiastically, received across the globe. Promoted by Osho International, which is uninterested in grand schemes for acquiring and settling land, Rajneesh's legacy has managed against considerable odds to rise above earlier controversies and, indeed, has never has been healthier.

FORGETFUL NATION

I conclude with a brief look at the other side of the settler dynamic, at the so-called natives of Antelope and Rush who felt their terrain had been encroached upon and desacralized by its newly arrived occupants. In Antelope, this registers clearly enough in the signs and slogans of the roadside demonstrators and in the local residents' anger, which escalated over the years and threatened the Rajneesh community in a variety of ways.[33] Adding another, colorful layer of local identity and entitlement is the fact that the Big Muddy Ranch also happens to be the site where a number of John Wayne Westerns were filmed. The Rajneeshee takeover of this piece of land thus could represent, for some Antelope residents, a type of desacralization that added insult to injury. As noted by religion scholars, certain national sites in the United States are "saturated with a distinctive kind of patriotic sacrality" that encourage the myth of national unity (Chidester and Linenthal 1995: 21). It seems few national icons more enthusiastically celebrate this myth of national unity and the associated westward and global march of the American frontier than John Wayne.

After the rather sudden evacuation of the Rajneesh community in 1985, the Big Muddy Ranch regained its name and returned to its previously dormant state. In 1992 a millionaire industrialist from Montana named Dennis Washington bought the property, hoping to convert the ranch into an educational center. But when petitioning to change the zoning laws so he could use and improve on the buildings on the property, he found that the locals, still reverberating from the Rajneesh "invasion," preferred to let the land and its amenities revert to tumbleweeds. For several years Washington used the property for cattle grazing and eventually tried, un-successfully, to sell it. He subsequently attempted to give the property away for free, yet memories of Sheela's poisonings created rumors, all unsub-stantiated, that stockpiled toxins had tainted the groundwater. In 1997 a Christian organization called Young Life finally accepted Washington's donation and, after assuring locals that they were not extremists, were granted permits to renovate the ranch buildings in order to run summer camps for teens.

In 1999, Big Muddy Ranch thus became Wildhorse Canyon Camp. Jay McAlonen, property manager for Young Life, expressed his determination that the camp be run in a way that would "help heal" a still shell-shocked community. Reflecting the understanding that the land was to be used for a sacred purpose at odds with an earlier spiritual community, McAlonen spoke of the need to cleanse the property and its buildings through prayer. As he put it, "We believe that there was a real presence of the enemy on the property. I'm not a person that normally has this type of discernment, but you would go into [Rajneesh's] house and it just plain gave you the creeps" (Moor 1999: 22; see also Egan 1995: 14; Rattlesnake-Heaven 1992).

The fact that Antelope residents took over a decade to accept a new group of settlers at the Big Muddy Ranch seems perfectly understandable. As Euroamerican descendants of settlers and immigrants, Antelopians cannot exactly claim native status—yet this should not minimize the re-percussions of being harassed, politically overthrown, displaced, and nearly poisoned by a group they regarded as invaders. The Rajneeshee invading presence—and, more importantly, Antelopian resistance—will likely never be forgotten; it is formative to Antelope history and identity. Memorialized and framed as such, a plaque sitting at the base of the Antelope post office flagpole reads: "Dedicated to those of this community who through the Rajneesh invasion and occupation of 1981–85 remained, resisted, and re-membered" (Duin 1999).[34]

In Rush, New York, town council members and select residents—all Euroamerican—resisted the arrival of a Hindu place of worship. In a move familiar to the Rajneesh story, they managed, at least initially, to block a public uses permit that would allow for construction of a building designed for public access. This obstruction was attempted even though a few years earlier, one block away, a church had been granted permission for the same permit. This anticipation of foreign invasion in reaction to newly settled Hindu temples, based on fear rather than fact, is not unique to Rush; it has occurred in other parts of the country as well.[35] Local resistance to the Rush temple may have been partially cultural, but most of the antagonisms experienced by temple members have been expressly religious in tone. At the temple's inception, a few conservative Christians in the neighborhood simply were—and still are—afraid of what non-Christians might do to the neighborhood. An elderly woman who lives across the street from the temple is the daughter of the farmer who once cultivated the sixty-four acres of land that is now temple property. As an evangelical Christian, she represents local religious resistance most poignantly. To compensate for her complicated loss, she and her sister used to place fire-and-brimstone pamphlets under car windshield wipers during temple festivals and, in a couple instances, stood at the end of the temple driveway to disperse literature to exiting temple members.[36]

Rush residents' anticipation of settler invasion where there is none represents a variation on a xenophobic theme prevalent in the United States from the time of European settlement to the present. Aiya, cognizant of suspicions currently aimed at Middle Eastern and South Asian immigrants, heightened after 9/11, has managed to earn numerous friends, alliances, and even admirers in his neighborhood. Well aware of those who continue to keep their distance, he chalks it up to fear of the unknown. In his typical dramatic style, Aiya painted a vivid picture of this culturally laden trepidation:

> I've heard sentiments like, "Oh, this place is going to become like a trailer park." [They believe] people are going to be hanging around, half-naked brown kids are going to be running around all over the place, and it's going to depress the property values. And these people are going to be singing their native songs and screaming their heads off—and drumming and doing all these things. That's what the fear is about.

Despite the xenophobic refrain ringing through the centuries—acted on by settler practices such as the displacement and extermination of Native Americans, the importation and exploitation of African slaves, and the subjugation of newly arrived immigrant groups—U.S. nationhood manages to found itself on a myth of welcome.[37] As historian Ali Behdad explains, this myth defines U.S. immigration as a form of national hospitality, a reinvention that requires a certain historical amnesia about the economics of immigration, a forgetfulness that "the nation's open-door immigration was born of a colonialist will to power and a capitalist desire for economic expansion" (2005: 3). To be fair, forgetfulness is pivotal to the foundation of any nation, and the United States is no exception. Histories of nation are necessarily triumphant narratives—much like John Wayne Westerns— that repress the brutality through which nationhood is achieved.

This negation of competing discourses, fundamental to colonizing and nation building, recalls the settler utopianism—and its many hidden ironies and contradictions—upheld by the Oregonian Rajneeshees. Not only did the Rajneesh settlers disregard the competing needs and land rights of local "natives"; their benign myth of origins, rife with euphemisms, also masked their exploitative intent (Wolfe 1999: 29). The Share-a-Home project that bused in homeless men from around the country was motivated less by philanthropic concern for the poor than by an ongoing battle for zoning rights. The organization dubbed the Peace Force who patrolled Rancho Rajneesh's grounds were heavily armed and often troublesome to the residents of Antelope. Most fundamentally, Rajneeshee sannyasins' harassment of locals was construed as "therapy," purportedly holding up a "mirror" enabling townspeople to see themselves as the angry racists that they really were.

As mentioned at the outset of this chapter, an analysis of sacred space in postsettler United States should attend not only to how space has been ritualized and interpreted, but also to how it has been appropriated, contested, and "stolen back and forth in struggles over power" (Chidester and Linenthal 1995: 16). A comparative archaeology of Hindu diasporic and Rajneeshee strategies for making and staking sacred terrain, exploring scenarios in which this ongoing back-and-forth takes place, uncovers vastly different relationships to land and to co-inhabitants that, in turn, are supported by religious frameworks used for very different purposes. Most simply put, the multilayered sacred terrain acknowledged by Hindu diasporic temple communities is built on a South Asian propensity for religious duplication, bolstered by a religious pluralism commonly espoused by members of mainstream diasporic Hinduism. This pluralism, lending itself to benign relations with coexisting religious and secular realities, also no doubt reflects a certain practicality among South Asian immigrants, one that ensures that religious transplants be accepted, not rejected, by foreign hosts.[38] It seems no better stage could be set for postcolonial heterotopia than a religious tradition that lends itself to duplication, possessed by pluralistic leanings, bolstered by political realism, and reliant on sanctified terrain for its existence. Although the Oregon Rajneeshee community's religious worldview was indeed eclectic, this apparently was not enough to prevent them from resorting to a rhetoric of exclusivity; their performance of agricultural miracles on the arid eastern Oregon landscape did not preclude them from an abstracted, unrealistically shallow engagement with the surrounding land and its inhabitants. The Rajneeshee settlement, an excellent example of what eventually became a utopian "no place," may have been better suited for a bygone colonial era or, more accurately, for colonial might that can afford to violently excavate heterotopian realities and their sacred artifacts without the risk of being run out of town.

Interestingly, Foucault's seminal essay on heterotopia ends not with an earthbound metaphor, but with a waterbound one. Here he envisions heterotopia par excellence as a ship, a concrete place encapsulating and floating between serial histories and destinies. Foucault contends that, without heterotopian ships, we're sunk. Describing a scenario that sounds very much like the demise of the eastern Oregon settlement, he warns, "In civilizations without boats, dreams dry up, espionage takes the place of adventure, and the police take the place of pirates" (27). My guess is that Rajneesh, if given the chance to reflect on this, would have to agree.

CHAPTER 4

✧

Embodying the Extraordinary in Iceland and India

The Difference Spirits Make

Switching our focus from earthly terrain to human bodies, we now consider the sanctification of a different type of materiality. We leave behind religious traditions that made their marks on the same North American continent and juxtapose here Neo-Vedanta in India and Spiritualism in Iceland.[1] Although perched on nearly opposite corners of our planet, intersecting roots and routes ultimately position these far-flung traditions on the same side of the ideological fence.

Planting Neo-Vedanta and Spiritualism most sturdily in ideological proximity is the fact that both traditions arose in response to a late-nineteenth-century scientific revolution that appeared, to many, to pose a threat to religion. Rather than competing with science, viewing it as the enemy or disavowing the "supernatural" altogether, these traditions bridged the science/religion gap by adopting scientific method to explain and validate their practices and beliefs—most particularly, to explain and validate extraordinary human abilities shared by both traditions. I cautiously refer to these heightened abilities—claimed capacities to predict the future, to read the hearts, minds, and past lives of others, and to heal—as "extraordinary" precisely because Neo-Vedantans and Spiritualists see them as scientifically verifiable and thus not as supernatural. Such phenomena suggest, instead, expanded conceptions of the natural world that are supported and verified, in turn, by the principles and practices of these traditions. Because these abilities augment ordinary existence, infusing it with power and meaning authenticated by established spiritual systems, practitioners understand such capacities—despite their scientific measurability—as tapping into sources appropriately conceived of as sacred. This chapter thus describes, from yet another angle, ways in which sacred efficacy is inextricably bound to, and in many ways reliant on, the earthly realm.

These extraordinary abilities, known as *siddhis* by Neo-Vedantans and *skyggnigáfa* by Icelandic Spiritualists, ground the sacred through similar dissolutions of the science/religion divide, blurring perceived supernatural and natural, material and spiritual, realms. Yet explanations as to *why* and *how* these abilities exist could not be more at odds. Most fundamentally, Neo-Vedanta typically upholds *siddhis* as hard-won evidence of a practitioner's discipline and dedication, while Icelandic Spiritualism understands *skyggnigáfa* as emerging unwittingly from an inborn—and often undesired—openness and access to the spirit world.

Rooted in the human abilities each tradition promotes, we thus discover drastically disparate cosmologies—one that takes for granted productive spirit interactions, and another that decidedly does not. Different ethical expectations moreover emerge when the insistent participation of spirits within Spiritualism draws practitioners into relationships bound by mutual need and assistance that run between earthly and spirit realms. Icelandic Spiritualists operate not only within an augmented empirical world, as do Neo-Vedantans, but within an expanded community of care that creates, at times, a heightened calling for those with extraordinary abilities to bridge ordinarily perceived gaps.

Icelandic Spiritualism and Indian Neo-Vedanta, founded on layers of similarity—on parallel histories and epistemologies that have nurtured similar philosophies, abilities, and goals—cultivate, in the end, different expectations for human practitioners due to drastically different bodily encounters with the sacred. The uncompromising presence—and absence—of spirits, framed by extraordinary abilities and experiences, invites us, as I see it, to reverse our analytical lens. Rather than speculating further on the societal and historical forces that have engendered these religious experiences and practices, this chapter finishes by considering how bodily engagements with the sacred are forces of influence in themselves. By comparing their impact on practitioners, we discover the roles they play in leading otherwise similar traditions into different conceptual and ethical directions. This final chapter thus explores not only how different religious traditions form and reform qualities and varieties of the earthbound sacred but, more basically, how experiences of material sacrality steer and form traditions themselves.

SETTING THE STAGE: SPIRITUALISM, THEOSOPHY, AND NEO-VEDANTA

Although the experiential differences between Neo-Vedanta and Icelandic Spiritualism can be traced to older indigenous traditions,[2] the movements themselves are thoroughly modern. They emerged during an era of heightened global interaction between India, Britain, and the United States in which Hindu reformers and Spiritualists frequently exchanged ideas and arguments with Theosophists, Christian missionaries, and scholars of religion.[3] Through print media as well as in public lecture forums, these groups were not only intimately aware of one another's ideas; their views—in response to shared scientific, religious, and political upheaval—were often refuted and transformed in the process (Kent 2010).[4] In this section's exploration of conversations and connections between Spiritualism and Neo-Vedanta (from which modern yoga springs), I set the stage for a subsequent comparison of philosophies and understandings of extraordinary abilities. I include Theosophy, too, as an important bridge between the two traditions. Historically rooted in Spiritualism, it shares many features with Neo-Vedanta and emerges from similar political and philosophical contexts and concerns. Theosophy has further relevance when we consider its direct and lasting influence on Icelandic Spiritualism, contributing to its remarkable resilience and setting it apart from British and American Spiritualisms.

Spiritualism in the United States and Britain

The birth of Spiritualism is typically dated at 1848, credited to the Hydesville, New York, Fox sisters, although some trace its origins to the mystical writings of Emanuel Swedenborg a century earlier.[5] Nonetheless, the Fox sisters' purported communication with spirits provoked an unprecedented Spiritualist boom, likely due to the religious rebuttal it offered to scientific advancements of the time. Many thousands chose to affiliate with Spiritualism because, for them, the tradition did not rely on blind faith; rather, thanks to mediums who claimed contact with the spirit world, it demonstrated and proved certain religious beliefs, particularly the existence of life after death.

Early Spiritualism's appeal to the modern masses was bolstered through its impressive membership roster, which included well-known writers, intellectuals, and scientists. The most famous Spiritualist scientist was Alfred Russel Wallace, known for his role in developing the theory of evolution. Convinced that the spirit world displayed natural forces that were empirically measurable and provable, Wallace argued that seemingly supernatural phenomena simply demonstrated our current ignorance of nature's laws. In *Miracles and Modern Spiritualism*, he writes,

> Many phenomena of the simplest kind would appear supernatural to men having limited knowledge. Ice and snow might easily be made to appear so to inhabitants of the tropics....A century ago, a telegram from three-thousand mile's distance or a photograph taken in a fraction of a second, would not have been believed possible, and would not have been credited on any testimony except by the ignorant and superstitious who believe in miracles. (Wallace [1896] 1975: 39)[6]

Other prominent Spiritualist scientists include Sir William Barrett, founder in 1881 of England's Society for Psychical Research, of which a sister society in the United States was established in 1885. Both societies were built on the premise that Spiritualism represented yet another break-through in modern science and were dedicated to determining empirically the authenticity of spirit phenomena (Swatos 1990).

Within a decade of the Fox sisters' rise to fame came an avalanche of Spiritualists in the United States and Britain who claimed mediumistic powers. Shortly afterward, many mediums in pursuit of fame and fortune were exposed as frauds. Those dedicated to uncovering fraudulence in-cluded psychical researchers, many of whom strove to weed out the charla-tans from those they believed were authentic (Hess 1993: 18).[7] In the wake of numerous public unmaskings in the late nineteenth century, Spiritualism eventually shrank into relative obscurity in both England and the United States, with the exception of a brief resurgence during and after World War I.[8] William Swatos, a sociologist who studies Spiritualism in Iceland, argues that the tradition floundered in the United States and Britain despite its tremendous initial appeal due to an overreliance on scientific method that neglected religious themes. As Swatos sees it, the "negative logic of scien-tific truth-testing" could not sustain a religious movement without the "positive affirmations of faith in the unseen." The scientific proof that ini-tially gave Spiritualism its electric appeal thus seems to have ultimately precipitated its downfall (Swatos 1990: 476; see also Barrow 1986).[9]

Part of the reason British Spiritualists tended to steer clear of estab-lished religion is that many ascribed to an anti-Christian secularism linked to anticolonial politics. This anti-Christian anticolonialism, emerging among the British working class during the latter half of the nineteenth century, was in response to the failed promises of imperialism, prompted by the Indian mutiny of 1857 and news of subsequent atrocities performed by both Indian subjects and Christian missionaries in India (van der Veer 2001: 59–68).[10] Detailed below, Icelandic Spiritualism's homegrown anti-imperialism, tied to its own independence movement, had the opposite effect, strengthening its ties to the state Church and ensuring that Icelandic Spiritualism was not cut loose—at least initially—from formal religious validation.

Theosophy

Helen Blavatsky and Henry Olcott, founders of the Theosophical Society, met in New York in 1875 when both planned to deepen their involvement with Spiritualism. Blavatsky saw in Spiritualism the potential for combating the present-day threat of scientific materialism and for furthering her fascination with occultism. Blavatsky's occult interests initially focused on ancient mystical traditions that included early Christianity, but her writings soon shifted to include anti-Christian polemics that compared modern Christianity unfavorably to Hinduism and Buddhism. From late 1875 on, Blavatsky identified herself solely with Asian traditions, eventually proposing that Western ignorance be replaced with Eastern wisdom (Goodrick-Clarke 2007: 5–6; Pearson 2006: 25). Olcott and Blavatsky both contrasted the mystical East with the inept rationalism of Western science, arguing that while the latter debunked Oriental mysteries as superstition and accused holy adepts of fraudulence, these holy "frauds" were proof that ancient knowledge could unlock truths Western positivism could not (Goodrick-Clarke 2007: 14).

This praise of a richer, wiser mystical East, one of the founding ideologies of Theosophy, echoes antiestablishment tendencies of the time, witnessed in the newly opened field of comparative religions and in a more general interest in the treasures of non-Western traditions. This was a period "when the Other—found in China, India, or Persia—was used to help critique the intolerance, violence, and hypocrisy of Christianity" (van der Veer 2001: 60).[11]

By turning their attention eastward, establishing the Theosophical Society in 1878 and soon thereafter moving its headquarters to India, Blavatsky and Olcott sought answers to the mysteries sparked by the Spiritualist tradition, which by that time they had dismissed as an unsophisticated preoccupation with spirits. They felt that Indian traditions such as Vedanta and yoga could better explain and more effectively harness the paranormal and spiritual phenomena found within Spiritualism. They regarded Spiritualism's focus on spirits of the dead as short-sighted since, as they saw it, the living had spirit forms as well. Drawing on theories of yogic *siddhi* powers, Theosophists aimed to learn, for themselves, how to project these subtle, more flexible, bodies (Goodrick-Clarke 2007: 9; Kent 2010: 15–16). Theosophical Society members who hoped to develop abilities for astral projection were instructed by Olcott and Blavatsky to consult the teachings of Yoga Vidya, translated into English as "Science of Yoga," based on their understanding that extraordinary yogic abilities were scientifically observable and measurable (Goodrick-Clarke 2007: 9; Kent 2010: 18).

Blavatsky's confident imposition of modern science upon Indian philosophical systems conveys a conviction that her grasp of both science and religion was superior to that of established authorities (Kraft 2002: 156). In *Isis Unveiled* Blavatsky claims to have plumbed the philosophical and scientific depths of Hindu texts more deeply and accurately than prior readings. She remarks that Indians have in fact misinterpreted their religious texts; if they would read them more closely and less literally, they would find that their ancient authors were also in fact scientists who had anticipated Darwin (Brown 2007: 438; Viswanathan 2000: 3).[12] After converting to Theosophy, Annie Besant likewise appeared to reclaim the riches of Hinduism for Indians. She attributed India's social problems to their adoption of Western ideals and felt that Theosophy was "sent" to help Hindus realize the treasures of their tradition and to show how the West owes its wisdom to Hinduism (Prothero 1996: 161). Theosophical praise of a mystical, spiritually superior East that could save the West from its destructive arrogance was espoused by many Indians themselves and played a significant role in the Independence movement. A number of prominent players in the struggle for Independence joined the Theosophical Society, if only briefly.[13]

Despite the collection of Hindu reformers and politicians who ascribed to and built on Theosophical philosophies, the society did not receive unquestioning support in India. Hindu reformer Dayananda Saraswati was a particularly strident detractor. Blavatsky and Olcott's initial plan was to run the Theosophical Society in partnership with Dayananda, yet as he learned more about Blavatsky and Olcott's beliefs and practices, particularly their channeling of spirits and, later, of Masters of the Universe, Dayananda broke with the society. In 1881 he published a flier entitled *Humbuggery of the Theosophists*, in which he accused Olcott and Blavatsky of trickery and irrationality, claiming that they were simply interested in putting on a show with little serious understanding of Hinduism's scientific nature (van der Veer 2001: 55; see also Goodrick-Clarke 2007: 17).[14]

Neo-Vedanta and the Science of Yoga

The best-known Hindu reformer to promote the scientific nature of Hinduism was Swami Vivekananda (1863–1902). Largely responsible for developing what is now referred to as Neo-Vedanta or, as he labeled it, Practical Vedanta, Vivekananda championed a scientifically verifiable spiritual system suitable for all people and all religions in the modern day. Vivekananda insisted that Neo-Vedanta was not reliant on faith or religious leadership but, similar to scientific method, could operate independently of religious structures. Vivekananda's aim of uniting all religious traditions, his high estimation of Hinduism's global potential, and his scientific, anticlerical, and anticolonial approach were not only familiar to Theosophists but also resonated with a range of Indian reformers and thinkers. Vivekananda first introduced his Neo-Vedantic teachings to the West when he enthralled participants at the 1893 World Parliament of Religions in Chicago (Goodrick-Clarke 2007: 24; King 1999: 142; Rinehart 2008; van der Veer 2001: 68–69, 73).

Along with his younger contemporary, Swami Rama Tirtha, Vivekananda lectured on Neo-Vedanta in the United States during a time when Spiritualism and other new movements were popular. Audiences for the swamis were often sympathetic to, if not practicing members of, these traditions. Yet judging from their lectures, it appears the swamis were skeptical. Rama Tirtha's San Francisco lecture, entitled "True Spirituality and Psychic Powers," describes contact with the dead to be nothing special regarding spiritual progress. Training for mediumship, as he saw it, was as mundane as training to be an engineer. He considered Christian Scientism and Spiritualism to be lower paths than Vedanta, useful perhaps in leading practitioners to explore superior levels of Vedantic truth. Vivekananda's critique was leveled primarily at U.S. mediums, purported miracle workers who charged the public for their "sleight-of-hand tricks." This he contrasted with Indian "wise men who do not go about the country performing their wonders in the market places for pay." Vivekananda denounced the medium entertainment industry as typical of materialistic America: "The people of this Christian land will recognize religion only if you can cure diseases, work miracles, and open up avenues to money; and they understand little of anything else" (Rinehart 2008: 28–32).

The swamis' promotion of Hinduism over Christianity was partly in response to ongoing Christian missionary critique of Hinduism. Simultaneously refuting what seemed to be modern science's challenge to all religions, reformers often argued for the viability and, furthermore, superiority of Hinduism's scientific rationalism. Vivekananda reasoned that while Christianity traditionally separated religion and science, science-centered Neo-Vedanta united them, providing a higher spiritual truth more suitable to the modern era (Rinehart 2008: 28, 36). Like Blavatsky, Indian leaders stressed that Western scientific discoveries were already "hidden" or "prefigured" in the great texts of Hinduism and Buddhism (van der Veer 2001: 81). Similar to the Spiritualists, they argued that abilities that seemingly contradicted natural law were not in fact supernatural but only indications that we had yet to discover aspects of the universe that could explain them.

Icelandic Spiritualism

The early-twentieth-century founding of Spiritualism in Iceland is attributed to national poet and newspaper editor Einar Kvaran.[15] Historians speculate that Einar was first exposed to Spiritualism through the Icelandic immigrant community in Manitoba, Canada, where he lived briefly.[16] On his 1903 return to the town of Akureyri in northern Iceland, Einar was inspired to start conducting his own Spiritualist experiments after reading the Spiritualist classic *Human Personality and Its Survival of Bodily Death* by Frederic Myers.[17] It was not until he moved to Reykjavík in 1904 that the movement finally got off the ground (Swatos and Gissurarson 1997: 57–63; Gissurarson and Haraldsson 2001: 29).

Einar had no structural models by which to conduct his psychical experiments and no seasoned Spiritualists in Iceland to help guide him. In a 1934 interview with Reykjavík newspaper *Morganblaðið*, seventy-five-year-old Einar recalls the disorder that reigned during the first few months:

> Here we started to sit at tables and the tables started moving. This received a lot of attention. Men gathered around tables and the tables shivered and danced. I discussed this with Reverend Haraldur Níelsson and he seemed encouraged if this indeed was offering some proof. But then many others began experiments with table dancing and automatic writing and as a result everything became one big mess. For example, one girl wrote an exact description of the nature of her uncle's death in a distant region. People believed this tale and were grieving for the dead relative. We didn't have phones at that time but in the next post the happy news was delivered that nothing had been wrong with the man. Nonsense of this nature scared people away. Haraldur Níelsson was losing interest. I heaped upon myself books about Spiritualism, read them, and was determined that we would move forward. ("Frá Landamærunum" 1934: n.p.)

It is possible that Spiritualism in Reykjavík would have remained "one big mess" if Indriði Indriðason had not arrived on the scene in 1905. Indriði had moved recently to Reykjavík from the country to work as a printer and lived with an uncle whose wife was an enthusiastic Spiritualist. Einar described twenty-two-year-old Indriði's dramatic entrance into a Spiritualist session, precipitated by his aunt: "One time she sat at the table when Indriði was there and asked him to participate in the experiments. But Indriði had hardly sat down when the table reacted forcefully and started moving. Indriði became frightened and almost ran out. From then on, the experiments with Indriði started" ("Frá Landamærunum" 1934: n.p.). Experiments with Indriði, the human centerpiece for early Icelandic Spiritualism, lasted four years; they were terminated in 1909 due to his failing health.

In 1905 Einar and Haraldur Níelsson established the Tilraunafélag, or Experimental Society, whose members tended to be academics, politicians, and other prominent members of society. Indriði performed sittings twice a week, was paid a salary by the society, and eventually received free lodging as well (Gissurarson and Haraldsson 2001: 30). Indriði's mediumistic feats multiplied as time went by, enthralling and sometimes unnerving society members. Einar describes Indriði's early trance states: "After some time had passed, Indriði began to fall regularly into trance. The first time he fell into trance, those of us present became a little frightened because we had never seen that sort of thing and we didn't know when, or if, he would ever wake up again" ("Frá Landamærunum" 1934: n.p.). Indriði's other abilities attributed to spirits, often while in trance, included the movement of large objects, the appearance of spirit forms, the projection of voices across the room, and the illumination of lights. Once while in trance, Indriði appeared to have temporarily lost his arm (Gissurarson and Haraldsson 1969: 56–79). During his five-year involvement with the Experimental Society, Indriði was arguably one of the biggest celebrities in Iceland. For some he offered undeniable support for the existence of the spirit world and validation for the Spiritualist tradition. For others he was an object of scorn and derision (Gissurarson and Haraldsson 2001: 36). Between 1905 and 1908 newspapers in Reykjavík hotly debated the relative merits and demerits of Spiritualism, some of them supporting the movement and others suspecting Indriði and the society of sorcery and extortion (Gissurarson and Haraldsson 1969: 132–34).

Haraldur Níelsson, a highly esteemed Lutheran priest, professor of theology, and nephew of the Icelandic bishop, was also key to Icelandic Spiritualism's success. Of particular influence were his poetic, passionate, and convincing sermons delivered between 1914 and 1928. Crowds that gathered to hear him grew so large that people regularly had to be turned away. Haraldur also influenced a generation of seminary students through his professorship at the University of Iceland until 1928 (Fell 1999: 249).

Haraldur began his career as a conservative scholar and defender of Lutheran orthodoxy yet eventually switched to the liberal wing of the Icelandic Church that resisted the imperial Danish Church's dogmatism and doctrines of eternal damnation. Literalistic and rigidly orthodox, official Danish Church theology grated against Spiritualist teachings, while liberal theology's optimistic view of human potential and its emphasis on the goodness of the individual melded well. Yet liberal theology rejected biblical and contemporary accounts of the supernatural—a perspective that was, for Haraldur, a product of the "great enemy," materialism. Spiritualism's revalidation of so-called miracles provided Haraldur with a corrective to what he felt to be liberal theology's flaw, offering a dimension he considered essential to faith (Fell 1999: 243–47; Swatos and Gissurarson 1997: 165–66).

While Spiritualism aimed to give scientific credibility to seemingly supernatural phenomena, Haraldur's theology gave Icelandic Spiritualism religious depth and legitimacy—dimensions largely missing from Spiritualist traditions outside Iceland. As Swatos and Gissurarson explain, "Icelandic spiritualism was not credulity in things unseen but assurance from things seen that there was more to the knowable world than positivistic science had subsumed under its rubrics" (1997: 155). At the same time, Haraldur adamantly insisted—similar to Vivekananda's approach to Neo-Vedanta— that Spiritualism was not itself a religion, fending off accusations that he was forming a new sect. Instead, he saw it as a form of scientific research that would help to support and correct religious understandings (Swatos and Gissurarson 1997: 175).

The resilience of Spiritualism in Iceland thus can be attributed in part to Haraldur's assurances that the tradition would not compete with the liberal wing of the Icelandic Church, thus maintaining its support. Also helping to strengthen the movement was its critique of Danish orthodoxy, positioning Spiritualism as part of the struggle for independence from Danish rule, in full swing at the time (Swatos and Gissurarson 1997: 51). Not only did Spiritualism's theological optimism and mediumistic practices challenge the Danish Church; some members of the Spiritualist movement also accused the Danish clergy of being antimodern in their inability to accept the scientifically verifiable truths of Spiritualism.[18] Thus while the explicit aim of Icelandic Spiritualism was research, its religious implications offered beneficial alliances with liberal theology, the Icelandic State Church, and the independence movement (Swatos and Gissurarson 1997: 69). Heated debates about Spiritualism waged by Reykjavík newspapers during this time fell across explicitly political lines and included accusations that Haraldur and Einar were using Spiritualism for political ends (Gissurarson and Haraldsson 1969: 132).

Also important to the Experimental Society was the scientific legitimacy it received from Guðmundur Hannesson, a professor of medicine who agreed to conduct tests during Indriði's trance meetings to determine whether his physical phenomena lay outside ordinary empirical explanation. Guðmundur held a post at the University of Iceland in Reykjavík from 1911 to 1946 and was widely respected for his scientific impartiality. He reportedly was skeptical of Spiritualism before he began conducting research on Indriði yet emerged, in the midst of his studies, a believer. The fact that he published papers on his findings and was made professor of University of Iceland only after publishing them demonstrates the degree to which the public found his study acceptable (Gissurarson and Haraldsson 1969: 102–26).

It was not until the many pieces and players fell into place—among them Indriði's seemingly unparalleled mediumistic capabilities, Haraldur's elegant appeal to religious sentiment, ties to the Independence movement, and Guðmundur's scientific support—that the general Icelandic public warmed to Spiritualism. The journalist who interviewed Einar decades later remarked on this palpable shift that occurred in the 1920s, and Einar responded,

> Yes, you could say that. Those [early] years I just told you about, we had to endure comments and put-downs. My children and Haraldur's children couldn't get peace on the street due to nasty comments because of our involvement in these matters. But the people came to our side. Reverend Haraldur's sermons had a great effect. The journal *Morgun* had done their bit to steer people's thoughts in this direction. ("Frá Landamærunum" 1934: n.p.)

When Indriði died of tuberculosis in 1912 at age twenty-nine, the Experimental Society dissolved. Einar and Haraldur established the Sálarrannsóknarfélag Íslands, the Icelandic Society for Psychical Research, in 1918, holding positions of president and vice president, respectively, until their deaths. Compared to the Experimental Society, the Society for Psychical Research was, at least implicitly, religious in character and somewhat less research-minded. Helping boost its popularity was the fact that many founding members were clergy, and the leadership and most mediums involved were male. This contrasts with Anglo-American Spiritualism, which, unhinged from organized religion, eventually became a tradition of women and the power-deprived (Swatos 1990: 479). By the mid-1930s half of the Icelandic clergy were sympathetic to or supportive of Spiritualism, and in 1938, when Icelanders first elected their own bishop, they chose, by a narrow margin, a man who was sympathetic. The election of an orthodox bishop in 1959 marks a turning point and an era of neo-orthodoxy in the Icelandic Church. Since then the official Church has remained critical of Spiritualism, though this is not necessarily the case for individual priests (Swatos and Gissurarson 1997: 185–87).

While the religious and political support enjoyed by Icelandic Spiritualism helps explain its success through the middle of the twentieth century, this does not account for the current health of Spiritualist practices that, in recent decades, seem to be on the rise. Swatos attributes this renewed interest to the New Age movement and, given the incorporation of Spiritualist practices into alternative healing traditions like reflexology, Reiki, and cranial sacral therapy, New Age eclecticism undoubtedly bears some responsibility for its continued strength.[19] Yet the tenacity and importance of early influences that formed Icelandic Spiritualism should not be underestimated. Current Spiritualist beliefs that are well supported in a New Age environment such as reincarnation and a pluralistic approach to world religions can also be traced to earlier Theosophical and, by association, Neo-Vedantic influences.

The influence of Theosophy on early Icelandic Spiritualism can be surmised from the simple fact that it has been a strong presence, arriving in Iceland in 1900 and inducted as a formal society in 1913 (Pétursson 2002: 16). By 1947 Icelandic membership in the Theosophical Society was the highest per capita in the world (Swatos and Gissurarson 1997: 159). Not only was Theosophy influential while Spiritualism was developing in Iceland, the exchange between these two Societies, unlike the global conversations, was not argumentative. Icelanders were often simultaneously members of both Societies. Aðalbjörg Sigurðardóttir, instrumental in establishing the first Icelandic Theosophical Society in Akureyri, was Haraldur Níelsson's second wife and a committed Spiritualist. Jakob Kristinsson, the first president of the Theosophical Society, was a Lutheran priest and a member of a Church hierarchy that was supportive of Spiritualism at the time (Fell 1999: 250; Péturson 2002: 16, 18).[20]

OVERLAPPING PHILOSOPHIES: NEO-VEDANTA AND ICELANDIC SPIRITUALISM

Given the intertwined roots of Neo-Vedanta and Icelandic Spiritualism, it is not surprising that the philosophical proclivities and aims of these two movements overlap as well. Most broadly speaking, the primary aim of

Neo-Vedanta is to rid oneself of ego-identification, to realize one's essential Self, or *atman*, as identified with the universal consciousness, or the Brahman. By shedding the ego and realizing one's true identification, enlightened practitioners ultimately merge in bliss with this One Reality. Advanced adepts, reaping the benefits of multiple earthly incarnations and after many years' dedication, ideally will get a taste of this bliss, a hint of a state to come, through yogic practices of mind and body discipline. Although Vivekananda pitched "Practical Vedanta" as a scientifically verifiable path superior to other religious traditions, particularly Christianity, a distinguishing feature of the movement, reflective of its modern origins, is a pluralistic approach to religions. Vivekananda's pluralistic view, construing all religions as streams leading to the one oceanic Source, was one of his lasting legacies and is still central to Neo-Vedantic thought.

These basic Neo-Vedantic motifs promoting religious pluralism, spiritual development through the relinquishment of the ego, reincarnation, and ultimate identification with a universal consciousness are core to Icelandic Spiritualism as well. These similarities are attributable to a range of factors impossible to extricate and isolate, ranging from turn-of-the-century global influences that spawned Neo-Vedanta, Theosophy, and liberal theology, to contemporary New Age inclinations that some would argue are rooted in these same turn-of-the-century global exchanges (Hess 1993: 20; Tingay 2002: 247).

During my conversations with Icelandic Spiritualists in the northern town of Akureyri in the summer and fall of 2009, these beliefs repeatedly asserted themselves despite their challenge to conventional Christian theology, particularly as packaged by today's conservative Icelandic Lutheran Church. Most fundamentally, Spiritualism's view of spiritual development departs from conventional Protestant conceptions of salvation; most people I spoke with related to Jesus less as a savior figure than as a model for spiritual advancement and master at executing extraordinary abilities. The expectation that we spiritually progress through our own efforts rather than a savior's, promoted also by Neo-Vedanta and Theosophy, can be traced to turn-of-the-century liberal theology as well. One of liberal theology's radical challenges to Lutheran orthodoxy is the rejection of a judgmental God who requires the death of his son to redeem humanity. For liberal theologians God is eternal and unchangeable, thus divine benevolence is constant rather than conditional. Redemption, as a result, is in the hands of humans themselves. This optimistic view that humanity is capable of redeeming itself is based on the belief that, as theologian Pétur Péturson expressed it, echoing Neo-Vedantic philosophies, you have something of God inside yourself. You are made in the image of God.... So you can choose; you can do something that can affect your own salvation. It's you that has to change. You do not have some dogma or some confession requiring you to say, "Yes, I accept this and believe in that" in order that you will have the blood of Christ save you. Haraldur [Níelsson] would say that God is goodness, kindness, and forgiveness. And God would never have planned for his only begotten son to suffer and to be killed. And this is the center of Spiritualism.[21]

Many Icelandic Spiritualists today are churchgoing Lutherans, more still invoke Jesus as an inspiration, and the Society for Psychical Research in Akureyri is filled with Christian imagery (Figure 4.1). Yet while Spiritualists often frame their practices in Christian terms, their larger outlook is uniformly pluralistic, supported from the start by liberal theology's decentering of Christian salvation and likely bolstered by the deep religious eclecticism of the surrounding Theosophical and New Age movements. Icelandic Spiritualists' pluralism is further enhanced by encounters with spirits who, as healers, guides, and protectors, hail from around the globe and represent a variety of religious traditions. Whether one is aided by a Catholic nun, a Native American warrior, a Tibetan monk, or an Icelandic doctor, religious affiliation seems to have little impact on a

Figure 4.1
Country Lutheran church and graveyard, outside Akureyri, Iceland.

spirit's abilities and dedication. Catholic monks and nuns are some of the most commonly encountered spirit participants, something that struck me as notable given the Catholic Church's official disdain for Spiritualism. When I occasionally commented that Catholic teachings don't seem to have a lasting effect on the spirit world, people thought this was perhaps interesting but had not given it much thought. The disjunction seemed to simply underscore what they already knew—that religious dogma was, in the end, irrelevant to human-spirit interactions.

Most Icelandic Spiritualists seem perfectly aware of how some of their views might conflict with orthodox Christian teachings, although this seems to have more of an impact on older participants. Lilla, in her mid-seventies and deeply involved with Spiritualism for decades, reflected on how her pluralistic tendencies might challenge traditional belief:

> If you were to ask me what religion I was, I probably wouldn't be able to answer you. The thing is, I believe in this *alheimsorka* [life force]. That's what I believe in, not some man with a beard and a book. I don't fit in a category of any religion, so maybe I'm a heretic. There's some good in every religion, throughout all of humanity. That's how I see it. I don't see the person with the gray beard. The *alheimsorka*, what I'm talking about, how is it controlled? If the energy had one huge computer to control the world and our existence, then God is like the computer.[22]

Sensing that the term God or Guð may be too limiting, many Spiritualists, like Lilla, interchangeably or exclusively use the term *alheimsorka*, meaning "life force" or, more literally translated, "universal energy," to accommodate their broader perspective.

Þórhallur, a full-time medium who hosts a weekly television program for a studio audience, described well this pluralistic position. Demonstrating a typical Icelandic Spiritualist disdain for conferring judgment, he explained,

> Of course God is a universal force. I'm not saying like President Obama, or anything like that. But the God we talk about is a universal force, *alheimsorka*. People are linking into it in their own way, differently, tuning into things in different ways. Because in the end all religions go into the same force [Þórhallur shows with his hand a wide space that moves forward and narrows to a point]. There is no doubt about that. Of course I respect the Hindus and the Muslims and everything—and Buddha. I like Buddha. I like all kinds....I'm Christian; I go to the church. I like to go to the church, but only up to a point....But one thing is for sure, and that is that God is a universal power. And we accept that.

As for the spirits, collectively they embody religious diversity; moreover, their views, believed to be expressed directly through trance mediums, are often pluralistic. On several occasions during trance sessions I heard spirit sentiments expressed through mediums in praise of religious tolerance. One of the most memorable was when Haraldur Níelsson himself came through Bjössi, a trance medium in his mid-sixties who owns a painting company. Haraldur wanted to discuss with me, among other things, the importance of learning from all religious traditions. To illustrate the importance of this matter, even in the spirit realm, he commented,

> What I want to say about the work here in the spirit world is that I am working among many others to produce a big book about religions across the world. And I really do expect that I will succeed in writing this with the help of a leader from each religion. And with that we'd like to make a frame for uniting all the religions in the world.

Haraldur went on to admit that such an ambitious project will certainly take time to complete and then added, smiling through Bjössi, "But we have plenty of time here."

In regard to ultimate spiritual goals, Spiritualists are willing—for obvious reasons—to describe in detail some of the conditions one might expect to find on departing the earthly plane. For Neo-Vedantans, absolute departure with no further need to reincarnate implies that one has reached a blissful state of perfection that defies description. This ineffability is not for lack of exposure (albeit fleeting) to blissful union but because the experience itself lies outside the sensory realm and simply cannot be put into words. Neo-Vedantans are willing to describe, however, the basic mechanics of reaching this final state in which the enlightened one's essence or *atman* merges with *Brahman*, the eternal, unchanging Reality. Other branches of Hinduism argue that our final goal is union with Divinity in which the *atman* remains separate and in an eternal, blissful state of devotion. Although Spiritualists may speak easily about ongoing development on the spiritual plane, people had difficulty hypothesizing about its culmination, likely due to the tradition's abiding pragmatism and aversion to dogmatic abstraction. Since no one—not even spirits—can claim to have arrived at this final state, my attempts to hear people's views on the matter were often met with thoughtful silence, a shrug of the shoulders, or, in some cases, resistance.

Ragnheiður, who has worked at the Society for Psychical Research in Akureyri in a variety of capacities and has also served as its president, expressed well this practical stance. When I asked her if she could describe the developing soul's final status, she was not willing to go out on a limb: "Well, I haven't been there, so I don't know." When I inserted that this was certainly fair to say, Ragnheiður steered the conversation back to more solid ground—to the topic of ongoing spiritual development:

> But of course our goal is to get closer to God, to get into the light. The way I look at it is that at a certain age in our life we go to a school. Some of us have to go long distances to a boarding school. I look at life like it is one big boarding school. If we look at eternity and our lifetime, it's not a very long period of time here in relation to eternity. So it's the same thing—you go to a university or a college, you go away and stay in the dorms by the school; you stay there for four years before you go on.... We are here and we're learning and then we go back home.

Reflecting on her answer, I suggested that even the spirits who communicate through mediums have not yet reached their final destination; everyone we talk to is in process, even if they are high, high beings. Ragnheiður agreed, "Yes, and unless God comes down to us and talks directly to us—or Jesus Christ or Mother Mary—we don't know. Because we are limited. We are only human."

While no one claimed to have a definitive sense of this final state, some offered their best guesses based on their encounters with the spirit world. Bjössi addressed the issue by first establishing what he considered to be the goal of our earthly lives: to be in loving connection with those around us. In the same way that we bring love to others on earth, Bjössi added that our aim should include bringing spirits into the light of love and peace through compassionate connections with the earthly realm. As he saw it, the end point of our development is that we *become* these aspirations, become light and pure love: "My opinion is that we're on our way toward the light. And in the end when we're done with the material world and we have developed true, pure love, then we are not dependent on anything at all. And we will be that light."

Similar to Bjössi's view that we eventually become the compassion-filled light to which we aspire, most Spiritualists I spoke with felt that our final goal would be a type of union with God, light, or *alheimsorka*. Given that this sounds like the Hindu view of final union with the *Brahman* or Divinity, I asked some people to humor me by entering more deeply into conjecture and weighing in on the classical Hindu debate as to whether this union is a complete merging with the universal energy or one in which we maintain our individual identities. The answer was consistently an "all of the above" compromise position. Guðbjörg, who currently makes her living as a full-time medium, described our final state as residing "in the light with God.

So by the time your light is so bright, you will be the light of God." Asked if she thought we would completely merge with God, she responded that we would become one with God but that we would continue to exist as separate souls. The reason for our continuation as individuals, consistent with Spiritualist altruism, was, as Guðbjörg put it, "because if God needs to use you, he can still send you to do this and that."

Þórhallur similarly described the culmination of all our earthly lessons to be unconditional love associated with the relinquishment of the ego. In that perfected state, he proposed that we will be joined with the universal energy, *alheimsorka*. When I asked if this meant that we would be one with this energy or if we would remain separate, he responded,

"I can accept both but see it in a different way. We are using our hearts in the *alheimsorka*. Our unconditional love unites us with *alheimsorka*. In this way we would be connected through our hearts with the *alheimsorka*," yet at the same time, as Þórhallur described it, "We are still separate people. . . . And so you become like a blossom. You are like a flower. You join and you give."

Another theme shared by Neo-Vedanta and Spiritualism that played through many of my conversations had to do with the importance of squelching the ego for spiritual advancement. Within Spiritualism this difficult task becomes further complicated when spirits enter the picture. Most basically, trance mediums are challenged by the necessity, as one medium put it, to "get out of the way" in order to allow the spirits through to do their work. Matti, a grounds worker at the University of Akureyri, related similar sentiments in the context of his reflexology practice. During a session he conducted in Reykjavík he recalled,

> Everything I was finding through my work with the woman was that there was something wrong with her appendix. But my [spirit] helpers were telling me that there was something wrong with her fallopian tubes. I just didn't listen and thought I was right, that it was the appendix. So two days later this woman passed through Akureyri on her travels somewhere else. She stopped by and had a reflexology session and the same thing happened. My helpers were telling me that it's that little tube there and I am saying no, it's the appendix. I can feel it right there [in the corresponding area on her foot, according to the principles of reflexology]. It's the appendix. So four days later this woman is hospitalized because there was a twist in the tube.

When I asked if this kind of mistake happens often, Matti responded that it has only happened to him three times. Asked if he now pays more attention to the spirits than to the feet, he replied, with a chuckle, "Not always," then added, "I think each and every one of us has to go through a phase where you have to put aside your ego so it doesn't get pushed down your throat again."

A set of Icelandic Spiritualist beliefs that seem more expressly Hindu than Christian involves the principles of karma and reincarnation. A shared assumption among Icelandic Spiritualists is that individuals develop through a series of earthly existences that are mapped out karmically in response to positive and negative actions performed during past lives. Departing from Neo-Vedanta is the view that one's personality can continue to develop—and assist the earthly realm—once it enters spirit form. Icelandic Spiritualists support their belief in reincarnation through communications with spirits and with the understanding that spirit guides were often in close human relationships, from a prior life, with the people they accompany. Although reincarnation represents a rather radical departure from Christian teachings, no one I spoke with—except a Lutheran priest inclined toward Spiritualism—seemed particularly concerned about this disparity. It appears that a belief in reincarnation was widespread in the early days of Icelandic Spiritualism as well, setting this branch apart from global Spiritualism, which officially does not, even to this day, support the doctrine of reincarnation.[23]

Siddhis and *Skyggnigáfa*: Packaging and Proof

Having established the historical and philosophical threads that connect and constitute Neo-Vedanta and Icelandic Spiritualism, we turn now to the extraordinary abilities that validate and further give shape to these traditions. Demonstrating how these abilities are anything but inconsequential to Neo-Vedanta-inspired Hinduism and Icelandic Spiritualism, my field notes from both the upstate New York temple and Akureyri, Iceland, are brimming with stories of extraordinary healings, feats, and prophecies, attributed to those understood to possess *siddhis* and *skyggnigáfa*.[24] These fantastical accounts, whether related in South Asian or Icelandic contexts, do not take credulity for granted. For all the wonder they may inspire, they are just as securely embedded in modern systems that rely—even if indirectly—upon the scientific frameworks promoted by their respective traditions. As such, Neo-Vedanta and Icelandic Spiritualism claim to have beat science-minded incredulity to the punch, deflecting criticism by playing by the rules of science itself. This have-one's-cake-and-eat-it-too scenario, defying the conventional notion that science and spirituality are ultimately incompatible, is a lasting point of pride for practitioners of both traditions.

In classical yogic and Tantric literature, *siddhis* are described at great length. According to these texts, the most common *siddhi* abilities include clairvoyance, clairaudience, thought reading, knowledge of the future, and fulfillment of ordinary desires (Bhagwat 1973: 45–59). According to the *Yoga Sutra*, examples of *siddhis* that extend beyond the ordinary include levitation, the ability to overcome hunger or thirst, and the capacity to manipulate matter and create a mind-made body (Brooks 1997: 204). *Siddhis* become available to yogis who practice systematic mind control and intensive meditation for many years and have achieved sharply focused levels of concentration. They must also have true faith and be free of ego-driven, mundane desires (Mathur 1998: 3; Bhagwat 1973: 43). According to the *Yoga Sutra*, people can possess *siddhis* at birth or can trigger them with mantras or with drugs. The prevailing view, however, is that the only realistic way to earn *siddhis* is to commit to a long-term practice of austerities and yoga (Mathur 1998: 4–6).[25]

The recognition of yogic powers has been a part of Indian traditions for millennia; Patanjali's *Yoga Sutra* is dated at around the second century CE and is based on even older oral traditions. Neo-Vedanta, responding to late-nineteenth-century challenges to religion, gave a fresh face to this ancient system by framing *siddhi* powers scientifically. Reminiscent of Neo-Vedantans—and Spiritualists—from a century ago, H. C. Mathur, an ex–United Nations Expert on Telecommunications, asserts that *siddhis* are scientifically explicable and appear miraculous only to the ignorant. *Siddhis* are no more miracles than the scientific gadgets like radios, TVs, or telephones that produce intelligent speech, music, or pictures out of nothing. Not only can the manifestation of *siddhi* powers be explained scientifically; the most scientific method for acquiring them, he insists, is the practice of yoga (Mathur 1998: 3–4).

Although the Shrividya tradition practiced at the Rush temple revolves around goddess worship, the ultimate aim of the tradition is, similar to Neo-Vedanta, union with a nonpersonalized divinity that transcends all identifiable gods and goddesses. Also in line with Neo-Vedantic ideals is the temple's promotion of religious pluralism and the scientific language Aiya uses to explain yogic powers. Aiya regularly expounds on these scientific principles, occasionally giving formal presentations on the physiology of meditation, complete with elaborate charts and illustrations that demonstrate the various bodily processes at work.[26] My first exposure to Aiya's scientific explanations of yogic powers occurred during an informal interview in 1998. While the two of us drank tea, he explained the mechanics of yogic practice and mental focus, without charts:

> The yogis have found that there are two separate nervous systems in the body. There is the sympathetic nervous system and a spinal nervous system. The spinal nervous system of course begins with the brain—with the attendant lobes and ventricles and the pineal stalk and all that and the brainstem. And it continues down as the spinal cord and it ends there behind the base of the spinal cord. And they have also found that there are places along that spinal cord where the important nerves meet. For example, the brachial nerve, right? Or the femural nerves—all these meet at various points. They have found that continued focus by the person who is trying to discover the truth of any particular religion will evoke, will create, particular reactions.

The scientific language Aiya used—incorporating, in the process, his religiously pluralistic view—took me by surprise at the time. It was the first of many such scientific interjections I was to hear from him over the years, functioning to explain but also validate a tradition that relies heavily on extraordinary powers, both human and divine.

As enthusiastic as Aiya may be to describe, in detail, the scientific underpinnings of *siddhis*, an open discussion of these abilities is taboo. This is not, of course, because he questions their value, but because his tradition strongly discourages preoccupation with them. Aiya maintains a fascination for powerful adepts he has encountered in his life; some of his favorite stories include wondrous tales of his gurus' abilities.[27] He is particularly free about discussing the *siddhis* of his first guru, and I suspect this is due in part to the fact that she is now deceased and it is safe to draw attention to them. For Aiya, impressive *siddhis* are not simply fodder for entertaining stories but are testimony to a person's lifelong commitment to the tradition, and as such they offer encouragement to his own students that the practice works.[28] But when I asked if he had any personal reflections to share on the workings of *siddhi* powers, he shied away from the subject and furthermore noted that if I were to come across spiritual adepts known to have great abilities and were to ask them about *siddhis*, they would invariably change the subject. The best approach, he suggested, would be simply to observe.

Icelanders who claim abilities associated with *skyggnigáfa* typically have no trouble talking about them. This stems from the fact that practitioners find themselves in possession of *skyggnigáfa* in a manner so completely different from the acquisition of *siddhis*. Whereas *siddhis* typically demonstrate decades of mind, body, and lifestyle discipline, *skyggnigáfa* is a talent or "gift" that is often undesired and typically discovered at a very young age. Ideally speaking, *siddhis* signify an ability to tap into an unbounded higher reality achieved after one's ego—or false sense of self—is successfully squelched. Speaking openly about these hard-earned abilities is akin to calling attention to one's accomplishments, potentially inflating one's ego, and ultimately risking access to realms where *siddhis* proliferate. Since those who claim *skyggnigáfa* have done nothing to earn their abilities (at least not in this lifetime), they are not particularly fearful of losing them. Firsthand accounts of *skyggnigáfa* that I heard while in Iceland were conveyed not only openly, but often with a sense of frustration and consternation, with humor and humility, and without concerns that they would be diminished.

The term *skyggnigáfa* does not translate well into English. *Gáfa* glosses fairly accurately but problematically into English as "gift" or "talent," and the standard translation of *skyggni*, "clairvoyant," does not do justice to its range of meaning in an Icelandic context.[29] Most basically, *skyggnigáfa* refers to an innate receptivity to the spirit world enabling a person to see spirits through internal or external vision and/or to hear or internally receive messages from them. This openness allows for a range of abilities fairly identical to those available to a yogic adept, including clairvoyance, clairaudience, telepathy, predicting the future, and healing. Some choose to incorporate their *skyggnigáfa* into public practice, most traditionally in trance or nontrance mediumship or as a member of a *hringur* or "circle" of participants that meets regularly to pray and/or support a trance medium's work. Other options include reading futures in Tarot cards or in patterns formed in a drained coffee cup, drawing people's auras or spirit guides, and healing with one's hands or with established systems like Reiki, reflexology, and cranial sacral therapy. In all cases, a person's spirit guides and helpers are understood to be an indispensable part of the process even if, for instance, a practitioner uses Tarot cards or applies the principles of reflexology.

Matti, referred to above as performing reflexology with the aid of spirit helpers, seemed destined to be open to the spirit world literally from the day he was born. Soon after his mother delivered him, a well-known medium who lived in the countryside came rushing to his house to deliver a message from a deceased Icelandic doctor named Mattías (with the common nickname Matti). The spirit doctor had come through her while in trance with the message that she should locate a particular house where a boy had just been born and tell the mother to name the baby Matthías, after him. As Matti put it, when telling the story, "My mom didn't dare call me anything else." From a very early age Matti remembers seeing people that others could not. His first recollection of a sighting was of a seaman: "I saw him often and I always ran and told my mom and my grandmother— I'd run off to get them—and told them that someone was there. But when they came…nothing." Eventually Matti's grandmother asked him to describe the man. When he did, she found a picture of his great-grandfather, and Matti confirmed that it was him. Among the regular team of spirits who helps Matti today in his healing practice is the doctor Matthías, his spirit namesake.

Rósa, a cook at a local school, remembers seeing spirits from the time she was around six. For the most part Rósa's *skyggnigáfa* gave her the uncanny ability to know the future. She accurately predicted the arrival of visitors and also, unnervingly, had premonitions about impending disaster and death. As Rósa describes it, a frighteningly large and shadowy spirit would always be the bearer of bad news, making her jumpy as a child.

> I was really afraid and always felt something was coming up from behind me, so I always put my back to the walls. Then I started saying things that I wasn't supposed to say—or know. Once a couple came to visit and when they were leaving I told my mom that we were never going to see the man again. My mom asked me to leave the room because she didn't want them to hear me say this. But we never did see him again, because he died soon after that.

Rósa, who lived in the country, would try to calm herself by going out to a place near the farm, two large stones that she called her "church." Sitting in the open near the stones she felt a certain peace and safety.

Difficulties arising from *skyggnigáfa*, similar to what Rósa describes, are not unusual. Although many mediums and healers I spoke with reported having family members who tried to keep their fears and confusion at bay, their *gáfa* seemed, to many, to be anything but a gift. People reported tremendous trepidation about the spirits they unwittingly encountered, about being judged by their peers as odd, and about the possibility that they might be crazy. In sharp contrast with highly sought-after *siddhi* powers, people with *skyggnigáfa* often sorely wished their abilities would simply go away.

Guðbjörg, a full-time medium mentioned above, recalls her sense of alarm on encountering spirits, as well as the solace brought by her mother's advice:

> I saw people and things and I didn't like it. I was very afraid of what I was seeing and I was very afraid of the dark. When I was eleven years old I saw a man who had hanged himself. I was so scared because it was in the place where we hung

our coats. It was a deep closet and in the inner part there was this man. I was so scared, every time I would come home from school I would jump when I got to that area because I wanted to get by it quickly. It was very hard for me and I was very scared. I asked my mother about it and she said she'd ask around. She told me sometime later that there was a man who had hanged himself there in the coat room and that the only thing I could do is to pray for him. So every day I came home from school I prayed for him—for quite some time. Then one day when I came home I found that the closet was empty. Nobody was there. And I was so curious. Was nobody there? It seemed like my prayers worked.

When I asked Guðbjörg if this incident helped rid her of her fears, she said it didn't: "Because if I didn't know who it was that I saw, I was scared. My mother told me once, 'Don't be scared of the people who are already dead. You should be scared of the people who are not dead.' So this helped me a little, knowing this."

Of the various accounts I heard of *skyggnigáfa* being less than a welcomed "gift," the most dramatic example was related to me by Jón, a shop owner in his late twenties. Jón described his early years as sleepless and fear-filled due to the spirits he felt and saw only fleetingly. Although he sensed that the spirits around him were benign, like his grandfather who often accompanied him, he still suspected they were playing tricks on him. "I felt like I was in a horror movie—just scary stuff—even though there were good things around me. I felt something but just didn't know what it was. It was like something was trying to attack me." Worried that he might be crazy, Jón shied away from telling people what he perceived. As a teenager he continued feeling frightened and alone, and his life took a turn for the worse.

> When you have an openness like me, you're scared, you're angry, you can do things like I did. I did drugs, I was drinking. I was fighting with someone who wasn't there and I was in a state that . . . hatred came in. Instead of bringing love, I hated people, I hated everything about me. I had so much hatred just because I didn't know what was going on.

After a several-year roller-coaster ride of rehab, commitment to a mental health unit, and still deeper plunges into despair and substance abuse, Jón finally emerged. With the help of prayer, Alcoholics Anonymous, and a community of support, he now sees his *skyggnigáfa* as a gift rather than a curse. Nearly a decade after his emergence from despair, Jón's resolve to dedicate his life anew includes his determination to tell his story openly so that others who struggle with this "gift" can take heart.

Further demonstrating the extent to which *skyggnigáfa* can be unnerv-ing, contrasted with *siddhi* powers that are a welcome affirmation of one's spiritual success, are stories of attempts to avoid or close these abilities entirely. Hrabba, a teacher at an Akureyri high school who works as a trance medium, told me that she had tried to steer clear of her abilities—and the responsibilities they brought with them—many times. Hrabba's *skyggnigáfa* brings with it a range of abilities, but like her mother, Rósa, she was un-settled by her knowledge of future catastrophe. As Hrabba described her early experiences, "I was at peace with some aspects of it. Dreams, they were okay. The healing part was mostly okay. But this information, where someone was trying to get messages through to my best friends, that was really hard." Since the messages often came in the form of bad news, Hrabba struggled over whether or not to relate them. Some of her peers ostracized her, out of fear, but thankfully others accepted her abilities and have re-mained friends to this day.

When Hrabba was in her mid-twenties, she felt pressure to work as a trance medium. As she describes it, "Some people say that the energy just builds up—lots of energy—and it's not healthy for your body." When Hrabba tried ignoring this pressure to make use of her abilities, she ended up getting sick. "I thought that something was happening because I lost my balance—I couldn't walk for a few weeks—and my doctor kept telling me that it was just a migraine." In 2000, when Hrabba was around twenty-seven years old, she finally gave in to the pressure. She joined a *bænahringur*, or prayer circle, her health returned, and she felt a great sense of relief. As she described it, "I started in a prayer circle to get peace. It was the only time during the week that I heard myself breathing, I think. And then the information got clearer. And then I met Garðar, from Akranes. And he said that I should try trance. I thought it was really creepy to get someone inside my body and speak for them." Hrabba is now comfortable with her trance work and appreciates making productive use of the energy within her and the spirits around her. She emphasizes that one of the biggest benefits of embracing her abilities is that she, like Jón, can help young people who likewise struggle with their *skyggnigáfa*.

Matti, comfortable with his ability to see spirits when he was young, became fearful as a teenager, particularly when he traveled between gigs as a drummer for a rock band. He found himself regularly unsettled by the people he alone saw walking along remote Icelandic roads and in the moun-tain passes. When he was seventeen he visited a famous medium, Einar frá Einarsstöðum, who lived on a farm east of Akureyri. As Matti put it, "I asked him to let things close. And he did." Matti then added, looking above himself, "Or they did." Matti's life subsequently went downhill, and during the next seven or eight years he was in and out of the hospital, the doctors seemingly unable to help him.

Eventually he decided to revisit the spirit world and look, as he put it, "into healing, and into God." A medium in Reykjavík reopened him in a trance session, during which, as Matti recalls, Einar, who had since died, came through the medium. Einar admitted that closing Matti was a mistake and suggested, as Matti phrased it, "that maybe it would have been better to lead me through a different path, not close it—maybe lead me through a path where he would have been guiding me." Once Matti's abilities were open again, they manifested in a different, less unnerving way. He now sees people through mental images rather than his outer vision. He can also feel them, as he describes it, through his heart. When Matti's abilities were reopened, he chose to use them primarily for healing, although he also now organizes a *hringur* where he serves as a trance medium who trains others to develop their trance abilities.

Indriði Indriðason, the medium largely responsible for launching Icelandic Spiritualism, also seemed to have unwittingly possessed *skyggnigáfa* abilities that transformed once he made use of them. It is important to note, however, that the range of abilities claimed today by Icelandic Spiritualists cannot be compared with those associated with Indriði. His apparent capacity to induce spirits to materialize, to speak or sing from disembodied voices, to move heavy objects, and to project lights secure his place in the rare category of physical medium, reportedly representing a one-time event in Iceland (Gissurarson and Haraldsson 1969: 56).

In Indriði's day, proponents of Icelandic Spiritualism took pride in their conviction that his physical phenomena could be scientifically tested and verified. It was also a time when, compared with today's Spiritualism, experimentation—and ridicule—loomed large in public discourse. Haraldur Níelsson, undeniably the most respected public voice of early Icelandic Spiritualism, took pains to thwart detractors by demonstrating that rational thinking and scientific method guided the Spiritualist approach. On May 18, 1913, Haraldur responded to widespread accusations of witchcraft and deception by delivering a lecture in Reykjavík entitled "Why Do You Hit Me?" Here Haraldur explained that he and Einar Kvaran were never convinced of any phenomena "unless we could touch it ourselves. We were like Thomas, we needed to put our fingers in the nail marks to believe and we wanted to put forth a lot of effort so we could, in truth, be able to feel it." Haraldur went on to insist that their society was modeled after the English psychical research society and was never intended to be a religious club filled with believers, as people had mistakenly presumed:

People were allowed to be members no matter what their opinion of the phenomena was. The only objective was to look for these phenomena and research them. I think it is likely that most of us have considered that the Spiritualist explanation is, in the end, the most probable explanation of the most spectacular phenomena and we are convinced that a connection with the deceased is attainable. (Kristjánsson n.d.: 138)

Spiritualism in Iceland today, negligibly concerned with officially orchestrated experiments,[30] maintains the Sálarrannsóknarfélag Íslands—the Icelandic Society for Psychical Research—as its formal society, with centers scattered throughout the island. Sálarrannsóknarfélag implies that the society (*félag*) focuses on soul (*sál*) research (*rannsókn*), yet it has, nearly from its inception in 1918, served more as a meeting place for healing sessions, trance and nontrance medium sessions, prayer groups, and workshops. Today these events are founded on the assumption that spirit communication is available to those gifted with special abilities. While the society's primary aim is to provide communication with the deceased and to offer aid to those on earth and beyond, this does not mean that proof is inconsequential to practitioners. Once established, however, it simply sets the tone for a host of other tasks.

Icelandic Spiritualists have never made use of scientific terminology to the elaborate extent that Hindu adherents have to validate *siddhis*. With the exception of Guðmundur Hannesson's laboratory-like studies of Indriði, proof of *skyggnigáfa* tends to be more anecdotal and streamlined—in some cases verified simply because it manifests in such surprising and unsolicited ways. For instance, a small child who insists she sees people that others cannot is rarely accused of being crazy or deceitful. Adults who work with the public as mediums or Tarot card readers must meet certain standards, considered genuine only if their readings are sufficiently specific and accurate. Healers must regularly affect cures or improvements that otherwise appear to be medically inexplicable. Since contemporary debates about Spiritualism in Iceland tend to be less charged than they were in the early 1900s, skeptics—who are not in short supply—feel little need to assert their views in ways that make practitioners publicly defensive. Although Icelandic skepticism is not uncommon, it appears that many more Icelanders maintain a noncommittal attitude toward Spiritualist phenomena.[31] This may be because *skyggnigáfa* is such a pervasive theme in Iceland, emerging regularly in family lore, literature, and pop culture, that many find it hard to discount it entirely.[32] It seems that, since the days of Indriði and early Spiritualism, agnostics and believers alike are less concerned about the scientific validity of Spiritualism as a whole than with the authenticity of individuals—ranging from young children to famous mediums—who claim extraordinary abilities.

INTERCONNECTIVITY AND ETHICS: THE DIFFERENCE SPIRITS MAKE

For the Icelandic public, the legitimacy of Spiritualism largely rests on the credibility of purported *skyggnigáfa*; for Spiritualists, the existence of *skyggnigáfa* in turn relies on earthly human interactions with the spirit realm. Neo-Vedantans may share Spiritualism's concern for empirical proof associated with extraordinary abilities, but they have absolutely no room for spirits, finding their existence a problem to be solved or, at very least, ignored. As to be expected, the conspicuous absence and presence of spirits result in a world of difference between these two traditions. In particular, this difference forges divergent ethical imperatives for those understood to possess—and choose to make use of—these abilities.

Although Hindu religious frameworks do not preclude the possibility that the dead and their powers can be accessed by the living, many consider such practices to be unclean and inauspicious. Given that death is a highly polluting state for Hindus, particularly problematic for the so-called purer, higher castes, spirits of the dead are likewise considered potentially polluting and bearers of misfortune for the living. Classical Hindu belief generally allows two respectable options for the eternal *atman* or soul of the deceased: transmigration into a new body according to one's karmic path or, if one's karma is complete, arrival at the state of *moksha* or final union/identification with the Divinity/*Brahman*. Given this framework, meandering in the spirit world is not a desirable option; elite Hindu traditions consider lingering spirits to be troubled or troubling, off track, and largely to be avoided.[33] Caste-conscious Hindus likely are distanced further from low-caste practices involving spirits of the dead through the work of turn-of-the-century Hindu reformers, many of whom also advocated for Neo-Vedanta. One of the aims of reform was to sanitize Hinduism, purging it of elements British colonizers considered superstitious; such unsuitable elements would have included a number of low-caste practices such as invocations of the dead.

An example of typical Hindu aversions to spirit encounters was the reaction I received from Aiya when I described to him my proposed fieldwork in Iceland. When I broke the news that I would be spending time in Akureyri studying a tradition of extraordinary abilities similar to *siddhis*, Aiya was intrigued and encouraged that Icelanders cultivated such practices. Anticipating his next reaction, I then explained that people in Iceland usually understood these abilities to derive "from the other side," from spirits of the deceased. To this bit of information, Aiya said nothing; he simply looked at me and grimaced dramatically. I couldn't help but chuckle at his reaction, but Aiya stayed serious. No more need be said. The traditions he has cultivated at his temple, although unconventional in many ways, are nonetheless founded on orthodox Hindu principles. Aiya does not doubt that spirits can linger and communicate with the living. Yet given that lingering spirits have not been reincarnated and have not achieved final divine union, he considers them to loiter close to the earthly realm for reasons other than good.[34]

Skyggnigáfa's heightened human-spirit interconnectivity is also—in a very different way—counterintuitive for Icelanders, running contrary to the expected individualism of the New Age movement, of a Northern European Protestant nation, and of Icelandic culture itself. Icelandic Spiritualist practices furthermore augment the human-spirit relations presumed by *skyggnigáfa*, supporting a multilevel web of interdependence that finds no parallel in Neo-Vedantic contexts. Although *siddhis* are often gained through the guidance of a guru or monastic community, they are almost exclusively a product of one's own efforts, whereas the acquisition of *skyggnigáfa* is anything but a solo affair. Emerging unbidden and initially severed from human agency, *skyggnigáfa* simply makes no sense without the cooperation, and sometimes insistence, of spirit entities. Similar to yogic adepts, whose *siddhis* grow and change over time, Icelandic mediums and healers may hone their abilities as well, but their success will depend, at least in part, on the particular talents and inclinations of the spirit "team" working with them. According to Spiritualists, although spirits are released from earthly restrictions, they possess, to varying degrees, strengths and limitations like anyone else.

Although yogic adepts cannot acquire *siddhis* except through their own efforts, they do engage with the wider human community when, similar to Spiritualist mediums and healers, they opt to use their abilities to benefit the public through counseling or healing practices. Furthermore, Neo-Vedantic reformers have shaped their tradition more communally than conventional Hinduism, resulting in an ever-growing number of guru ashrams dedicated to public outreach aimed at uplifting impoverished and marginalized members of society. The religious rationale for this modern emphasis often stems from the view that all life-forms are manifestations of and united through the same divine source. This divine interconnectivity creates a religious imperative to work toward the well-being of all.

When spirits enter the picture, however, understandings of interconnectivity and "public outreach" expand considerably, and, as a result, so do ethical considerations. Not only are spirits integral to Icelandic Spiritualists' public service of counsel and healing, but the flow of aid also goes in more than one direction. Guðbjörg's successful delivery of the hanged man out of her closet, described above, offers a dramatic example of spirit dependence on the living. This partially explains why those who try to ignore or close their openness to the spirit world, witnessed by Matti, Hrabba, and Jón's accounts, ultimately fail. Once people with unwanted *skyggnigáfa*, harassed (so it seems) by insistent spirits, give in to spirit "pressure" and begin to work within the Spiritualist framework, their relationship to the insistent dead tends to become, although perhaps still challenging, much less unwieldy.

Of course exceptions abound: needy spirits can come unbidden to those who have already consented to working with their *skyggnigáfa*, as when Matti discovered an anguished—and anguishing—spirit in his new apartment. After many unsuccessful attempts to pray for the spirit, to bring him into the light, Matti agreed to allow him come through him while in trance. As is typical of trance mediumship, Matti does not remember the session but was told by members of his *hringur* that the spirit was of a man who had died of leprosy long ago. He explained through Matti that he had been wandering in the dark, unable to go toward the light because of his shame: half of his face was gone, and he felt that no one who could see him would want him. As Matti's *hringur* members understood it, the man's agonizing self-judgment prevented him from moving forward. They eventually succeeded in convincing him that his disfigurement was not his fault and that he was indeed worthy of basking in the light. He no longer haunts Matti's apartment, although he sometimes comes through him while in trance to express his gratitude and to offer updates on his progress.

Spiritualist practitioners who work most deliberately and diligently to deliver the dead from the darkness of self-hatred are trance mediums and *hringur* members who arrange their weekly meetings like counseling sessions, designed to convince the disturbed deceased that they are worthy of light and love. This approach reflects one of the central tenets of Icelandic Spiritualist theology, preached by Haraldur Níelsson, informed by his liberal theology, and something I encountered repeatedly during my stay in Akureyri: God is pure love and light. When our earthly lives are over, God does not judge us, we only judge ourselves. Eternal damnation does not exist, only darkness due to our own self-hatred. When we forgive ourselves we can be delivered, sometimes with help from the living. The logic that trance sessions can be of particular help to lost souls has to do with the idea that those trapped in regret and self-loathing are mired, in one way or another, in the material world and earthly regrets. Those still existing on the material plane who are open, loving, and nonjudgmental thus become important mediators and conductors of earthly healing energy, potentially convincing spirits—if they are receptive—that they can advance to a better place. According to Icelandic Spiritualists, the act of simply inhabiting a trance medium's physical body can help a spirit move forward, as can consoling conversations with the *hringur's* human participants.

Hrabba, whose *hringur* often dedicates itself to ushering disturbed spirits into the light, works to ease not only spirit self-loathing but also the shock and confusion of those who have died suddenly and violently. With the help of Hrabba's spirit guides, her *hringur* often seeks out victims of natural disasters such as earthquakes, fires, and avalanches. As Hrabba sees it, her job is easy compared to that of her *hringur* members who take on the emotional task of interacting with profound sadness and upheaval, something she hears about only after the fact. Reflecting on the process of easing spirits' guilt, most excruciatingly felt by those who have taken their own lives, Hrabba noted, "It's really strange how much it does for people just to be listened to. They have to tell somebody why they made this decision—and that they regret it. So then they can go into the light to get some peace."

Near the end of my interview with Hrabba, reflecting on the fact that her trance sessions basically go on without her, I asked if there was anything that her work as a trance medium has taught her about the world or about herself. She responded, immediately, that she has been taught not to judge. She then described to me what she referred to as one of the most difficult experiences of her life when helping a young man who had committed suicide. The first time he came through her into her *hringur* he expressed profound regret, yet, as Hrabba put it, "he didn't see any other way out. [His life] was just darkness and he couldn't see any happiness. He told us that he didn't have one happy thought even though he had children." When Hrabba was preparing for her next trance session—feeling, deep down, that there is always something worth living for in life—this man's spirit came to her and asked if she would take on his emotional state when he decided to end his life. Hrabba agreed and remembers crying nearly all day long as a result. As she described it, "It was really, really, *really* hard. So [I learned] I'm not supposed to judge." Aside from learning not to judge others, Hrabba's work with troubled spirits has taught her that one of the greatest challenges—in earthly life and beyond—is self-forgiveness.

Trance sessions dedicated to helping spirits in need, such as Hrabba's and Matti's, are not unusual in Iceland. In fact, all six trance mediums I spoke with geared their sessions significantly, if not exclusively, with this kind of work in mind. The expansiveness of this human-spirit interdependence seems a far cry from the early days of Icelandic Spiritualism, in which spirits appeared to work in the service of the living—and in cooperation with science—offering tangible proof of life after death. Yet according to Einar Kvaran's 1934 recollections of the movement's early days, the needs of troubled spirits seemed to have asserted themselves from the start. Einar describes an incident when Konrad, Indriði's spirit controller, speaking through him while he was in trance,[35] precipitated a begrudging change in direction:

> We were once surprised when Konrad told us that he had come with a man who we had to pray for. We hadn't had any inclination to have these meetings be prayerful, so we responded half-heartedly. We asked why [the spirits] could not do this themselves, if that would not be just as effective. But they insisted and explained that this man was not aware of [the other spirits]. We asked them if we might just as well pray for him in silence. But we got the answer that this was not enough because he needed to hear us. Haraldur Níelsson then recited a very beautiful prayer. When that was over, Konrad said that the prayer did a lot of good. And after that, many more came to us asking for the same thing. This led to the meetings becoming different than before. Hymns were sung and people joined together in this prayerful mentality. ("Frá Landamærunum" 1934: n.p.)

Today's emphasis on helping troubled spirits does not, of course, negate the continued need, established at the start of the Spiritualist movement, for reassurances from the beloved departed and proof of life after death. Such tasks—in addition to counseling and healing practices for the living—remain central to Spiritualist clients, and significant to practitioners as well. The work of praying for and counseling troubled spirits is noteworthy, however, in that it does not offer the same dividends as other kinds of Spiritualist work—or of outreach work performed by guru ashrams. Spirit-helping sessions with trance mediums tend to be performed in darkened private spaces; success stories are appreciated only by the spirits themselves and by the small group who dedicate their time and energies to assisting them. So quiet is this work that I found, to my surprise, that *hringur* members and trance mediums were often unaware that an otherwise familiar *hringur* had a similar emphasis. Many were under the impression that they were among the very few groups who specialized in this approach. This leads me to believe that, although spirit-helping sessions may have been carried out from the beginning in Iceland, once Konrad had requested them, their prevalence—and the urgency with which they are performed—is fairly new.[36]

This focus on tending to the needs of the dead, drawing from Icelandic Spiritualism's foundational emphasis on nonjudgment and forgiveness, relies not only on the existence of *skyggnigáfa* but on those who choose, altruistically, to use this gift in a low-profile way. As I see it, return for this kind of work, largely hidden from (living) public view, is that it offers a profound if not cosmic sense of purpose. Outreach to the departed in crisis, labor that is admittedly difficult and draining, fulfills an ethical imperative that is, for those with whom I spoke, richly gratifying.

The established goal of Spiritualism, envisioned as progressing with compassion and forgiveness toward the eternal light of *alheimsorka*, is not so different, ideologically speaking, from the Neo-Vedantan goal of achieving ego-free enlightenment and union with universal consciousness. Yet practitioners' bodily experiences of this pathway toward light/enlightenment, framed by extraordinary abilities that, in turn, bring spirits into (or out of) the picture, could not be more different. While meandering spirits can be a hindrance or, at very least, disconcerting to Neo-Vedantans in search of enlightenment, the spirit world is no less than integral to Icelandic Spiritualists' aim, ethic, and—in contrast to Neo-Vedanta—collective sense of purpose. Moreover, from the perspective of lost or troubled spirits themselves, *skyggnigáfa* could not be more different from *siddhi*s, whether the latter are hard-earned or not. Seen from this angle, *skyggnigáfa* is a "gift" not just for the living but also for the dead, made possible by those willing to assume the challenges of offering it over. Sacred redeeming power in this context breaches divides in ways unlike any other described in this book, unequivocally and necessarily earthbound, offered for the sake of the unearthly.

༄

Postscript

Unanticipated Adventures in Ritualized Ethnography

I conclude this book's adventures in comparison on a slightly different note. Here, rather than exploring strategies for accessing the earthly sacred across religious and cultural divides, I juxtapose ritual and ethnography to view how these activities, "lofty" enterprises in their own right, are nevertheless formed by earthly concerns and constraints.[1] Humanizing qualities that I argue are intrinsic to both endeavors—bodily knowledge, reflexivity, and indeterminacy—structure the following reflections. Also, in contrast to the other chapters in this book, here I reflect on an actual—rather than an intellectual—collision of two systems, provided by one of my more surreal fieldwork experiences. By bringing to light observers of religion alongside religions observed, ethnographers alongside ritual practitioners, I hope to even the stakes a bit, to conclude by considering how the limitations and possibilities of our earthbound state inform and deepen not just the religions we study but our scholarly trade as well.

Historically speaking, the disciplines of ethnography and ritual studies find themselves on similar footing as both underwent dramatic revision somewhat simultaneously during the second half of the twentieth century. Yet their respective shifts—rooted broadly in challenges to a taken-for-granted European and North American Protestant order—moved them in opposite directions. While ethnography's crisis prompted some scholars to question the legitimacy of an enterprise that claimed to represent and categorize the Other, ritual gained new respectability. Whereas ritual once was considered to be a mindless, static, and mechanical agent of an outmoded, status quo, it is now commonly attributed with creative, transformative, and ethical properties. This shift largely coincides with the reframing of ritual as a mode of performance.[2] Further casting a positive light on ritual performances are statements by theorists who understand the healthy state of ritual studies to be contagious, potentially invigorating the academy itself. Gavin Brown's discussion of ritual performance optimistically posits that, "for many scholars, performance has become the conceptual hammer with which to break down disciplinary boundaries and traditional conceptual frameworks formerly demarcating the study of a broad range of human cultural activities" (2003: 31). Catherine Bell suggests that the study of performance can be mutually beneficial among practitioners of ritual and ritual studies, invoking, as she puts it, "a new sense of community between theorists and actors, characterized by modest, mutual dependence and shared problems of meaning, epistemology, and critical self-reflection" (1998: 54).[3]

The flesh-and-blood event on which I build this postscript provides a conceptual hammer of sorts that unwittingly breaks down categories and divisions between people, forging a community composed of theorists and actors whose performative roles become somewhat interchangeable. Enabled by this shared mode of performance, it is an encounter that enfolds ethnography into ritual (and now, as I reflect, back into ethnography), enacting role inversions by turning a typical observer-interpreter (me) into a ritual actor and ritual actors into observer-interpreters of a text that, in turn, recounts and interprets ritual performances.

RITUALIZED ETHNOGRAPHY

This swirling mix took place in January 2004 at the Rush temple in upstate New York. I had just finished writing a book manuscript about the temple and was scheduled to travel to Rush from Wisconsin around the same time for a weeklong visit.[4] Aiya, the head priest/guru at the temple, aware of the status of the manuscript, asked that I bring it with me before shipping it off for review. Since he is a ritual enthusiast, to state things mildly, I anticipated involving the manuscript in a temple rite of some kind. Most likely, we would lay the pile of papers next to the temple goddess before *puja* started, where it would receive blessings in the form of appropriate *slokas* and perhaps an extra wave of camphor flame.

This was not, however, what Aiya had in mind. Late morning on the day I arrived, a group of us were sitting and chatting outside the main temple in front of *homam* fire pit when, seemingly out of the blue, Aiya asked me to fetch my manuscript. When I returned, 320 pages in hand, he patted the floor next to him, indicating where I should sit. Wondering how one might ritualize a manuscript in this setting, I plunked myself next to him. Aiya then motioned to the Goddess *murti* facing us on the far side of the con-joining temple. Chiseled from black granite, she was dressed, as usual, in a fine sari, wore a garland of flowers from the previous afternoon's festivities and, on this day, looked somehow expectant (Figure 5.1). He announced, as though I knew what was coming, "Okay. Now you can read." I laughed, thinking he must be joking, to which he gently asserted, "Go ahead and read it, Amma." When it became alarmingly clear that he wanted me to read the entire book, I protested that I likely would drone on for days, monopolizing all otherwise interesting and important conversation. But Aiya stood firm. I tried suggesting that a chapter or a few chapter selections would certainly suffice, but still he wouldn't budge. So, with a mixed sense of em-

Figure 5.1
Rush temple Goddess, Sri Rajarajeshwari.

barrassment, intrepidation, and gratitude I read for the divine and human audience over a three-day period. Once the rather theoretical introduction was behind us, the human audience became more participatory, occasionally commenting on ideas and events, becoming particularly animated when someone among them was referenced or quoted.

To further thicken the plot, it so happened that at the tail end of the manuscript recital, as I inhaled to begin the first sentence of its final page, my graduate adviser Ann Gold and her husband Dan stepped out of a fierce snowstorm and into the temple. I put down the manuscript, greeted them, and introduced them to Aiya. Since they were first-time visitors, a small group of us took them on a tour of the temple, and afterward we sat together to read the final page. As Ann and Dan left the temple later that afternoon, Ann noted to me, in a prophetic aside, that I would probably write about this one day.

The morning after I finished reading, the temple held a special *puja* in honor of Shiva. Aiya asked me once again to fetch my manuscript so that the work could receive the deity's blessings. This was more like what I had imagined: a pile of papers adorned with a dab of red *kumkum* and a flower became an offering amid flame, bell ringing, chanting, and copious clouds of incense. Those at Oxford University Press who shortly after received the innocuous-looking manuscript likely had no idea what it had just been through—though I imagine a lingering whiff of incense may have tipped them off.

EMBODIED KNOWLEDGE

This story of a ritual and ethnographic mega-collision was made possible, in part, by the fact that both endeavors require bodies that, moreover, are instrumental to the process of conveying and receiving knowledge. Distinguishing ritual and ethnographical performances from other types of religious and academic pursuits is not only their involvement of the body in a particular space and time, but the varieties of perception— cognitive, kinetic, and emotional—engaged through bodily channels. Performance as a genre can also be applied to both ritual and ethnography in that it involves bodies but also a tradition of commonly acknowledged codes and procedures, a sense of collective action that is deliberate, and a communal awareness that these actions are different from ordinary events (Sullivan 1986: 5). Framed as such, ritual and ethnography are performances in that they are embodied, orchestrated multisensory events containing agreed-upon parameters of conduct.[5] The key difference between them lies in the fact that while contemporary ethnographers have begun in earnest to appreciate and investigate a range of emotional and sensory experiences associated with the ritual practices of others, taken-for-granted ethnographical codes of conduct prevent them from analyzing, with equal enthusiasm, the multisensory experiences embedded in their own work.[6]

Offering an example of bodily knowledge conveyed through ritual performance is the Shrividya Tantric tradition practiced at the Rush temple, one that explicitly connects bodily senses, movement, and emotions to bodily learning and discipline, consciously reflected on and enhanced in a number of ways. For temple participants, ritually prescribed movements, sounds, and smells are not only conduits for communication with and reception of divine activity; in some instances they trigger important emotions honed through experience and memory. Appreciative of these associations, Aiya insists on using camphor flame in temple rituals even though it blackens surfaces and stubbornly remains in crevasses. He reasons that the smell of camphor invokes memories of worship among Sri Lankan temple participants; memories steeped in a particular scent invite them deeper into their devotion. Likewise, ritually prescribed bodily movements known as *mudras* give power and purpose to rituals and their officiants and, just as importantly, instill a sense of devotion in members of the congregation for whom these actions are familiar. When instructing his students, Aiya explains that *mudras* must be performed with devotion and care, both for the benefit of the ritual and to inspire devotion in those observing.

Not only does Shrividya ritual engage types of bodily knowledge—kinesthetic, sensual, and emotional—for the purposes of devotion; the physical body can also act as a means for identification with divinity. In the *shricakra puja*, a ritual central to the tradition, the practitioner's goal is to bodily identify with the goddess residing in the three-dimensional *meru*. The *nyasam* chanted at the beginning of the ritual literally describes the body according to its physiological systems and components. While it is commonly thought to be a rite of bodily protection, creating an impenetrable shield for the ritual performer, Aiya considers the *nyasam* to also be an invocation that associates the body—from its individual systems to the smallest of cells—with divinity:

> When you initiate the *nyasam*, that deity on whom you are focusing your energies is the priest [who is chanting]. Analyze this statement in terms of what you know about the body. What is the body? The body contains 6.4 billion cells. Right? You have nine different broad-based systems in your body. That is why it

is called Nava Avana *puja* [another name for the *shrichakra puja*]. The Devi takes control of those nine systems (Aiya counts on his fingers): nervous system, muscular system, skeletal system, endocrine system, digestive system, respiratory system, urinary system, excretory system, right? Cardiovascular system...one more is there, lymphatic system. You've covered the whole body [Aiya chants the *nayasam* to demonstrate].... That's why when I talk about the Devi I always say that she gives five components to the body and Shiva gives four.... So now what is happening? All these cells have already been differentiated; they've already formed tissue systems. But each cell is alive and kicking. Therefore each cell can be described as a deity—a *gana*, a *yogina*. Right?

Such understandings of the body's multilayered emotional and physiological engagements are indeed welcomed by ethnographers who consider bodily knowledge and expression foundational to ritual performance. The fact that, despite this appreciation, ethnographers themselves only sporadically reflect on how the body and its senses engage with their own fieldwork performances seems, to some, inconsistent. In his article "Magical Laments and Anthropological Reflections" James Wilce notes that the pull toward scholarly distancing and objectivity continues relatively unabated despite current academic trends. He identifies select scholars of ritual who nonetheless unconsciously embed emotion—reflecting something akin to ritual expression itself—in their writing. The fact that these embedded emotions emerge only unwittingly is something Wilce sees as indicative of contradictions and inconsistencies in the field. He thus appeals to ethnographers to be more self-aware and forthright about their embodied work that must, by nature, be emotionally engaged (2006: 891).

Respondents to his article—particularly those whose work he heavily cites—take offense at this interpretation, viewing it as a paternalistic portrayal of naive anti-intellectualism. However one respondent, Margaret Trawick, defends Wilce by arguing that likening anthropological reflection to ritual expression is insulting only when one erroneously equates ritual with the nonmodern and the nonrational. Trawick furthermore argues that anthropologists naturally, and at their best, will be affected by what they study. It should thus come as no surprise that scholars deeply engaged in translation and analysis will be transformed by their work: "Good ethnographic writing is necessarily always mimetic, always an attempt at accurate reflection, and through the act of mimesis, the act of reflection, the mime and the mirror are changed" (2006: 909).[7]

In an effort not only to own up to the ways bodies and senses reflect and inform the study of ritual but also to promote the importance of bodily knowledge that emerges from such engagements, Kimerer LaMothe encourages scholars to train their bodies and senses so they can best be used as tools appropriate for study. As a student of ritual dance, she in fact suggests that religion scholars take up dance to hone their sensory empathy and deepen their analytical frameworks.[8] Clearly aware of her audience, LaMothe hedges her suggestion by adding that, certainly, not all scholars will or should take up dance. For those of us who study more standard types of ritual performances, we also may not opt—nor have the option—to train in the rituals we write about, but as fieldworkers we cannot help but bring our bodies with us to the site. As such, one could argue that we have no choice but to involve a range of perceptions that potentially enables us to empathize more deeply with embodied aspects of our study. Whether or not we consciously choose to reflect on these bodily forms of knowledge—and how able we are to translate them to language—is another matter.

REFLEXIVITY

This cycle of knowing—of the ways in which embodied knowledge embedded in the process of our study can reflect and inform the study itself—points the way to the participant-observer dialectic known as reflexivity. Generically speaking, reflexivity can be understood as a process of mirroring and enfolding, demonstrated fairly dramatically by this chapter's opening vignette, in which ethnography collapses into ritual and vice versa, turning the traditional observer into a ritual actor and ritual actors into observers. While typical ethnographic reflexivity does not mirror with quite so many permutations, ethnographers tend to be familiar with the push and pull of the process and with ongoing debates regarding its benefits and excesses. Questions about ritual's potential for productive reflexivity, however, are less well known.[9]

At one end of the spectrum, anthropologists Myerhoff and Ruby warn readers of the limits of ritual reflexivity, positing that religious performances often "parade as other versions of 'reality.' [...] They masquerade as different versions of truth into which individuals may come and go without realizing how contrived it all is." They argue that, in fact, rituals have a way of discouraging reflexivity, since they typically involve repetitive actions that are "mindless and frenetic," keeping the body "too busy to allow the mind to criticize. [...] Precariously, a ritual may march along the edge of discovery of its own contrivances, producing not reflexivity but reflections" (1982: 3–4). Although Myerhoff and Ruby identify ritual as a human activity that is most likely to be contrived and least likely to encourage true reflexivity, they also, to be fair, note that most of us under normal circumstances teeter between a completely unexamined and an achingly clear understanding of life.

At the other end of the spectrum, a number of religion scholars release ritual from obligations to produce similar types of knowledge—and therefore similar types of reflexivity—as other, particularly academic, endeavors. As Theodore Jennings argues, ritual action can lead to profound reflexivities, particularly when it conveys paradigms of the community or, most radically, ontological or cosmogonic praxis. In full disagreement with Myerhoff and Ruby, Jennings submits that in such instances ritual participation is intrinsically reflexive, since its enactment is "to know how the world acts, how it 'comes to be'" (1982: 121).[10] Catherine Bell and Lawrence Sullivan similarly argue for the naturally reflexive nature of ritual performances, inasmuch as ritual offers opportunities for people to stand back and assess the creation of culture or identity, allowing participants to become "an audience to themselves" (Bell 1992: 75; Sullivan 1986: 13).[11]

Augmenting this understanding of ritual as inherently reflexive, as enfolding subject and object and dissolving self/Other dualities, are the ways in which a religiously charged emotion, wonder, invites reflexivity and, moreover, wider ethical concern. Like ritual, wonder is conventionally associated with mistaken notions of cause and effect and with unreflective receptivity and passivity yet, as reframed by Robert Fuller, wonder can also evoke creativity and a deeper connection to one's surroundings. Fuller emphasizes wonder's capacity to expand our "field of peripheral vision," encouraging reflection on the ways individual objects and people are connected to a greater whole. He notes how wonder is ultimately nondualistic in its capacity to move others' concerns into one's own sphere of interest; it is unmatched in its potential for engendering true empathy and compassion. Admitting that too much wonder could indeed encourage a world of fantasy and illusion, Fuller concludes that "while it is true that wonder-driven thought carries considerable philosophical risk, so too does thought wholly devoid of wonder" (2006: 384).

Again drawing from Rush temple practices, we find that reflexivity is tied to ritual performance and theology in a variety of ways, fueling and fueled by a sense of wonder. Most basically, consistent with Jennings's description of ritual performances as orchestrated enactments of communal and cosmic realities, Rush rituals are reflexive events in and of themselves. Aiya's readily offered interpretations of ritual mechanics and theology, of praxis and reflection on this praxis, represent a more cognitive mode of reflexivity that encourages participants to be audience to themselves.

Finally, rituals at Rush are reflexive in that they both appeal to and create divinity, requiring ritual performers to assume the status of devotee and object of devotion. The aim of ritual is thus to produce a dialectic, religiously reflexive relationship between subject and object, actor and benefactor, ideally transforming both in the process.

Although Rush temple rituals often involve the generation of and engagement with infinity and divinity, fine distinctions remain between different ritual forms. For instance, at *homam* fire rituals practitioners most explicitly create, through the fire, the deity to whom offerings are given. In the case of *puja* rituals performed to the granite temple *murti*, the energy of the deity, generated from the *yantra* beneath the image, is maintained rather than created from scratch. Meditation practices, internal rituals of sorts, most radically blur the distinction between devotee and object of devotion or, more accurately, help practitioners realize that no distinction in fact exists to begin with.

During the summer of 2007, I asked Aiya to reflect on the ways meditation erases dualities, to which he responded that the practice is simply a matter of bringing one's awareness to an ever-present, unchanging reality:

> Whether you like it or not, the Mother is connected to you from inside. Because otherwise you would stop breathing. You're not aware of it. So if you are not aware of the divine presence inside of you, that does not mean it is not there. It's there! It is the One that is running the whole show and you're absorbing it. Sometimes you have to remind yourself of that. When you internalize that [through meditation] then you know: "Okay, this is happening. I owe everything to Her."

Applying this principle of identification to other temple rituals, I asked, "So do you ever think about how performing any kind of ritual or *homam*, for instance, is a devotion to something you just created that already exists that is you? I mean, so you can collapse all that, actually?" Aiya, nodding his head while I was talking, responded,

> Mmm hmm. Ultimately, that is what the *homam* comes down to. Finally you say, "I offer all of this to my Mother." And who's Maha Tripurasundari [a title for the great goddess of the Shrividya tradition]? She's my consciousness. So I'm giving it to my consciousness. So that will be there. And just because I have entered the cycle somewhere and done this ritual, she is the one who is taking, she is the one who has it, she is the one who owns it, she is the one who has actually commis-

sioned the ritual, she is the one who has actually performed the ritual. Therefore, let her bless everybody with whatever the ritual has been. That's the whole idea.

As described above, the *shrichakra puja*, central to the temple's Shrividya tradition, enfolds devotee and object of devotion in explicitly physiological ways. The main focus of this *puja*, the *meru*, is a three-dimensional representation of the *shrichakra yantra* that encapsulates associations with the human body as well as with multifaceted divinity. On one level, when practitioners undertake the four-hour-long *shrichakra puja*, they perform ritual to their own bodies in the form of the *meru*. The large *meru* at the temple—submerged beneath another *meru* in 2005—was in fact made especially for Aiya's physical body, measured to correspond to the 206 bones in his frame. At the same time, the *meru* is understood to contain the power of the Goddess, who in turn contains the entire cosmos. In the following exchange, occurring during the summer of 2007, Aiya portrays the *meru* and its multiple frames of reference as continuously folding into one another. The resulting description is of a ritually layered, reflexively collapsing reality that might be difficult to follow if one were not somewhat familiar with Shrividya theology. Aiya begins his depiction of the *shrichakra meru* as follows:

> The *meru* is a representation of the microcosm that is inside you. When you're performing the ritual, obviously because of the fact that you are performing it, there is already duality. So you place something in front of you; you have placed your consciousness out, which is the beauty of the entire universe, which is God; you have placed that entity visually [in the form of the *meru*], you have visualized that you have placed that entity in front of you and now you are performing your devotions to it.

Aiya pauses to see if I am following him. I nod and respond, "Right," and he continues:

> When this is happening, here is the performer; here is the deity [Aiya places his hands, each facing the other, about a foot apart]. There is an act of the performance. So there is one end of the triangle and the other end of the triangle here [again with two hands facing one another] and in between there is the apex of the triangle [the point above the two initial points] which, as the ritual is being commissioned, is encompassing everything that is outside of you in the universe, and it's involving the causal power. It's a subtlety lost on most practitioners because they focus exclusively on the *meru* and on the body.

I interject, "And not the apex." Aiya continues,

Yeah, not on the apex of the thing. But when you're performing it, gradually through practice, as Shrividya tells you, gradually through practice you will begin to be able to experience the universal being's participation in the ritual. So it's taking place on three different levels. On the physical plane and, if you're visualizing something, on the mental plane and, because of your concentration in the physical and the mental plane, it's performed on the causal plane also [Aiya shows the apex with his hand]. It's performing here at the same time. So the ritual does not focus on the *meru* itself. Its focus is on you—on your body—on the *meru*, and on the universe.

For clarification, I add, "And sometimes the *meru* represents both your body and the cosmos. And your body also represents the cosmos. And the causal plane connects those two and encompasses those two." Aiya, nodding, responds, "Right. And so, there's a triangle that will ultimately collapse into a point."

"And that's the *bindu*."

"Right."

Aiya's description of the *shrichakra*'s triadic identifications, of complex reflexivities acknowledged and collapsed through ritual, is corroborated in the work of Douglas Brooks, a scholar of the Shrividya tradition: "Ritual is the key to reading the śricakra as a divine map and to gaining access to the divine presence, for it is in ritual that the śricakra is elevated from being divinity's self-generated pattern for reality to divine presence (sadbhava)....These achievements, however, are contingent upon the adept identifying in body and soul with the śricakra and Śrividyā" (1992: 118). Brooks describes the point of collapse beyond identification, the *bindu*, as "the nondifferentiated state of being that precedes manifest creation," a state that depends, as Aiya explained, on a triadic formulation of knowing and reality. As Brooks puts it, "This 'triadic' shape symbolizes the world's basic epistemological and ontological patterns; for example, reality depends on the triadic relationship of subject, object, and process of cognition....In Śrividyā's world view, epistemological dualism is not binary but tertiary" (1992: 123).

Recalling Myerhoff and Ruby's assessment of ritual as tending toward the mindless and frenetic, obscuring true reality, it is interesting to note that their assessment of ethnographical reflexivity uses language loftily reminiscent of Shrividya ritual theology. As they describe it, it is not enough for us to hold up a single mirror to be reflexively engaged: "The mirrors must be doubled, creating the endless regress of possibilities, opening out into infinity, dissolving the clear boundaries of a 'real world'" (1992: 3). This endless regress of subject-object reflection might be likened to the process of cognition—identified by Aiya as the causal plane beyond all thinking and being—that, according to *shrichakra puja* theology, engages when subject and object, self and *meru*, identify. Analogous to dissolving "real world" categories, as posited by Myerhoff and Ruby, the *shrichakra* triad of identification ideally collapses to form a *bindu* representing a "nondifferentiated state of being." Despite Myerhoff and Ruby's assessment of ritual as a diversion from reality, the language they use to describe reflexive reality seems perhaps more at home in ritual than in ethnographic settings. I suspect Wilce would claim this as yet another example of unwitting spillage of ritual language into the ethnographical realm.

The religiously laden language shared between anthropologists and a Hindu guru might encourage us to think about the ways ethnographic reflexivity potentially challenges conventional conceptions. Here I refer to processes that, described by Aiya, extend beyond our everyday state of thinking and being, stemming yet separate from subject/object identification. Although I wouldn't go so far as to ascribe these processes to divine awareness, I suggest that they nonetheless represent forces that lie outside our cognitive control and, in the best of instances, give vitality to our work.

THE RISK AND POTENTIAL OF INDETERMINACY

Speaking of forces outside our cognitive control, we arrive at the final point of shared concern for ritual and ethnographic performances: indeterminacy. As described by Gavin Brown, performance at its heart is precariously fraught with indeterminacy in that it relies on a preexisting script that nevertheless must take place in the realm of human action. As such, "a performance represents a creative tension between the 'what should be' of the script and the 'what happens' of the actual performance" (2003: 5). Performances are furthermore indeterminately risky, since participants might read meanings into them not intended or sanctioned by the script. Religious performances add another layer of indeterminacy due to their contact with powerful and possibly capricious forces (Howe 2000: 67). Viewed from this perspective, the ritual reading of my manuscript suggests multilayered, multidisciplinary risky indeterminacies—from possible mistakes in recording facts or analyses, to misconstrued receptions of readers or listeners, to an offering rejected by the goddess.

With ritual studies' turn toward performance, rituals become necessarily unique with each enactment, and indeterminacy becomes less a liability than an asset. From the perspective of performance, departures from the script are what give ritual its dynamic quality and transformative power. As Gavin Brown explains, if we understand ritual as rigidly scripted and bound by original intent, "we are settling for what ritual is designed to achieve rather than what it may achieve in each and every moment of its performance" (2003: 11). In cases where ritual performances depart from convention in socially transgressive ways—such as when Shrividya rituals are performed by women and non-Brahmans at the Rush temple—additional layers of meaning and power can accrue. Furthermore, the "risk" that an audience might not understand the ritual as it was originally intended disappears, since, as literary theory tells us, such "misreadings" are unavoidable. The fact that the meaning of a text/ritual cannot be found with the author but must instead be forged by the reader amounts to privileging the performative moment. Reading/participating is thus not passive consumption but becomes performance in itself. Rituals, like texts, articulate meanings that emerge through action and interaction rather than simply reflecting that which is predetermined.

A similar argument could be made for ethnography. Not only is an author's intention somewhat up for grabs once her book is in the hands of a reader; ethnographical writing is itself an act of interpretation that admittedly, like ritual, has little hope of accurately duplicating an original encounter. If we are comfortable framing ethnography as creating culture—as ritual theorists seem comfortable describing ritual—we would not worry so much about the uncertainties of ethnographic performances. But the extent to which we stray from the live "text" that we study and the extent to which readers' interpretations stray from our intentions remain rightly on our minds during each stage of the process, as we perform fieldwork and write. No matter how careful we are, risks seem to loom as hazardous byproducts of inevitable indeterminacies.

I thus was given quite a start when, a few months after my book on the Rush temple was published, Aiya made a passing reference to its "little mistakes." Surprised and a little panicked that he would say this—as he had carefully read and commented on each section as it was being written—I reacted a bit dramatically: "Mistakes!? What do you mean? What were they?" Taken aback, Aiya assured me they were of little consequence and certainly not noticeable to anyone except a few temple insiders. When I pursued the issue, asking him for examples, he smiled reassuringly and said, "Don't worry about it, Amma, they're endearing." I puzzled over this word "endearing," and in July 2006 I brought the subject up again. Aiya told me that he could no longer recall the book's mistakes and reiterated that they were of no consequence. What mattered was the spirit of the book. He felt that my heart was in the right place and that this came through in my writing.

At the end of a day's interview that summer, I told Aiya that I felt the project of doing fieldwork is similar to ritual in that it is messy and prone to human foibles and misunderstandings. I asked him if, in the end, he felt fieldwork study was worth the effort. As someone who tends to color mundane activity with divinity, Aiya's response ended up conflating fieldwork with ritual, both of which he felt would be successful as long as we assume the right attitude:

> It's very worth it. Because anything you do on this planet, whether it is just a simple exercise like walking to the fridge and making a sandwich—taking the ingredients out and making a sandwich, consuming it and then washing the vessels and putting them away—just that action alone, if you can relate it to divinity . . . as you're doing it, if you're thinking "I'm feeding the divinity that is within me, therefore I'm making these preparations," then it becomes ritual. It's a ritual. So the other side of it is, whether you realize it is a ritual or not, it is a ritual that the divine being within you is participating in. . . . At some level, however mundane it may appear, it is a ritual. And if you consciously offer the ritual, you're offering it to Her.

For clarification, I interjected, "So if your mind is in the right place . . ." to which Aiya responded, "Your mind has to *be* in the right place. Like I told you, if it's in an egotistic place, if you think [Aiya's voice sounding self-important], 'I have learned all this. I know how to do this. These fellows should be coming and falling at me,' then you're in trouble."

Aiya's reference to ego relates to a previous conversation we had about the risks of performing ritual incorrectly. Although ritual practice is a highly honed skill under Aiya's tutelage, he maintains that the biggest mistake a practitioner can make is not technical error but, rather, temperamental imbalance. Rituals become risky not because the deity is displeased with incorrect execution but because the executioner's overblown ego misdirects or abuses the ritual's power.

The following day when I asked Aiya to revisit the topic of ritual mistakes, he brought the conversation back to the divine Mother:

> Because the omni-compassionate Mother knows that her little child can make a mistake in the commission of the ritual, she's not going to say, "Oh, you idiot, that's not the way to do! Come here!" [Aiya smacks one hand with the other] and

whack you. She's not going to do that. You have to be very clear about that. That is the fear complex that those in the know have instilled into the people just to prevent them from getting into the inner loop.

I responded, "Right. They say that mistakes are dangerous. But it's not that. Why would someone misuse ritual power? What's at the bottom of that?"

Because they want their own power.... People want others to look at them and say, "Oh, this guy's really good." Big deal. So that's ego. And that's the one thing that we're trying to destroy and then you go back and do it anyway [laughs]....It's that Catch 22, yin-yang thing. You go in one direction and it'll push you back into the black area.

Aiya and I later agreed that if one performs ritual with the right disposition, with the view that everything, including the power gained from the ritual, emanates from the goddess, one is humbled. If one forgets who is ultimately in control, one easily commits the gravest ritual mistake of all by becoming arrogant. So ritual power is, as Aiya termed it, a "yin-yang thing," harboring potential for opposite dispositions.

Attention to disposition above all does not mean—particularly in the Shrividya tradition—that following a ritual script is not important. While Aiya encourages innovation among his students and appreciates that every *puja* will be different, individual variation constitutes accessory more than substance. When students inadvertently diverge from some of rituals' more crucial elements, it is understood that the goddess will nonetheless honor the offering. Adding further cushioning against ritual mistakes is the guru lineage. Before a ritual is performed, the officiant will invoke the guru *parampara* so that it can, as Aiya puts it, "absorb the mistakes" and ensure the absolute benefit of the ritual.

Like ritual performers, those of us who perform fieldwork and write about it are bound by community code to learn and follow the basic—and sometimes elaborate—academic conventions at our disposal and, within certain parameters, to innovate. A foundational component of ethnographic indeterminacy—one that creatively enlivens our work—is that no two people will engage with or write about a particular cultural phenomenon in the same way. Yet our fellow academics and audience rightly care about certain types of accuracy, and I would argue that our hearts are in the right place. Our academic *parampara* might help us regain legitimacy when out on a limb or, in some cases, may share some of the negative effects of our work's indeterminacies. But they cannot, alas, absorb them into nonexistence. Ethnographies riddled with inaccuracies are (if and when those inaccuracies are discovered) fairly useless, and fieldwork undertaken from a position of detached and depersonalized arrogance is, as Aiya and reflexivity advocates would agree, hardly worth its while.

THE MISSING PIECE

Let me finish by admitting to an episode that I had consciously left out of my tale about reading to the temple goddess, an omission I considered appropriate when embarking on this essay in order—so it happens—to stave off accusations of anti-intellectualism and, related to this, to protect my ego. I have since changed my mind, for obvious reasons. The event appropriately features sensory understandings born of reflexive identification and shifts my musings about ethnographic indeterminacies into a different register—one that reflects on internal experiences lying outside our cognitive control and considers what they can teach us about ways of knowing and being.

As I mentioned in my story at the start of this chapter, I was initially appalled by Aiya's suggestion that I read my entire manuscript for all to hear. I not only hated the thought of monopolizing endless hours of conversation but was also afraid that members of the audience might take offense. Perhaps I would reveal "mistakes" in fact or interpretation that would disappoint or hurt someone. Yet I experienced a conflicting sense of gratitude at the same time that, as I didn't mention earlier, quickly upstaged my fears. As I fumbled through the first paragraphs of the introduction, I was bombarded with a sense—not thoughts—of the sheer weight of the manuscript. I was hit by telescoped feelings of intimacy, generosity, trust, faith, and plain hard work that were packed into the pile of papers in my lap. Triggered by the presences around me, I was awash in gratitude for the many who had entrusted me with things held so dear to their hearts and who had helped me feel part of a vibrant community despite my never-quite-dissipated status as the researcher with her tape recorder. The feelings that spilled over me at that time I have put into words only upon writing this, and clumsily so, at that. Their original unordered, unnamed, and unintellectualized state seemed to give them all the more impetus.

As a result, I became choked up when I began reading the manuscript, during an introduction that, believe me, is nothing to get choked up about. My strategy was to read quietly so as not to burst into tears and embarrass myself until Aparna, sitting behind me, piped up, "Corinne! You need to read louder; I can barely hear you!" As I turned to explain that I was trying not to cry, to my great dismay, the floodgates opened. I handed Aparna the manuscript so she could read while I sobbed. By the time she finished the introduction, I was ready to read on. Interestingly, no one sitting around the *homam* pit asked me why I was crying. My emotions, for all to see, likely reflected the depth of my investment in the temple and its members—something that is probably good for my audience, temple members and beyond, to know.[12]

Another reason this episode is worth relating is that it viscerally demonstrates how ethnography can function, although humbly so, like ritual. Similar to the causal plane or apex that Aiya describes as emerging amid repeated subject-object identification, the layers of reflexivity embedded in fieldwork—fortified by years of painstaking work, discipline, and focus—can reveal a third realm that operates within and beyond our cognition and control, harbored in our minds and bodies. Angled differently, rituals are often understood to represent potent microcosms of larger realities, demonstrated by *shrichakra puja* practitioners whose bodies explicitly enact microcosms of the cosmos. Such ritual performances are not simply symbolically dense but, if doing their job, are meant to be physically, emotionally, and spiritually packed as well. Likewise, ethnography is not, at its heart, simply an intellectually dense house of reflexivity mirrors lodging potential misrepresentations of misunderstandings. As a sensually and emotionally laden performative process, it can offer—at its best and in often unanticipated ways—something more.

Stretching established convention and expectation, earthbound religious encounters described throughout this book suggest an array of sacred possibilities enhanced by and for the human condition. In the case of ritual and ethnography, their humanizing qualities likewise enrich our engagements, offering further glimpses into the deeply entangled ways that we—whether in religious or academic arenas—find efficacy and meaning.

NOTES

INTRODUCTION

1. I take my cue here from an edited volume conveniently entitled *A Magic Still Dwells*, the first sustained and, for my particular approach, currently the most important response of religion scholars to the comparison controversy. The title of the volume is borrowed from Jonathan Z. Smith's essay "A Magic Dwells." Also helpful to me has been a recent issue of the journal *Numen* 48.3 (2001) dedicated to discussing and defending comparison as a viable, important, and often inevitable approach to religious studies. Religious studies scholars who are more theologically and philosophically inclined have recently tackled the comparison debate in ways that, although less pertinent to my work, are helpful in thinking about larger issues at stake. See especially the Comparative Religious Ideas Project, noteworthy for its richly collaborative comparative process involving a working group of six specialists of six major religious traditions, four generalists, a number of graduate student assistants, and editor Robert Cummings Neville (2000). The project ran for several years and produced three volumes: *The Human Condition*, *Ultimate Realities*, and *Religious Truth*. See also Francis Clooney's *Divine Mother, Blessed Mother: Hindu Goddesses and the Virgin Mary* (2005), an excellent comparative work based on textual and theological reflections.

2. Since I am referencing children's games, allow me to add that this seems to be a bit like—albeit on a cosmic level—"Calvin ball," the game that cartoon characters Calvin and Hobbes played in which the rules constantly changed in order to give advantages to whoever made them up. Needless to say, Calvin ball always ends badly.

3. The English signifiers "history of religion," "history of religions," "science of religion," and "comparative religion" were used interchangeably by nineteenth- and early-twentieth-century scholars. See Chidester (1996), Masuzawa (2005), Paden (1988 [1994]), and Sharpe (1986) for extensive histories and descriptions of comparative religion as an academic discipline.

4. Comparative theology, a field that emerged alongside comparative religion, was likewise indebted to understanding non-Christian traditions yet argued expressly for Christianity as providing a final answer to questions raised by partial answers

given by non-Christian "ancient" traditions. For a discussion of the subsequently neglected nineteenth-century field of comparative theology and the ways it was, in the end, not unlike the purportedly scientific new field of religious studies in its Christian-centric approach, see Masuzawa (2005). See also Locklin and Nicholson (2010) for an excellent argument for the return—or admission—of fluid boundaries currently between comparative religion and comparative theology, one that answers well to the critique of postmodernism.

5. For Müller's science of religion see Müller (1872). Müller's quote about religion, "He who knows one, knows none," is a phrase he borrowed from Goethe, who used it in reference to languages.

6. Robert Segal (2001) cites James Frazer and William Robertson Smith to argue that despite these early scholars' understandings that their work borrowed from evolutionary theory, this was not necessarily the case. Since Frazer's religious categorizations were not geographically contiguous and therefore attributed independent invention rather than cross-cultural influences, he was not strictly borrowing from evolutionary theory. Furthermore, Segal notes that Frazer tended to blur his categorizations of primitive and civilized religion, particularly as they existed within modern-day religions. Not only did Frazer identify contemporary religions as rooted in primitive belief and behavior; he also argued that these primitive elements remained into the present day. By contrast, William Smith seemed to understand religion's progression in a more strictly evolutionary sense. As a devout Christian he understood contemporary Christianity to be completely devoid of primitive elements—a feat he found remarkable and therefore, as he saw it, divinely influenced.

7. In his discussion of the South African settler context, David Chidester describes how the process of comparing religion by European settlers during the early 1800s, using Protestant Christianity as their benchmark, helped those on the frontier to label local tribes—perceived as barbarous, superstitious, and without religion—as ultimately dangerous, aiding the cause of colonization. The taxonomies that Europeans invented for Africans, supporting the process of settlement, were taken up in the latter half of the nineteenth century by comparative religionists in London, Amsterdam, Paris, and Berlin who, at that time influenced by Darwinian theories, involved themselves in arranging religious systems in an evolutionary sequence from primitive to civilized. See Chidester (1996: 26–29, 98–102). See also Long (1986: 3–4) and J. Z. Smith (1990: 34).

8. Wach's concern that religious studies not be confused with "godless" perspectives also arises from his anticommunist stance, a view shared by his successor at the University of Chicago, Mircea Eliade. (My thanks to an anonymous reader for bringing this to my attention.)

9. For an overview of scholarly critique of Eliade, see Rennie (1996: 179–212). For a more specific overview of scholarly critiques of Eliade's purportedly scientific methods, see Olson (1992: 14–26).

10. The postmodern critique of comparison largely follows from the work of anthropologist Clifford Geertz, one of the most celebrated opponents of comparativism. Geertz argues against the explanatory approach typical of early comparativists in favor of interpretive approaches to culture that require attention to particularity (see Segal 2001: 342–43).

J. Z. Smith's equation of the comparative endeavor with scholars' magic has to do with what he understands to be the problem of similarity. He bases this claim on E. B. Tylor's first comparative work, *Researches in the Early History of Mankind*

(1st ed. 1865), in which Tylor observed that the logic of magical practices is upheld by the "principle of association." J. G. Frazer builds on Tylor, saying that "homeopathic magic is founded on association of ideas by similarity; contagious magic is founded on the association of ideas by contiguity" (quoted in J. Z. Smith 1990: 25). Smith posits that the same applies to the enterprise of comparison in the human sciences: "For in scholarship, comparison has been chiefly an affair of the recollection of similarity. *The chief explanation for the significance of comparison has been contiguity.* The procedure is homeopathic. The theory is built on contagion. The issue of difference has been all but forgotten" (J. Z. Smith 1990: 25–26, italics in original).

11. This political charge against the comparative method is founded on the idea that comparison abstracts and that abstractions are "construed as a political act aimed at domination and annihilation; cross-cultural comparison becomes intrinsically imperialistic, obliterating the cultural matrix from which it 'lifts' the compared object" (Patton and Ray 2000: 2). In an interview with Lawrence Sullivan, Patton also references Adorno and Horkheimer as saying that comparison as a category is oppressive. It engenders "abstraction as a form of killing by distortion because of the radical destruction of the context surrounding that which is abstracted" (Patton 2000b: 221). See Patton (2000a) for an extensive comparativist response to particular postmodernist concerns. See also Eckel (2000: 56).

12. J. Z. Smith (2004, 2010) notes that Eliade had in fact intended to write a companion volume dedicated to historical context that may have quelled many of his detractors' critiques.

13. Related to this connection between politically and religiously imposed universalisms, postcolonial scholar Terrence Brown notes how the occult and cultural nationalism can involve a similar desire for blurring differences and for the rediscovery of a common ancient essence of nation/humanity, a spirit that unites:

> Both involve belief in hidden realities which must be made manifest. The idea that the spirit of the people, geist, which survives through countless ages and vicissitudes to link a modern democratic Christian people with their putative ancestors in pre-history involves a fair measure of simple credulity which can only be fanned into ardent faith by appropriate forms of incantation in a sacred language, often the national tongue, perhaps itself lately rescued from near-extinction: incantations in song, in drama and poetry and in heady political rhetoric. Then and only then can a people be mesmerized into the curious conviction that they have more in common with the denizens of a dim antiquity and the world of myth than with their near neighbors across a narrow sea or over a border but recently established.... It also takes, I think, an odd kind of visionary sense of the world to hold to the conviction that one's fellow citizens, the grocer as well as the prophet, the baker, the candlestick-maker, as well as the poet or composer, are possessed in all their activities by the national essence, the spirit of the nation. (Brown 1996: 222)

14. For a feminist critique of Eliade, see Carol Christ (1991). Although Christ does not take issue with Eliade's universalizing tendencies (something she tends toward herself), she does critique his perpetuation of an androcentric paradigm in which the male represents the universal norm for humanity and the female a deviation from this norm.

15. Eckel notes how Smith himself engages in an inventive process of comparison when he juxtaposes Jonestown with the cargo cult of New Hebrides and the Dionysiac festival in Euripides's *Bacchae*. As Eckel explains,

   I am not aware that the comparative procedure in this article has been given a name, but I am inclined to say that Smith proceeds in a style of "imaginative and ironical juxtaposition," in which dramatically different phenomena are set down side by side in such a way that they suggested common features. How "real" are these common features? That is unclear. But they are a useful imaginative device to remove the sense of uniqueness that makes the events at Jonestown seem unintelligible. This process of investigation is "magic" transmuted into understanding (if not into science) by the use of the "imagination." (2000: 57)

16. J. Z. Smith notes this inevitability when viewing comparison not only as a lifelong companion to the study of religion but as intrinsic to human thought itself. Comparison is, as Smith describes it, "a fundamental characteristic of human intelligence. Whether revealed in the logical grouping of classes, in poetic similes, in mimesis, or other like activities—comparison, the bringing together of two or more objects for the purpose of noting either similarity or dissimilarity, is the omnipresent substructure of human thought. Without it, we could not speak, perceive, learn, or reason." This statement is almost immediately followed by the sentence "It is unfortunate that relatively little work has been done on the history of the use of comparison in scholarship and that deeper questions of method and the underlying philosophical implications of comparison have been ignored by many disciplines including History of Religions" (1978: 240). Smith's frustration with a clear lack of purpose and contribution to the study of religions is one to which he repeatedly returns in subsequent addresses and publications, central to his critique of comparativism, as I mention below.

17. Jensen (2001) likewise discusses religious studies' basic reliance on generalizations. He argues that if juxtapositions of certain properties were not available for analysis, the "study" of religion would not make any sense. He argues, however, for the comparison of etic categories of analysis in order to understand emic categories intrinsic to religion. For a discussion of the inevitability of comparison, vital to certain activities of the mind brain, see Saler (2001) and Eckel (2000: 56).

18. See also Dempsey (2002, 2005) for a similar discussion of the problems of rigidly asserted religious labels.

19. Susan Sered, who conducts a cross-cultural study of twelve women-dominated religious traditions across the globe, understands that, without comparison, anthropology ceases to be the study of human culture and becomes "merely a technique for collecting exotic customs" (1994: 10).

20. Kimberly Patton likens comparative religion's admittedly tricky balancing act to juggling torches, although risky it can be significantly rewarding. While on one hand we might get burned, if we juggle the torches with skill, our faces "will begin to glow." Patton goes on to argue in defense of the comparative method that

   even if we conceded, with Bryan Turner, that "[t]erms, concepts and categories are inextricably meshed in social contexts and institutional arrangements; they can only be extricated from their social settings by great ingenuity and stealth." The fact remains that it is not a totalitarian—or even a silly—thing to try.

Stealth it shall be, and sensitivity, and humility. But not surrender of the whole comparative enterprise just because it is hard to do it right. (2000a: 168)

21. Laurie Patton likewise asserts that comparison—whether modern or postmodern—"reinforces ethical relations between scholars and their objects of study" and that "the comparative move and the ethical move can be one and the same" (2000: 204).

22. Eagleton similarly argues that certain postmodern preoccupations with finding difference are, in their extreme, promoting "a kind of shamefaced universalism. To argue that you want to fashion a society in which everyone is incommensurate with everyone else is inevitably to make a totalizing, universalizing claim" (1996: 119).

23. Huston Smith also notes the importance of a carefully contextualized comparativism that ideally counteracts today's overemphasis on difference that severs human communities. Smith insists that an important conduit for encouraging human understanding, an importance likewise denied by many theorists, is religion. "Religion, *religio*—presumably religious studies' primary reference point—has to do with being connected. Are deconstructionists, cultured despisers of metaphysics that they are, aware of how (to quote Lyotard one last time) their call to 'wage war on totality [and] activate differences' pulls against connectedness?" (2000: 180).

    David White similarly proposes that a historically grounded comparativism can provide an important corrective to extreme positions within postmodern and postcolonial studies and the kinds of comparativism that, according to Lyotard and other postmodern critics, neglect "cultural specificity in favor of theoretical comprehensiveness." Drawing from Antoine Meillet's *Comparative Method in Historical Linguistics*, White notes two types of comparison with very different goals—one is to find universal laws and the other historical information. The first system, which is "patently deductive, interpreting particulars on the basis of universal principles," assumes a "timeless, immutable system." The other system, "whose goal is to interpret historical data, is diachronic, inductive, and as such, most attentive to différence" (White 2000: 50). White advocates this latter system for creating a new comparativism, one in which "difference is not explained away, but rather mustered to thicken the description of similarity" (2000: 52).

24. As described by Diana Eck, this determination to support responsible interactions between scholars and the people they study is, realistically and most productively, reflexive. As such, she considers comparison to involve a type of interreligious dialogue, yet not as typically configured: "Rather, I mean that the study of religion is itself a form of dialogue involving not only encounter with our subjects of study, but continued reflection on the personal, religious, or intellectual presuppositions that shape the intention and direction of our own study." Without this ongoing process of self-interrogation, the study of religion and, in particular, religious comparison runs the risk of becoming "merely political or polemical" (2000: 140, 142).

25. Viewing this irony from the perspective of the currently troubled category of the sacred, Huston Smith considers the revival of the sacred as a category of analysis to be vital to the newly revised study of comparative religion if it is to offer an effective means for understanding and promoting human connectedness. While agreeing that careful contextualization is necessary for understanding how the meanings that inform our lives are solidly grounded in human particularities, Smith posits that the "shadow side" of strict contextualization is that we could

end up "limiting our meanings to the communities that generate them and questioning the possibility of trafficking between them." He furthermore argues that "the providential feature of the human religious heritage is its consistent refusal to stop there—indeed, its refusal to let human connectedness stop anywhere short of Reality itself. That is the final explanation for religion's power" (2000: 180–81).

As described by Robert Orsi, postmodernity's rejection of the transcendent "sacred" as irredeemably problematic is preceded by modernity's rejection of sacred presence—a rejection still felt today. As Orsi sees it, it is the tangible, contextualized presence of the sacred that contradicts modernity more than any other quality of religious experience, creating a "deep antipathy between modern cultures all over the world and the practice and experience of sacred presence.... The modern world has assiduously and systematically disciplined the senses not to experience sacred presence; the imaginations of moderns are trained toward sacred absence" (2005: 12).

26. Just as some religion scholars have appealed to the flexibility of their discipline, demonstrating how a revised comparativism can challenge and correct earlier approaches, so also can postmodern theory adjust to current conditions and concerns, theoretical and real. For instance, Malcolm Eckel describes anthropologist Gananath Obeyesekere's appeal to rediscover an earlier manifestation of Sri Lankan Buddhism in order that it respond more compassionately to the country's ethnic conflicts. Eckel notes that, if he understands Obeyesekere correctly, he is arguing for a "new essentialism," based not on substantive identity but on pragmatism that has drawn Obeyesekere back into old modernist debates about the nature of Buddhism itself. Eckel considers whether Obeyesekere has found "a way to smuggle the old myths of 'reason,' 'progress,' and 'identity' back into the study of the tradition," thus deflecting postmodern critique. Rather than being bothered by this, Eckel expresses an appreciation for "this uneasy, hybrid character in postmodern scholarship," in which modernist myths may buckle but they do not disappear, coexisting "instead with the rediscovery of traditional patterns of life and thought that were considered long since out of date." In the end, Eckel finds cause for hope in "the complexity, eclecticism, and irony of the situation" and of the serious work of scholarship as well (2000: 61).

27. Eliade goes on to describe Freud's theory of the origins of social organization, lived out through a primordial "totemic banquet" in which the son kills and eats his father. As described in Freud's *Totem and Taboo*, this banquet repeatedly celebrates a God who is "nothing other than the sublimated physical father." Eliade notes that although many ethnologists in Freud's time tried "in vain" to demonstrate the absurdity of this theory, "Freud was not in the least troubled by such objections and this wild 'gothic novel,' *Totem and Taboo*, has since become one of the minor gospels of three generations of Western intelligentsia" (1965: 23–25).

28. For recent, theoretically thematic studies that, like mine, are written by single authors who attend to ethnographic contextualization (and beyond), comparing across significant cultural and geographical divides, see especially Gananath Obeyesekere's *Imagining Karma* (2002) and Susan Starr Sered's *Priestess, Mother Sacred Sister* (1994). For an extensive and historically grounded comparison of ancient Greek, Vedic, and Semitic cultures, see Kimberley Patton's *Religion of the Gods*, which works with, among other sources, material evidence from these traditions to explore meanings and motivations behind sacrifices performed by the gods. For an excellent cowritten cross-culturally comparative volume, see *Ritual*

and Its Consequences by Adam Seligman, Robert Weller, Michael Puett, and Bennett Simon (2008). Edited volumes are often a good source for well-contextualized cross-cultural treatments of particular religious themes, the comparative layer reliant on a strong introduction and/or conclusion. See Patton and Hawley's *Holy Tears* (2005) for a particularly strong introduction attendant to comparative themes.

29. Examples of comparative studies of geographically proximate traditions are on the increase, particularly in the richly pluralistic context of South Asia. Kent and Kassam's edited volume includes chapters that deliberately set out to investigate boundaries between religions as sites that impel or propel the religious Other and blur or underline the religious demarcations that distinguish them. See also Dempsey (2001); Flueckiger (2006); Gottschalk (2000); Khan (1997); Gilmartin (2000); and Raj and Dempsey (2002).

30. See also Jonathan Z. Smith (1990: 51–53) for a discussion of natural versus unnatural acts of comparison.

31. As J. Z. Smith describes it, since "thought would be impossible without comparison, we could not stop comparing even if we wished to" (2004: 30). I submit that one advantage of comparative magic is that the pivotal scholarly choice of juxtaposition is positioned up front from the start, for all to see and, rightly or wrongly, to critique. Along these lines, James Clifford criticizes the tendency for ethnographers not to describe, up front, decisions and circumstances that led them to the field. They are often depicted as magically "there" in their writing, neglecting to remark on how their decisions and approaches got them there (1997: 23).

32. A similar critique was posited by anthropologist Clifford Geertz, a vocal critic of the comparative method. Geertz argued that comparativism not only sacrificed accuracy and detail, it created generalities that, when sufficiently self-evident, were vacuous and meaningless (1973: 25). See also Segal (2001: 342–43) and Paden (2001: 277).

33. See Asad (1993).

34. See Charles Taylor (2002) for an overview of the new materialist approach.

35. William Sax observes this dynamic in his discussion of sacred landscape. He notes that while many social scientists tend to ignore the specifically religious dimensions of sacred places, religion scholars continue to use nonempirical categories—such as "the sacred"—to describe and analyze their subject. Together these inclinations create an unhelpful dichotomy between religion and politics (2003: 177). (Thanks to Luke Whitmore for drawing Sax's observation to my attention.)

36. Many of the contributors to the edited volume *Religion: Beyond a Concept* take this both/and approach. See especially the introduction by Hent de Vries (2008).

37. Anthropologist Michael Lambek likewise notes this interplay between the study and phenomena of religion: "just as anthropology draws, by nature, from encyclopedist and genealogical elements, religions themselves move between universalizing ambitions and particularizing practices" (Lambek 2008: 138). Along these lines, Lambek (2002) argues more specifically that anthropology is resolutely comparative in that particular ethnographic accounts must be made to speak to one another in order that useful analytical frameworks emerge.

38. The same might be said about the category of religion itself. De Vries describes the category as enticingly vast and unwieldy, as something that "defies census and censorship, planning and strategy, markets and media, governmental control and political spin as well as overconfident distinctions between privacy and public-ness, individual empowerment and public nature, orthodoxy and heterodoxy, free

speech and blasphemy, decency and perversion promise and threat, life and death, immanence and transcendence" (2008: 7).

39. As the reader may recall from the discussion above, this is the same late-nineteenth-century revolution that prompted Max Müller to bill the new field of comparative religions as the "Science of Religion."

40. This manuscript was eventually published as *The Goddess Lives in Upstate New York* (Dempsey 2006).

41. With this in mind, it should be noted that each chapter in this book draws from ethnographical encounters on at least one side of the juxtaposed divide, admittedly adding embodied and emotional dimensions—often unequally distributed—to my processes of cognition and comparison.

42. In November 2007 I gave a paper at the San Diego American Academy of Religion Conference that compared ethnography and ritual processes in light of the Rush temple experience. I did not consider how well this comparative essay fit into this volume until I later presented an expanded version of this paper for the South Asia Lecture Series at Syracuse University in October 2008. I am grateful for an ensuing conversation with Anne Gold, who encouraged this possibility.

43. As described by William Paden, comparative patterns, ideally speaking, are not meant to be "timeless archetypes carrying ahistorical values or meanings which are simply replicated in historical material, but rather are exploratory and refinable" (2000: 186).

CHAPTER 1

1. For further description of the history and makeup of Syrian Christianity in Kerala, see Neil (1984, 1985).

2. For one exception found in written accounts, see Josetta (2009: 83). A notable and very visible exception, expressed in art rather than text, is the mural recently mounted both on Alphonsa's hilltop chapel and on the bank below depicting Alphonsa surrounded by children.

3. Alphonsa, configured as one who courageously accepted her difficult lot in life, also fits squarely and more generically in the number-one category for conferring saintliness on women: "fortitude in illness" (Weinstein and Bell 1982: 229).

4. Alphonsa's *imitatio christi* has inspired much artistic reflection and expression. Priest-poet Anniyil Tharakan poetically describes Alphonsa's renunciation of the world as "an act of sacrifice, and sacrifice for her was a process of making the world sacred. She left the world for the seclusion of the convent not because the world did not offer her anything beautiful and triumphant, but because she wanted to continue with Christ's redemptive process of sanctifying it through her sacrifice. She wanted to make the presence of Christ in the world all the more triumphant and be a sacrament herself for the grace of God to flow into the recess of it" (Tharakan 2008: 73).

5. This anticolonial reversal that depicts India as essentially spiritualized and superior to Europe and the United States was promoted most famously by Gandhi among other Independence leaders. It is also the basis for the Theosophical movement, which arose during the Indian struggle for Independence. I discuss the Theosophical position—its relationship to the scientific revolution and its connection to the Independence movement—in chapter 4.

6. Synge's representations appear more nuanced, portraying a sense of Irish cultural diversity. Most critics have read this play as promoting the prevalent binarism between the characters of the priest and tinker, between "civilized culture" and

"natural." On the surface the priest—sedentary, rule-bound, and religious—and the tinker—wandering, earthy, and capricious—are opposites. Yet Burke points to moments where Synge softens the binarism. The priest drinks and asks for money for a job for which he already is getting paid (Burke 2009: 66–74). Different than the drunken priest of folklore, the drinking and dishonest priest in Synge's play is not romanticized. His character cuts through the binarism of the Christian sedentary and the sinning wanderer by recalling motifs from the Church's itinerant past. The play describes a "shared moral weakness that bind Traveller and settled" (Burke 2009: 73).

7. Irish poet James Cousins, who spent much of his career in India, places similar hopes in India's spirituality as charting the course for Ireland's rediscovery of its foundational essence. Cousins furthermore was interested in following Rabindranath Tagore's lead in formulating a type of human universalism that would correct what he saw as the narrow nationalism of his countrymen. See Vishvanathan (2004). See also MacNeice (1967). Terence Brown makes a broader point about the natural affinities between nationalism and occultism's search for a unifying essence and spirit that has been lying dormant and awaits revitalization (Brown 1996: 222–23).

8. Yeats had a lifelong preoccupation with Asia, ranging from the Orientalism of the Theosophical Society, and the writings of Rabindranath Tagore, to the Japanese Noh theater. In his later years he worked with an Indian monk, Shri Purohit Swami, on a translation of the *Upanishads* (Rickard 1997: 96; see also Guha 1968).

9. This excerpt is from Yeats's "Pages from a Diary Written in Nineteen Hundred and Thirty" (see Rickard 1997: 105). Similar to Sr. Vengaloor's observation that more of value can be seen through the third eye than the microscope, Yeats describes the modern empiricist view as erroneously constructing identities limited to individual selves and a world known only through the senses. This sensory-constrained self Yeats describes as a sealed bottle. In his translation of the *Eesha-Upanishad*, he incorporates this metaphor and laments, "They have put a golden stopper into the neck of the bottle. Pull it Lord! Let out reality. I am full of longing" (quoted in Rickard 1997: 105). Yeats claimed that "in two or three generations it will become generally known that the mechanical theory has no reality, that the natural and the supernatural are knit together, that to escape a dangerous fanaticism we must study a new science" (Rickard 1997: 109). The *Upanishads* were clearly at the center of this new science, as were investigations into the occult sciences. For a while Yeats consoled himself with the belief that Indian philosophy was the source of this Indo-Irish "science," a pure well that could be drawn from to decontaminate the "poisoned rivers and filthy modern tides of Western culture" (Rickard 1997: 110).

10. This dynamic is described in detail in Dempsey 2001: 28–34.

11. Taylor and Inglis argue that the Irish Church's ambivalent position is, within the European context, unique to Irish Catholicism (Taylor 1990: 169–70; Inglis 1987).

12. The theme of ambivalent Western influences—and shifting centers of gravity from Europe to the United States—also emerged in a conversation about European saints stationed at the St. Mary Forane Church in Bharananganam. The first time I encountered these saints, I found most were immediately recognizable to me as an American Catholic. A particularly puzzling statue was of a priest whose plaque simply read, "St. John." He looked unlike any St. John I knew, so I asked a woman standing beside me, also looking up at the statue, if she could tell me. After a moment's consideration, she confidently replied, "John Kennedy." When I replied

that this didn't sound quite right to me, she stayed firm in her opinion, seemingly thinking me rather dull for having reservations. I found out later that this was indeed not John Kennedy, but rather John de Britto, a European saint with strong devotion in Tamil Nadu.

13. For descriptions of a similar process of priestly reform that took place among Irish immigrants living in Wales, see O'Leary (1996). As in Ireland, priests attempted to curtail the overconsumption of alcohol and to reform popular religious events such as funeral wakes, where the priest traditionally had no role.

14. It is interesting to note how priestly reform changed over time. Whereas early reform involved a clamping down on popular devotions of all sorts, including pilgrimage and rituals performed at sacred wells, the priests during the Irish Revival period began not only to support holy well practices but to lead pilgrimages and hold outdoor Masses. This had to do in part with a romanticization of old Irish practices and also reflected the extent to which the earlier reforms had successfully tamed such practices, making them palatable to the hierarchy.

15. Given shifting global power structures, the ubiquitous outside influences bringing immorality and materialism to India are understood as emanating primarily from the United States rather than Britain.

16. Alphonsa's powers also bring to mind *shakti* power, typically associated with Hindu women who live lives of discipline and sacrifice. Since *shakti* is so often associated with powers of married women, emerging within the domestic realm, *tapas*—a power associated with celibacy, typically associated with male ascetics— seems a better fit with Alphonsa's life story.

17. See Richards (1998: 102–8) for a description of the process of Irish identity-making as a flip-flopping of rejecting and embracing Euro-influenced modernity.

18. Classic postmodern studies that grapple with this issue of dismantling the intertangled colonial and postcolonial binarisms within the Indian context include the work of Edward Said (1993), Homi Bhabha (1994), and Ashis Nandy (1983), to name a few. Authors who have grappled more recently with similar dynamics in Ireland, often drawing from the above theorists to found their arguments, include Bachorz (2001), Graham (2001), Lloyd (1993), Richards (1998), and Smythe (1999). Much postcolonial theory about Ireland produced in the 1990s and afterward is written in response to the Irish Field Day Theatre pamphlets, written in the 1980s, which tended to present absolute "Orange/ Green" oppositions between colonizer and colonized. Kirkland (1999) argues that Field Day pamphlets were critical to setting the stage for later deconstructive analysis.

19. See Bachorz (2001) for an excellent discussion of Adorno's position in reference to Irish postcolonial theory.

CHAPTER 2

1. For a more detailed description of Aiya and the Rush temple, Dempsey (2006).

2. For a similar project that brings the principles of process theology into conversation with Hindu philosophies, see Long (2007).

3. The Christian community I studied, known as the Syrian or St. Thomas Christians, is located mostly in the Kottayam district in the inland areas of Kerala (see Dempsey 2001). The Syrian Christians, who have a history of landownership and trade, are typically a well-to-do community and therefore not the typical demographic for engaging with liberation theology. Kerala Christianity also includes a community known as the Latin Catholics who are predominantly coastal fisher-

folk and typically of a lower socioeconomic class. Although I found Syrian Christians largely uninterested in liberation theology, I am aware of its presence and significant influence in the Latin Catholic community.

4. See Ramanujan (1981) and Cutler (1987) for more on south Indian bhakti saints. For an overview of the north Indian bhakti tradition, see Hawley and Jurgensmeyer (1988). For a more detailed description of how Aiya breaks with convention, see Dempsey (2006: 83–146).

5. See Dempsey (2006: 83–86) for an elaboration on Aiya's story.

6. In a similar vein, Swan (2001) writes an overview of the forgotten early Christian Desert Mothers, overshadowed by the Desert Fathers. See also Buhrig (1993) for a wider treatment of the problem of women's invisibility in the Christian tradition.

7. An account of the unnamed woman to whom the Shiva lingam leaned is also left out of Sekkizhaar's *Periya Puranam* edited by Dr. N. Mahalingam. In this version, Mahalingam simply says that the lingam is leaning and that the king wanted to have *darshan* of a lingam "in the proper vertical position" (Sekkizhaar 1985: 510). He does not mention how it came to be that way.

8. Interestingly, this episode of Kungiliya Kalayar's life is prefaced by Mahalingam's note that very few saints mentioned in the *Periya Puranam* ever entered the sanctum sanctorum of a Shiva temple. The story of Kungiliya Kalayar recounts one instance in which a saint enters the sanctum to worship the Lord residing there.

9. In some written versions of the story, the sister is given the name Thilakavathiyar. She is nonetheless not given any other special recognition, nor is she given particular notice for healing her brother with sacred ash.

10. See Schüssler Fiorenza's (1990) argument that despite conventional biblical exegesis of Paul's letters, women missionaries played a significant role in the formation and mission of early Christianity. For a Christian feminist rethinking of Paul's seemingly misogynist bias, see West (1990).

11. A tangible example of this process, described by Selva Raj (2008), can be found within the caste-conscious Tamil Catholic Church, which, for decades, exclusively enlisted high-caste Vellalas as priests and bishops. Beginning in the 1980s and due to the influence of liberation theology, members of the Dalit community not only received ordination but were appointed to the rank of bishop. This shift helped the clergy to better represent the sizable Dalit Catholic population and to set aside the injustice of traditional caste elitism in the Church. Yet, as noted by Raj, a reverse caste elitism has emerged, "involving a new cast of characters, in that today dalits keep the doors closed to non-dalits and upper-caste clergy…According to some Vellala clergy, not only are all doors to key ecclesiastical offices are closed to Vellalas, they are now regarded as untouchables" (2008: 53).

12. For a summary and response to the highly critical 1984 document *Instruction on the Theology of Liberation*, written by Cardinal Ratzinger on behalf of the Congregation, see Segundo (1970). As Pope Benedict, Ratzinger continues his critique of liberation theology. He addressed Brazilian bishops on December 9, 2009, in honor of the twenty-fifth anniversary of the publication of the *Instruction*, claiming that "visible consequences" of the "deceitful principles" of liberation theology in the Church in Brazil have been "rebellion, division, dissent, offense, anarchy [that] are still being felt, creating amidst your diocesan communities great pain and a grave loss of living strength" (see Hilary White 2009).

13. In 1968, at the dawning of liberation theology, and decades before the Vatican leveled its official condemnation of the movement's Marxist utopian leanings, Gustavo Gutiérrez addressed an audience of theologians and Church workers in Chimbote, Peru. Here he quoted Marx's appraisal of Christianity as spiritualized and disconnected to social uplift:

    The social principles of Christianity preach the need of a dominating class and an oppressed class. And to the latter class they offer only the benevolence of the ruling class. The social principles of Christianity point to heaven as the compensation for all the crimes that are committed on earth. The social principles of Christianity explain all the viciousness of oppressors as a just punishment either for original sin or other sins, or as trials that the Lord, in his infinite wisdom, inflicts on those the Lord has redeemed. (Quoted in Gutiérrez 1968: 27–28)

    Gutiérrez juxtaposes this description of Christianity with a passage from Isaiah which reads,

    But be glad and rejoice forever in that which I create; for behold, I create Jerusalem rejoicing, and her people a joy... They shall build houses and inhabit them; they shall plant vineyards and eat their fruit. They shall not build and another inhabit; they shall not plant and another eat; for like the days of a tree shall the days of my people be, and my chosen shall long enjoy the work of their hands. (Isaiah 65:19–22)

    Rather than defend Christianity from Marx's assessment, Gutiérrez notes that— witnessed by Christian teachings and practices perpetuated over the centuries—Marx's description is not inaccurate or unfounded. He ends his address by appealing to his audience, asking whether the Christian community is capable of working toward the realization of Isaiah's prophecy or whether it will continue to contribute to and support Marx's countertestimony (Gutiérrez 1968: 28). Gutiérrez's appeal continues to resonate among liberation theologians, and an array of scriptural passages has been used in its support. Although directly stated indebtedness to Marx has faded in light of Vatican condemnation, the message of earthly redemption remains fundamentally the same.

14. For an overview of Tantrism's construction of an interdependent spiritual and material realm and a comparison with non-Tantric, non-goddess-centered Hindu theologies see Sherma (1998). For a comprehensive look at Hindu practices and ideologies and their relationship to the environment, see Chapple and Tucker (2000).

15. According to Douglas Brooks, Tantrism has not historically promoted an egalitarian worldview but tends to provide "a reaffirmation of the religious rights of a few over the many and the importance of ritual for living a truly meaningful life without renouncing the mundane. Tantra assumes that privilege and hierarchy is part of the divine plan" (1992: 183).

16. See McDaniel (2007).

17. See also Boff's *Cry of the Earth, Cry of the Poor* (1997). Paralleling liberation theology in a number of ways, process theology likewise asserts a divinization of humanity and all life. As such, humanity is understood to be, with God, co-creators of and accountable for the future well-being of our planet. See Christ (2003) for a recent accounting of an ecofeminist process perspective. Thanks to Don Fadner (personal communication) for reminding me of this theological strain.

CHAPTER 3

1. I am not the first to compare the Rajneesh Oregon community to settler coloniz- ers. Lewis Carter characterizes the conflict that arose between the Rajneeshees and locals as having the "features of previous range wars (poisoning, arson, threats), though with the addition of uniquely contemporary social weapons and tactics...not available in earlier land-use conflicts in the region" (1990: xv).

2. Similarly, cultural geographers recently have tended to frame culture as an ongo- ing process of conflict steered by related interests in symbolism and discourse analysis. Recent studies in geography and religion have taken their cue from this dialectical approach, such that "land and landscape become symbol-laden arenas in which human actors play out different religious cultures and their competing value systems" (Scott 2001: xxii).

3. Details in this section were gleaned from and corroborated by Carter (1990), Fitzgerald (1986a, 1986b), Gordon (1987), and Thompson and Heelas (1986).

4. See Thompson and Heelas (1986: 17–19).

5. For an overview of conflicting accounts regarding the Rajneesh community's tran- sition between Pune and Oregon, see Lewis Carter (1990: 128–35).

6. See Fitzgerald (1986a: 51–52, 55–58); Thompson and Heelas (1986: 88–89); Gordon (1987: 99–100).

7. See Fitzgerald (1986a: 51); L. Carter (1990: 90).

8. See Fitzgerald (1986a: 68–78); Thompson and Heelas (1986: 71–85).

9. For an analysis of Rajneeshpuram that argues, against Max Weber, that charis- matic authority can indeed be compatible with capitalist economics and hierarchi- cal control, see Hugh Urban (1996).

10. My framing of the Rajneesh community as colonizing in comparison with diasporic Hindu settlements is at odds with presentations of the Rajneesh com- munity as victims of local residents' religious intolerance (which of course they were as well), mentioned at the end of this chapter. For an account that elaborates on local bigotry and hysteria and places most of the responsibility of the failed Rajneeshee experiment on eastern Oregon "natives," see Braun (1984). See also Murphy (1986) and Brecher (1993).

11. In 2006, the Antelope Oregon population had grown to 115.

12. Probably the most serious broken promise on the part of the Rajneesh commu- nity had to do with the local Antelope school district, whose elementary school ended up being staffed entirely by Rajneeshee devotees (see Fitzgerald 1986b: 86).

13. Lewis Carter describes "hints" that the Rajneesh settlers planned on expanding their territory well beyond Antelope, as much as ninety miles away, as a means to build their new society (1990: 94).

14. See also Lewis Carter (1990: 203). Given their penchant for naming, the Rajneesh community also named their refuse. In what was perhaps accurately interpreted by locals as an act of desecration, their chosen site for the "Adolph Hitler Garbage Dump" was right next to the Antelope community church (L. Carter 1990: xvii, 93).

15. It seems the moral blindness and double standards set by the settler population at the time of decolonization were particularly dramatic. This generation of settlers, cut loose from the metrapole, reveled in the conquest of democracy over brutal fascism in Europe, yet within their own borders a completely different code of ethics prevailed. As historian Caroline Elkins recounts, "On the heels of their tri- umph over Hitler and Mussolini European settlers were perpetrating crimes that contemporary critics found Gestapolike" (2005: 218).

16. See Ashcroft, Griffiths, and Tiffin (1995a: 3, 213); Elkins and Pederson (2005: 3, 22); Johnston and Lawson (2005: 363). Stephen Slemon describes this settler ambivalence from the perspective of Second World postcolonial literature. As Slemon explains, in settler contexts resistance is grounded in "multiple and contradictory structures of ideological interpellation or subject-formation—which would call down the notion that resistance can *ever* be 'purely' intended or 'purely' expressed" (1995: 108). He continues, "The illusion of the stable self/other, here/there binary division has never been available to Second-World writers, and as a result the sites of figural contestation between oppressor and oppressed, colonizer and colonized, have been taken inward and internalized in Second-World post-colonial textual practice" (1995: 109).

17. The Peace Force was formed by six men and four women who took a ten-month training course at the Oregon Police Academy. All ten graduated in the top 10 percent of their class, and one was even chosen as the best of the seven hundred trainees (Fitzgerald 1986a: 65).

18. This view stems from *Manu Smrti* 2:22–24, which encourages members of the higher classes to live in lands extending between the western and eastern oceans that are considered "fit for the performance of sacrifice" (Narayanan 1992: 147).

19. On a related note, Joanne Waghorne observes that Hindu temples newly built in cities and/or in the diaspora often reflect a process of globalized localization. By this she means that particular divine powers and features associated with particular localities have been successfully transferred to new places, appealing to a variety of classes. Physical access to divine power, although seemingly in contradiction with scientific rationality, technology, and middle-class affluence, it turns out, is one of the key components to modern diasporic Hinduism's vitality (Waghorne 2004: 171–230).

20. An interesting twist in this pattern of conferring American landscape with Hindu divinity can be traced to 1872, when Clarence Edward Dutton conferred on the peaks and edifices in the Grand Canyon the names of Hindu gods Shiva, Vishnu, and Brahma (in addition to Manu, Buddha, and Zoroastra). Dutton accompanied John Wesley Powell, who, in a prior expedition, is understood to have been the first European explorer to discover the canyon, naming it "Grand" (Singh 2000).

21. Temples in India commonly have origin stories, often rooted in a distant past. For a detailed description of a more recent story of Shiva's dream appearance, prompting construction of a temple in the suburbs outside Chennai, India, see Harman (2008).

22. For more examples of the ways land has become sacred at the Rush temple, see Dempsey (2006: 156–62).

23. www.himalayanacademy.com/ssc/hawaii/iraivan/ (accessed April 6, 2010).

24. This ability of diasporic Hindus to recognize and peacefully superimpose sanctity on previously designated sacred terrain is not necessarily a Hindu attribute in all instances. In India a number of sacred sites are hotly and even violently contested; the most famous of these is Ayodhya. See van der Veer (1992) and Romey (2004) for overviews of the conflict and descriptions of how sacred history is (re)written into Indian terrain. For an example of a similarly contested Christian site of pilgrimage in south India, see Dempsey (2005).

25. A similar sharing of a sacred object involves a Trinidadian site in the town of Siparia that was originally sacred to natives. Catholics later dedicated the shrine to Mary as Our Mother La Divina Pastora. When Hindus subsequently settled, they offered devotion to her as well, so much so that the shrine today is called Sipari Mai. A week before Easter, devotees move Mary from the altar to another

room so she can be worshipped in an explicitly Hindu manner. On Good Friday she returns to her station in the church (Prorok 2003: 291).

26. A religious shift in emphasis away from locality and toward temporality can be seen in the early Christian community, performed as a unifying strategy. As Jonathan Z. Smith puts it, the liturgical year, marked by saints' feast days, enact "the celebrations of those heroes whose feast days are marked out in time, rather than being distributed in different places, [and] supply the unifying occasions. It is through structures of temporality, as ritualized, that the divisiveness and particularity of space are overcome" (1987: 94–95).

27. An understanding of Utopia as an abstracted ungrounded ideology is appropriate, as the word "Utopia," based on the Greek and coined by Thomas More, means "no place" or "nowhere" (Sheldrake 2001: 94).

28. I follow Sheldrake and Chidester and Linenthal's understandings of Foucault's heterotopias. Not surprisingly, other interpretations abound. See Soja (1995) and Genoccio (1995) for examples.

29. LaDuke presents excellent examples of an ongoing process of desacralization, epitomized by the controversy raging over Arizona's Mt. Graham, in which the Apache and environmentalists are at odds with the University of Arizona and the Vatican about the building of a giant telescope that will desecrate a sacred mountain central to Apache identity (2005: 31; see also Taylor 1995: 100–125). Greene describes a rather extreme version of this process in which British colonizers ridiculed, ignored, and or selectively appropriated sacred sites in Ghana, resulting in a lasting shift in which bodies of water are no longer attributed with the capacity for divine access and human bodies are no longer considered conduits for spiritual power (2002: 6–7).

30. For a discussion of Hindu duplications, see Eck (1993: 57–61).

31. See also Lewis Carter (1990: 84–85) and Jonathan Z. Smith (1987: 28–29).

32. The breakup of the community began with a warrant for Sheela's arrest, which led her to flee to Germany. She was eventually arrested and returned to the United States, sentenced to twenty years imprisonment for a host of crimes, including attempted murder, second-degree assault (poisoning), and fraud. She was released from prison after serving only twenty months and moved to Switzerland, where she took on the job of managing nursing homes.

33. A similar observation from a different angle was made by some of Lewis Carter's research assistants who, as ethnic minorities, felt that the limited access they experienced when visiting Rajneeshpuram was not unlike experiences of marginalization felt in "normative" small-town American society (1990: 32).

34. Residents have placed a similar plaque outside the city courthouse of Dalles, in eastern Oregon. It reads: "Dedicated to all who steadfastly and unswervingly opposed the attempts of the Rajneesh followers to take political control of Wasco County. 1981–1985" (L. Carter 1990: 127). For a brief local history of how the Big Muddy was transferred from Native American tribes to European trappers, then to Rajneeshee devotees, and to its current inhabitants see Stark and Harding (2006).

35. See Dempsey (2006: 176–84) for more examples of local obstructions to Hindu temple construction.

36. For more details regarding neighborly resistance to the building and presence of the Rush temple, see Dempsey (2006: 177–81).

37. On a related note, Braun ends his book on the Rajneesh community with a twenty-four-stanza poem reflecting on inconsistencies between what he considers

American hospitality toward foreigners and its religious intolerance. The first stanza reads:

> Give me your poor,
> your tired and downtrodden.
> Your helpless, hungry and impure.
> Give me your Cuban misfits,
> criminals, insane and derelicts.
> Send me your Asian boat people,
> your Soviet dissidents, defectors
> and all your other displaced souls.
> But please don't send religious leaders
> unless they walk the same path as we
> and dare not espouse a different idea. (1984: 233)

38. The ability of the Rush settlement to acknowledge, at least in part, heterotopian realities, inscribing layers of religious meanings into the land, likely emerges from their status as a minority group working to fit in rather than take over. This adaptive quality assuages but unfortunately does not protect them entirely from non-heterotopian discourses in their midst.

CHAPTER 4

1. I use the term "Neo-Vedanta" because it is recognizable, although "Modern Vedanta" may be more appropriate. Vedantic philosophies have been reinterpreted and reframed for centuries, making so-called Neo-Vedanta simply one of the most recent permutations. Those who resist singling out Neo-Vedanta as particularly "new" feel that the label lends a certain inauthenticity to the movement. (Thanks to Reid Locklin, personal communication, for this insight.)

2. Swatos and Gissurarson describe the proliferation of spirits and ghosts in the Icelandic sagas and Eddas long before the rise of twentieth-century Spiritualism. They argue that although Spiritualism is a unique, modern movement and not just a continuation of an older tradition, earlier Icelandic traditions provided fertile ground (1997: 39–42). Neo-Vedanta, likewise a thoroughly modern movement, nonetheless draws on ancient traditions found in Vedantic and yogic practices and scripture.

3. I also refer to this period of exchange in the introduction, when I describe the origins of comparative religions established as a "science" of religion.

4. This goes against what scholars of New Age say about the accelerated mixing of international beliefs. Frisk notes that the New Age seems to differ from historical transnational religion due to "the accelerated eclecticism and emphasis on an inner experience of unity of multicultural elements. This 'open' worldview, without too much emphasis on ideas or belief systems, has become more attractive as the plausibility of the traditional religious metacultures has been undermined" (2001: 33).

5. Robert Fuller argues compellingly that, although the Fox sisters are usually given the credit for starting the mid- to late-nineteenth-century Spiritualist movement, credit is more aptly given to Andrew Jackson Davis, who preceded the Fox sisters by several years. Davis claimed trance states that allowed him to channel spirits, including that of Emanuel Swedenborg, whose teachings became foundational to American and, later, British Spiritualism (2001: 38–44).

6. Carl Jung likewise appeared interested in producing empirical evidence for traditional religious claims and the survival of the human personality after death. This concern led him to base his doctoral dissertation on a case study of a spirit medium (Main 2002: 199).

7. Professional magicians, including Harry Houdini, were particularly active in exposing frauds. Houdini claimed not to disbelieve the possibility of mediumship but felt particularly affronted by those who consciously deceived the public, in contrast to magicians who admitted to trickery (Hess 1993: 22).

8. Hazelgrove (2000) argues that a resurgence of Spiritualism in Britain between the First and Second World Wars had to do not simply with a need to contact the newly dead but also with Spiritualism's ability to absorb and organize an array of popular practices.

9. Iceland is one of the few places where Spiritualism still thrives, as does Spiritism in Brazil, in part because these traditions tend to be more holistic rather than simply scientific. Spiritism, developed by Allan Kardec in late-nineteenth-century France, connected scientific research with philosophical principles and Christian morality. He also borrowed from Eastern philosophy—as does Icelandic Spiritualism—the ideas of reincarnation and karma (Hess 1993: 18).

10. See Oppenheim (1985) for a fuller description of British Spiritualism's appeal to turn-of-the-century agnostics. See also Tromp, who argues that séances in England, especially those performed by women who materialized foreign spirits, reflected British anxiety about the uncontainable colonial Other and ambivalence toward the imperial project (2006: 75–96).

11. As mentioned in the introduction, the comparative study of religions often led—or threatened to lead—to secularism, since, for many, comparison undermined the truth claims of all religions. Theosophists, however, used the secularists' methods to argue the opposite. They sought to discover common ground between all religions without necessarily subscribing to any particular religion. In the process, rather than undermining religion, they argued for a divine consciousness underlying all of creation (Viswanathan 1998: 132, 193; Viswanathan 2004).

12. In addition to Indians, who were naturally affronted by Blavatsky's bold claims to more accurate interpretations of Eastern philosophies, Max Müller critiqued her work via publications meant for European and American audiences. In an essay entitled "Esoteric Buddhism" he wrote, "If I were asked what Madame Blavatsky's Esoteric Buddhism really is, I should say it was Buddhism misunderstood, distorted, caricatured. There is nothing in it beyond what was known already, chiefly from books that are now antiquated. The most ordinary terms are misspelt and misinterpreted" (quoted in Oppenheim 1985: 163–64).

13. Van der Veer discusses various confluences between the Theosophical Society and the Indian nationalist movement. He mentions Motilal Nehru and Jawaharlal Nehru, his son, as two of the most notable members of the nationalist elite that joined the society, if only briefly (2001: 76–77).

14. British and American Spiritualists likewise considered Theosophy's penchant for mysticism and secrecy to be unscientific, in contrast to what they understood to be Spiritualism's open-eyed rationalism (Oppenheim 1985: 159–62). Blavatsky and Olcott, already disdainful of Spiritualism, became critical of Arya Samaj as well when Blavatsky discovered that the group accepted Dayananda's infallible authority and viewed the Vedas in a way that reflected a Vedic fundamentalism and hostility to other religions. Olcott, as a result, officially called off the proposed merger with Dayananda (Goodrick-Clarke 2007: 14–15).

15. At this time, Einar was still using his patronym, Hjörleifsson, which he soon afterward changed to Kvaran.

16. Because Spiritualism arrived relatively late in Iceland, by way of Canada and England, it appeared relatively unscathed by earlier scandalous fraudulence in the United States and Britain.

17. Akureyri happens to have an early history with alternative religious movements. Jón Hjaltalín, who had translated Swedenborg into Icelandic in the 1880s, lived in Akureyri, and the first Theosophical Society was established there.

18. Thanks to Pétur Pétursson for this insight (personal communication).

19. Hess mentions Theosophy, established in 1875, as a more direct precursor to the New Age movement because of its interest in ritual, magic, astrology, and Eastern religion and reincarnation (Hess 1993: 20). Following this, Blavatsky has even been referred to as the "Mother of the New Age" (Tingay 2002: 247; see also Brown 2007: 437). Key elements of the New Age movement as described by Heelas and Main further reflect Theosophical aims and interests. For instance, like Theosophy, the New Age movement has defined itself in resistance to processes of modernization and secularization, yet it is also Romanticist and thus a product of modern society (Main 2002: 186–89; Heelas 1996: 5, 27).

20. Contrasting this with the ongoing fracas between Spiritualists and Theosophists outside Iceland, recall Blavatsky's disdain for Spiritualist's short-sighted preoccupation with spirits. An 1884 investigation by the Society for Psychical Research, many of whose members were Spiritualists, accused Blavatsky, in return, of being one of the "most accomplished, ingenious, and interesting impostors in history" (Kent 2010: 17). Hess explains, "While Theosophy rejected Spiritualism as philosophically unsophisticated and uncosmopolitan, Spiritualists rejected Theosophy as unscientific occultism" (1993: 20). In addition to their anti-Christian, particularly anticlerical polemics, Theosophists in India were known to have worked directly against Christian missionary activity. Missionaries sometimes discovered that potential converts on the brink of conversion were convinced by Theosophists to remain Hindu (Kent 2010: 8).

21. Personal communication with Pétur Pétursson, November 2009.

22. References to computers and computer technology as a metaphor for metaphysical phenomena is something I heard several times in conversations with Spiritualists in Iceland.

23. In spite of this official stance, it is not uncommon for contemporary Spiritualists to ascribe to a belief in reincarnation.

24. See Dempsey (2006), especially chapter 3, as well as my forthcoming book on Iceland, for accounts of some of these stories. For classic accounts of yogic feats see Paramahansa (1946).

25. Brooks notes a distinction between secondary *siddhi*s, described here, and supreme *siddhi* known as *parama siddhi*. The supreme *siddhi*, the fully realized, merges individual consciousness with Supreme Consciousness and finds unbounded joy within, not identified with the ever-changing states of the body or limited ego. As Brooks describes it, this state "paradoxically incarnates within the human condition the freedom of the transcendent consciousness and the power of the realm of divine ecstasy" (1997: 204, 207–8).

26. Elsewhere (Dempsey 2008) I describe Aiya's temple science in considerable detail.

27. See Dempsey (2006: 57–60, 66–69).

28. In Independent India the debate changes. Thus while miracles had little place in colonial Practical Vedanta, they are now presented as legitimate "not because of superior

understanding of universal laws," but because they "prove something about the power of the person to whom they're attributed" (Rinehart 2008: 36–37).

29. In the foreword to his book *Lára Miðill*, which details the life and accomplishments of a medium in Akureyri, Sveinn Víkingur lists ten types of extraordinary human abilities often attributed to spirit assistance. He first lists *skyggni*, described as the "fairly common" ability to see the deceased. While this use of the word *skyggni* refers to people who "see," the term *skyggnigáfa*, an openness to the spirit world, allows for a much wider range of abilities, among which Víkingur lists *dulheyrnir*, the ability to hear voices that others cannot; *fjarhrif*, telepathy; *forvizka*, knowledge of events to come; *ósjálfráð skift*, automatic writing; and *huglækningar*, spiritual healing (Víkingur 1962: 10–21).

30. A significant exception to this is the work of Erlendur Haraldsson, a professor of psychology at the University of Iceland, who conducted research on paranormal phenomena. See especially Haraldsson and Stevenson's (1974, 1978) experiments with Hafsteinn Björnsson, a highly acclaimed Icelandic medium who died of a heart attack in the late 1970s.

31. See Haraldsson (1986) for his multinational study that compared general belief in psychic and religious phenomena. Interestingly, Iceland's relatively high levels of belief in spiritual phenomena are matched by relatively low church attendance.

32. Icelandic rock lyrics often include references to Spiritualist phenomena, and a popular Icelandic mystery series first airing on television in 2009 features a boy with *skyggnigáfa* and an occasional medium who solves important pieces of the puzzle.

33. See also van der Veer (2001: 56–57). Interesting exceptions to this tendency to avoid spirits abound, as well. Renuka, a Hindu girl in Kerala understood to have been healed by Sr. (now St.) Alphonsa, subsequently gained the ability to predicted future events, communicated to her by Alphonsa. Although this seems somewhat consistent with Catholic faith in Alphonsa, those who visited to Renuka in search of spirit-inspired prophecies were both Hindu and Catholic. See Dempsey (2001: 62–64).

34. Following the teachings of Blavatsky, early Theosophists also had misgivings about spirits and séances. Blavatsky maintained that the astral plane was inhabited by nonhuman entities and spirits of the lowest forms of humanity who deceived those who called on them into believing they were their loving departed. Similar to mainstream Hindu views of reincarnation, Blavatsky held that decent human beings departed to more rarified realms of existence than the spirit world (Oppenheim 1985: 165).

35. The term "controller" refers to the spirit who regularly performs a function similar to a Master of Ceremony for the *hringur*, organizing and introducing spirits who come through the trance medium.

36. It seems Icelandic Spiritualism's concern for the troubled dead is somewhat unusual. One rarely encounters descriptions of such work when reading about the Spiritualist movement in the United States and England. I have spoken with several American Spiritualists who were quite surprised by my descriptions of Icelandic medium assistance to spirits in need. In their opinion, this was potentially dangerous work that put living participants at risk.

POSTSCRIPT

1. This is not a new exercise for me. I have written elsewhere about intersections between mode and subject of fieldwork study and between the travel aims of tourists, pilgrims, and ethnographers. See Dempsey (2000; 2006: 209–14).

2. Rather than simply cementing the status quo, ritual performances, as framed by Jean Comaroff, can act as mediators between history and contemporary transformations, providing "an appropriate medium through which the values and structures of a contradictory world may be addressed and manipulated" (1985: 196; see also Bell 1997: 82–83). Tom Driver considers transformation to be the nature of ritual itself. Given that ritual performance is bodily enacted, its capacity to expose and transform social injustices and inequities are all the more potent and revelatory: "Performance makes present. Because it is performance and not verbal description or exhortation, ritual brings the far-away, the long-ago, and the not-yet into the here-and-now. Because it is performance, ritual produces its effects not simply in the minds but also in the bodies of its performers" (1991: 190). See also Durayappah and Dempsey's (forthcoming) descriptions of traditional Hindu ritual's potential to innovatively validate alternative lifestyles in North America.

3. See also Sullivan (1986), who argues that the academic study of culture could be positively informed or reshaped by studies of ritual performance.

4. See Dempsey (2006).

5. Lawrence Sullivan describes this sensory aspect of knowing in detail, referring to it as "synesthesia" (1986: 6–8).

6. Since ritual studies' turn toward performance in the 1960s, theorists indeed have attempted to expand their investigation of ritual knowledge to encompass bodily activities, senses, and emotions and to ascribe intellectual value to them as modes of understanding. As Theodore Jennings proclaims, it is not "that the mind 'embodies' itself in ritual action, but rather that the body 'minds' itself or attends through itself in ritual action" (1982: 115). Jennings notes how our cultural bias toward disembodied expressions of consciousness—rather than a plurality of modes of knowing—is embedded in redundant phrases such as "embodied consciousness," often applied to ritual (1982: 124). Similarly, Yvonne Daniel argues that ritual dance provides worshippers a vital means for sensing and learning an array of cultural values and meanings. Ritual dance is a form of embodied knowledge that is not only accumulated; it is constantly consulted (2005: 265). This is the case even though, as Daniel puts it, "physical/cognitive/emotional/spiritual knowledge—embodied through dance behavior—has been greatly belittled and often devalued" by academics (2005: 268).

7. Similarly arguing against conventional bias that ethical judgment emerges from detached intellect, Martha Nussbaum notes that emotions are "essential elements of human intelligence, rather than . . . supports or props for intelligence" (2003: 3). She argues that once we discern links between emotion and intelligence, we cannot, in serious attempts to find meaning, sideline them as irrelevant.

Catherine Bell agrees that locating common ground between performances of ritual and its analysis can be helpful in sidestepping mind/body, thought/action dichotomies. On the other hand, she warns against scholarly inclinations to collapse entirely the differences between "observing scholar" and "performing native," as this is likely to undercut the value of our study (1998: 219). She suggests, more modestly, that "we are entering an era in which what we want to learn cannot be learned if our terminology overdetermines the theater of engagement. It is an era in which our terms are best used as a minimalist set of props with which we can begin to engage ideas and inquire into practices that may well modify the surroundings" (1998: 220–21).

8. Likewise, as a dancer and ethnographer of ritual dance—a mirror to her subject of study—Yvonne Daniel argues for the potential for using multichanneled embodied knowledges as ethnographic tools: "In dancing or in the kinesthetic world, you rely on a simultaneous multisensory experience that is at once physical, cognitive, and emotional.... In simpler terms, dancing as an investigative method emphasizes the pragmatic approach to knowledge" (2005: 270).

9. Barbara Myerhoff and Jay Ruby work to fend off the critique that reflexivity is an exercise in myopic self-concern. Ideally they frame the process as something that "pulls one toward the Other ... breaking the thrall of self-concern by its very drive toward self-knowledge that inevitably takes into account a surrounding world of events, people, and places" (1982: 5). Along the same lines, Norman Denzin advocates autoethnography that obscures distinctions between self and Other by folding the ethnographer's reflections into the stories of others, making the self vulnerable to one's own experiences as well as to those of others. Similar to reflexivity described by Myerhoff and Ruby, attention to the self in autoethnography is meant to move the researcher into larger spheres of concern. As Denzin describes it, "Performance ethnography simultaneously creates and enacts moral texts that move from the personal to the political, from the local to the historical and the cultural" (2003: x).

10. Lawrence Sullivan notes that the pivotal difference between scholarly hermeneutics and ritual performance is that the hermeneutical circle deals with culture as human creation, whereas ritual performance often deals with "a quality of being that is imaginable as something other than human" (1986: 30). The latter affords ritual, according to Sullivan, a certain aesthetic richness and efficacy.

11. Bell and Sullivan furthermore note how this shared performative reflexivity provides a tentative link between scholars of ritual and ritual practitioners. Bell posits that the epistemological concerns of those who study ritual are similar to the concerns of those who perform it, since ritual's fusion of thought and action parallels the scholar's theoretical project and its object, ritual activity. Both generate meaning, first for the ritual actor and second for the theorist (1992: 75; 1998: 210). As Sullivan describes it, the hermeneutics of both the academy and of ritual practices are acts of interpretation that are, at the same time, based on performance. He argues that interpretation is itself an act of performance that is self-constituting, as is ritual. In other words, hermeneutics, like ritual, does not stand outside culture but is the work of understanding that makes culture. We learn by experience, and experience is communicated in the symbolic actions and forms of our culture. Closing the hermeneutical circle, one of the best ways of learning, Sullivan posits, is through our performative genres (1986: 28–29). Conflating ritual with art, Gilbert Lewis likewise notes that "in ritual as in art, he who devises or creates or performs is also spectator of what he does; and he who beholds it is also active in the sense that he interprets the performance. The value of ritual lies partly in this ambiguity of the active and passive for the creator, performer, and beholder" (1980: 38).

12. As Lawrence Sullivan puts it, tears in a ritual context, ineffably intelligible, represent "a symbolic vehicle for the full load of human experience" (1990: 52–53). Sullivan is also quoted in Patton and Hawley (2005: 3), an edited volume that explores the cross-culturally the religious resonance of weeping. See especially Patton and Hawley's introduction for the comparative significance of tears.

REFERENCES

Adamski, Mary. 2005. "Hindus and Hawaiians Build Truce." *Honolulu Star Bulletin*, March 25.

Adorno, Theodor. 1983. *Negative Dialectics*. Translated by E. B. Ashton. New York: Continuum.

Asad, Talal. 1993. *Genealogies of Religion: Discipline and Power in Christianity and Islam*. Baltimore: Johns Hopkins University Press.

Ashcroft, Bill, Gareth Griffiths, and Helen Tiffin. 1995a. "General Introduction." In *The Post-Colonial Studies Reader*, ed. Bill Ashcroft, Gareth Griffiths, and Helen Tiffin, 1–4. London: Routledge.

———. 1995b. "Introduction to Part XII." In *The Post-Colonial Studies Reader*, ed. Bill Ashcroft, Gareth Griffiths, and Helen Tiffin, 391–93. London: Routledge.

Bachorz, Stephanie. 2001. "Postcolonial Theory and Ireland: Revising Postcolonialism." In *Critical Ireland: New Essays in Literature and Culture*, ed. Alan Gillis and Aaron Kelly, 6–13. Dublin: Four Courts.

Barrow, Logie. 1986. I*ndependent Spirits: Spiritualism and English Plebians 1850–1910*. London: Routledge.

Behdad, Ali. 2005. *A Forgetful Nation: On Immigration and Cultural Identity in the United States*. Durham, NC: Duke University Press.

Bell, Catherine. 1992. *Ritual Theory, Ritual Practice*. New York: Oxford University Press.

———. 1998. "Performance." In *Critical Terms for Religious Studies*, ed. Mark Taylor, 205–24. Chicago: University of Chicago Press.

Bhabha, Homi. 1994. *The Location of Culture*. London: Routledge.

Bhagwat, A. L. 1973. *Mohini Vidyā Sādhanā and Siddhi: Hindu Way to Hidden Powers*. Bombay: Shree Gajanan Book Depot Prakashan.

Boff, Leonardo. 1979. *The Maternal Face of God: The Feminine and Its Religious Expressions*. Translated by Robert Barr and John Diercksmeier. San Francisco: Harper and Row.

———. 1981 [1986]. *Church, Charism, and Power: Liberation Theology and the Institutional Church*. Translated by John Dierksmeyer. New York: Crossroads.

———. 1986. *Jesus Christ Liberator: A Critical Christology for Our Time*. Translated by Patrick Hughes. Maryknoll, NY: Orbis.

———. 1995. *Ecology and Liberation: A New Paradigm*. Translated by John Cumming. Maryknoll, NY: Orbis.

———. 1997. *Cry of the Earth, Cry of the Poor*. Translated by Phillip Berryman. Maryknoll, NY: Orbis.

Bonino, José Miguez. 1975. *Doing Theology in a Revolutionary Situation*. Philadelphia: Fortress.

Braun, Kirk. 1984. *Rajneeshpuram: The Unwelcome Society: Cultures Collide in a Quest for Utopia*. West Linn, OR: Scout Creek.

Brecher, Max. 1993. *A Passage to America*. Bombay: Book Quest.

Brooks, Douglas Renfrew. 1992. *Auspicious Wisdom: The Text and Traditions of Śrīvidyā Śākta Tantrism in South India*. Albany: State University of New York Press.

———, ed. 1997. *Meditation Revolution: A History and Theology of the Siddha Yoga Lineage*. South Fallsburg, NY: Agama.

Brown, C. Mackenzie. 2007. "Three Historical Probes: The Western Roots of Avataric Evolutionism in Colonial India." *Zygon* 42, no. 2: 423–47.

Brown, Gavin. 2003. "Theorizing Ritual as Performance: Explorations of Ritual Indeterminacy." *Journal of Ritual Studies* 17, no. 1: 3–18.

Brown, Terrence. 1996. "Celticism, Cultural Nationalism, and the Occult." In *Celticism*, ed. Terrence Brown, 221–30. Amsterdam: Rodopi.

Bührig, Marga. 1993. *Woman Invisible: A Personal Odyssey in Christian Feminism*. Valley Forge, PA: Trinity Press International.

Burke, Mary. 2009. *"Tinkers": Synge and the Cultural History of the Irish Traveller*. New York: Oxford University Press.

Bynum, Caroline Walker. 1991. *Fragmentation and Redemption: Essays on Gender and the Body in Medieval Religion*. New York: Zone.

Carter, Lewis. 1990. *Charisma and Control in Rajneeshpuram: The Role of Shared Values in Rajneeshpuram*. Cambridge: Cambridge University Press.

Carter, Paul. 1995. "Naming Place." In *The Post-Colonial Studies Reader*, ed. Bill Ashcroft, Gareth Griffiths, and Helen Tiffin, 402–6. London: Routledge.

Chacko, K. C. 1948 [1990]. *Sister Alphonsa*, 6th ed. Bharananganam, Kerala: Vice Postulator, Cause of Blessed Alphonsa.

Chapple, Christopher Key, and Mary Evelyn Tucker. 2000. *Hinduism and Ecology: The Intersection of Earth, Sky, and Water*. Cambridge: Harvard University Press.

Chidester, David. 1996. *Savage Religion: Colonialism and Comparative Religion in Southern Africa*. Charlottesville: University of Virginia Press.

Chidester, David, and Edward Linenthal. 1995. "Introduction." In *American Sacred Space*, ed. David Chidester and Edward Linenthal, 1–42. Bloomington: Indiana University Press.

Christ, Carol. 1991. "Mircea Eliade and the Feminist Paradigm Shift." *Journal of Feminist Studies in Religion* 7, no. 2: 75–94.

———. 2003. *She Who Changes: Reimagining the Divine in the World*. New York: Palgrave Macmillan.

Clifford, James. 1997. *Routes: Travel and Translation in the Late Twentieth Century*. Cambridge: Harvard University Press.

Clooney, Francis. 2005. *Divine Mother, Blessed Mother: Hindu Goddesses and the Virgin Mary*. New York: Oxford University Press.

Comaroff, Jean. 1985. *Body of Power, Spirit of Resistance: The Culture and History of a South African People*. Chicago: University of Chicago Press.

Connolly, S. J. 1982. *Priests and People in Pre-Famine Ireland*. New York: St. Martin's.

Cutler, Norman. 1987. *Songs of Experience: The Poetics of Tamil Devotion*. Bloomington: Indiana University Press.

Daniel, Yvonne. 2005. *Dancing Wisdom: Embodied Knowledge in Haitian Vodou, Cuban Yoruba, and Bahian Candomble*. Urbana: University of Illinois Press.

de Vries, Hent. 2008. "Introduction." In *Religion: Beyond a Concept*, ed. Hent de Vries, 1–98. New York: Fordham University Press.

Dempsey, Corinne. 2000. "The Religioning of Anthropology: New Directions for the Ethnographer-Pilgrim." *Culture and Religion* 1, no. 2: 189–210.

———. 2001. *Kerala Christian Sainthood: Collisions of Culture and Worldview in South Indian Christianity*. New York: Oxford University Press.

———. 2002. "Lessons in Miracles from Kerala, South India: Stories of Three 'Christian' Saints." In *Popular Christianity in India: Riting Between the Lines*, ed. Selva Raj and Corinne Dempsey, 115–40. Albany: State University of New York Press.

———. 2005. "Nailing Heads and Splitting Hairs: Conflict, Conversion, and the Bloodthirsty Yakshi in Kerala, South India." *Journal of American Academy of Religion* 73, no. 1: 111–32.

———. 2006. *The Goddess Lives in Upstate New York: Breaking Convention and Making Home at a North American Hindu Temple*. New York: Oxford University Press.

———. 2008. "The Science of the Miraculous at an Upstate New York Temple." In *Miracle as Modern Conundrum in South Asian Religious Traditions*, ed. Corinne Dempsey and Selva Raj, 119–40. Albany: State University of New York Press.

Denzin, Norman. 2003. *Performance Ethnography: Critical Pedagogy and the Politics of Culture*. Thousand Oaks, CA: Sage.

Doniger, Wendy. 2000. "Post-modern and -colonial -structural Comparisons." In *A Magic Still Dwells: Comparative Religion in the Postmodern Age*, ed. Kimberly Patton and Benjamin Ray, 63–74. Berkeley: University of California Press.

Driver, Tom. 1991. *The Magic of Ritual: Our Need for Liberating Rites That Transform Our Lives and Our Communities*. San Francisco: HarperCollins.

Duin, Steve. 1999. "The Rajneesh Ranch Reborn." *Oregonian*, September 5. www.rickross.com/reference/rajneesh/rajneesh5.html.

Durayappah Sudharshan, and Corinne Dempsey. 2009. "Recasting Sexuality, Gender, and Family through Contemporary Canadian Ritual Innovation." Paper delivered at the Conference on the Study of Religions of India, Kalamazoo College, Michigan. June 18–21.

Eagleton, Terry. 1996. *The Illusions of Postmodernism*. Oxford: Blackwell.

Eck, Diana. 1993. *Encountering God: A Spiritual Journey from Bozeman to Banaras*. Boston: Beacon.

———. 2000. "Dialogue and Method: Reconstructing the Study of Religion." In *A Magic Still Dwells: Comparative Religion in the Postmodern Age*, ed. Kimberly Patton and Benjamin Ray, 131–49. Berkeley: University of California Press.

———. 2001. *A New Religious America: How a "Christian Country" Has Now Become the World's Most Religiously Diverse Nation*. San Francisco: HarperSanFrancisco.

Eckel, Malcolm. 2000. "Contested Identities: The Study of Buddhism in the Postmodern World." In *A Magic Still Dwells: Comparative Religion in the Postmodern Age*, ed. Kimberly Patton and Benjamin Ray, 55–62. Berkeley: University of California Press.

Egan, Timothy. 1995. "Oregon Ranch with a Troubled Past Faces a Dubious Future." *New York Times*, October 20: 14.

Eliade, Mircea. 1958. *Patterns in Comparative Religion*. Translated by Rosemary Sheed. New York: Meridian.

————. 1965. "Cultural Fashions in the History of Religions." In *History of Religions: Essays on the Problem of Understanding*, ed. Joseph Kittegawa, 21–38. Chicago: University of Chicago Press.

Elkins, Caroline. 2005. "Race, Citizenship, and Governance: Settler Tyranny and the End of Empire." In *Settler Colonialism in the Twentieth Century: Projects, Practices, Legacies*, ed. Caroline Elkins and Susan Pedersen, 203–22. New York: Routledge.

Elkins, Caroline, and Susan Pederson. 2005. "Introduction: Settler Colonialism: A Concept and Its Uses." In *Settler Colonialism in the Twentieth Century: Projects, Practices, Legacies*, ed. Caroline Elkins and Susan Pedersen, 1–21. New York: Routledge.

Fell, Michael. 1999. *And Some Fell into Good Soil: A History of Christianity in Iceland*. New York: Peter Lang.

Fitzgerald, Frances. 1986a. "A Reporter at Large: Rajneeshpuram—I." *New Yorker*, September 22: 46–96.

————. 1986b. "A Reporter at Large: Rajneeshpuram—II." *New Yorker*, September 29: 83–125.

Flueckiger, Joyce. 2006. *In Amma's Healing Room: Gender and Vernacular Islam in South India*. Bloomington: Indiana University Press.

Foucault, Michel. 1986. "Of Other Spaces." *Diacritics* 16, no. 1: 22–27.

"Frá Landamærunum: Einar H. Kvaran Segir frá Upphafi Sálarrannsókna Hjer á Landi." 1934. *Morgunblaðið*, 291. Tölublað. December 6.

Freire, Paolo. 1971. "Education as Cultural Action: An Introduction." In *Conscientization for Liberation*. Ed. Louis Colonnese. Washington, DC: Division for Latin America, United States Catholic Conference.

Frisk, Lisolette. 2001. "Globalization or Westernization? New Age as a Contemporary Transnational Culture." In *New Age Religion and Globalization*, ed. Mikael Rothstein, 31–41. Copenhagen: Aarhus University Press.

Fuller, Robert. 2001. *Spiritual but Not Religious: Understanding Unchurched America*. New York: Oxford University Press.

————. 2006. "Wonder and the Religious Sensibility: A Study in Religion and Emotion." *Journal of Religion* 86, no. 3: 364–84.

Geertz, Clifford. 1973. *The Interpretation of Cultures*. New York: Basic.

Genoccio, Benjamin. 1995. "Discourse, Discontinuity, Difference: The Question of 'Other' Spaces." In *Postmodern Cities and Spaces*, ed. Sophie Watson and Katherine Gibson, 35–46. Oxford: Blackwell.

Gilmartin, D., ed. 2000. *Beyond Turk and Hindu: Rethinking Religious Identities in Islamicate South Asia*. Miami: University Press of Florida.

Gissurarson, Loftur Reimar, and Erlendur Haraldsson. 1969. *The Icelandic Physical Medium Indriði Indriðason*. London: Society for Psychical Research.

————. 2001. "History of Parapsychology in Iceland." *International Journal of Parapsychology* 12, no. 1: 29–50.

Goodrick-Clarke, Nicholas. 2007. "The Theosophical Society, Orientalism, and the 'Mystical East': Western Esotericism and Eastern Religion in Theosophy." *Theosophical History* 13, no. 13: 3–28.

Gordon, James. 1987. *The Golden Guru*. Lexington, MA: Stephen Green.

Gottschalk, Peter. 2000. *Beyond Hindu and Muslim: Multiple Identity in Narratives from Village India*. New York: Oxford University Press.

Graham, Colin. 2001. *Deconstructing Ireland: Identity, Theory, Culture*. Edinburgh: Edinburgh University Press.

Greene, Sandra. 2002. *Sacred Sites and the Colonial Encounter: A History of Meaning and Memory in Ghana*. Bloomington: Indiana University Press.

Griffiths, Gareth. 2001. "Postcoloniality, Religion, Geography: Keeping Our Feet on the Ground and Our Heads Up." In *Mapping the Sacred: Religion, Geography, and Postcolonial Literatures*, ed. Jamie Scott and Paul Simpson-Housley, 445–61. Amsterdam: Rodopi.

Guha, Naresh. 1968. *W. B. Yeats: An Indian Approach*. Darby, PA: Arden Library.

Gutierrez, Gustavo. 1968. "Toward a Theology of Liberation." In *Gustavo Gutiérrez: Essential Writings*, ed. James B. Nickoloff, 23–28. Maryknoll, NY: Orbis.

———. 1973. *A Theology of Liberation: History, Politics and Salvation*. Translated by Sister Caridad Ina and John Eagleson. Maryknoll, NY: Orbis.

Haraldsson, Erlendur. 1986. "Representative National Surveys of Psychic Phenomena: Iceland, Great Britain, Sweden, USA, and Gallup's Multinational Survey." *Journal of the Society for Psychical Research* 53: 145–58.

Haraldsson, Erlendur, and Ian Stevenson. 1974. "An Experiment with the Icelandic Medium Hafsteinn Björnsson." *Journal of the American Society for Psychical Research* 68: 192–202.

———. 1978. "Further Experiments with the Icelandic Medium Hafsteinn Björnsson." *Journal of the American Society for Psychical Research* 72: 339–47.

Harman, William. 2008. "A Miracle (or Two) in Tiruchirapalli." In *Miracle as Modern Conundrum in South Asian Religious Traditions*, ed. Corinne Dempsey and Selva Raj, 105–18. Albany: State University of New York Press.

Hawley, John Stratton, and Mark Juergensmeyer. 1988. *Songs of the Saints of India*. New York: Oxford University Press.

Hazelgrove, Jenny. 2000. *Spiritualism and British Society between the Wars*. Manchester: Manchester University Press.

Heelas, Paul. 1996. *The New Age Movement: The Celebration of the Self and the Sacralization of Modernity*. Oxford: Blackwell.

Hess, David. 1993. *Science in the New Age: The Paranormal, Its Defenders and Debunkers, and American Culture*. Madison: University of Wisconsin Press.

Holdrege, Barbara. 2000. "What's beyond the Post?: Comparative Analysis as Critical Method." In *A Magic Still Dwells: Comparative Religion in the Postmodern Age*, ed. Kimberly Patton and Benjamin Ray, 77–91. Berkeley: University of California Press.

Howe, Leo. 2000. "Risk, Ritual and Performance." *Royal Anthropological Institute* 2: 63–79.

Inglis, Tom. 1987. *Moral Monopoly: The Rise and Fall of the Catholic Church in Modern Ireland*. Dublin: University College Dublin Press.

Jameson, Fredric. 1991. "Utopianism after the End of Utopia." In *Postmodernism, or, the Cultural Logic of Late Capitalism*, 154–80. Durham, NC: Duke University Press.

Jedrej, Charles, and Mark Nuttall. 1996. *White Settlers: The Impact of Rural Repopulation in Scotland*. London: Harwood Academic.

Jennings, Theodore. 1982. "On Ritual Knowledge." *Journal of Religion* 62, no. 3: 111–27.

Jensen, Jeppe Sinding. 2001. "Universals, General Terms and the Comparative Study of Religion." *Numen* 48, no. 3: 238–66.

Johnston, Anna, and Alan Lawson. 2005. "Settler Colonies." In *A Companion to Post-Colonial Studies*, ed. Henry Schwarz and Sangeeta Ray, 360–76. Malden, MA: Blackwell.

Josetta, F. C. C., Sr. 2009. *St. Alphonsa: A Flake in the Flame of Love*. Translated by Poovathilappu, Shijomon. Kottayam, Kerala: Franciscan Clarist Provincial House.

Karlen, Neal, with Mark Kirchmeier. 1984. "The Homeless and the Guru." *Newsweek*, September 14: 35.

Kazanjian, David. 2003. *The Colonizing Trick: National Culture and Imperial Citizenship in Early America*. Minneapolis: University of Minnesota Press.

Kent, Eliza. 2010. "Strange Apparitions: Visions of Indian Spirits by Protestant Missionaries, Theosophists and Early Scholars of Comparative Religion." Paper given at Williams College, conference entitled "Holy Spirits: Spiritualism and the Formation of Religious Studies," Williamstown, MA, January 21–22.

Kent, Eliza, and Tazim Kassam. (2012). *Lines in Water: Religious Boundaries in South Asia*. Syracuse, NY: Syracuse University Press.

Khan, Dominique-Sila. 1997. *Conversions and Shifting Identities: Ramdev Pir and the Ismailis in Rajasthan*. New Delhi: Manohar.

King, Richard. 1999. *Orientalism and Religion: Postcolonial Theory, India, and the "Mystic East."* New York: Routledge.

Kirkland, Richard. 1999. "Questioning the Frame: Hybridity, Ireland, and the Institution." In *Ireland and Cultural History: The Mechanics of Authenticity*, ed. Colin Graham and Richard Kirkland, 210–28. London: Macmillan.

Kraft, Siv Ellen. 2002. "'To Mix or Not to Mix': Syncretism/Anti-Syncretism in the History of Theosophy." *Numen* 49, no. 2: 142–77.

Kristjánsson, Benjamin. n.d. *Haraldur Níelsson: Stríðmaður Eilífðarvissunnar, 1868–1968*. Akureyri: Sálarrannsóknarfélag Íslands.

Kunnunkal, Hippolitus, O. F. M. 2006. "Preface to the English Translation." In *In the Footsteps of Alphonsa* by Eliseus Vengaloor, FCC, 5–6. Translated by Thomas Chavarany. Bharananganam, Kerala: Jeevan.

LaDuke, Winona. 2005. *Recovering the Sacred: The Powers of Naming and Claiming*. Cambridge, MA: South End.

Lambek, Michael. 2002. "A General Introduction." In *A Reader in the Anthropology of Religion*, ed. Michael Lambek, 1–18. Malden, MA: Blackwell.

———. 2008. "Provincializing God? Provocations from an Anthropology of Religion." In *Religion: Beyond a Concept*, ed. Hent de Vries, 120–38. New York: Fordham University Press.

LaMothe, Kimerer. 2008. "What Bodies Know about Religion and the Study of It." *Journal of the American Academy of Religion* 76, no. 3: 573–601.

Lanters, José. 2008. *The "Tinkers" in Irish Society: Unsettled Subjects and the Construction of Difference*. Dublin: Irish Academic Press.

Levine, Amy-Jill. 2004. "Introduction." In *A Feminist Companion to Paul*, ed. Amy-Jill Levine, 1–12. Cleveland, OH: Pilgrim.

Lewis, Gilbert. 1980. *Day of Shining Red: An Essay on Understanding Ritual*. Cambridge: Cambridge University Press.

Lloyd, David. 1993. *Anomalous States: Irish Writing and the Post-Colonial Moment*. Dublin: Lilliput.

Locklin, Reid, and Hugh Nicholson. 2010. "The Return of Comparative Theology." *Journal of the American Academy of Religion* 78, no. 2: 477–514.

Long, Charles. 1986. *Significations: Signs, Symbols, and Images in the Interpretation of Religions*. Philadelphia: Fortress.

Long, Jeffery. 2007. *A Vision for Hinduism: Beyond Hindu Nationalism*. London: I. B. Tauris.

MacNeice, Louis. 1967. *The Poetry of W. B. Yeats*. London: Faber.

Main, Roderick. 2002. "Religion, Science and the New Age." In *Belief Beyond Boundaries: Wicca, Celtic Spirituality and the New Age*, ed. Joanne Pearson, 173–222. Burlington, VT: Ashgate.

Masuzawa, Tomoko. 2005. *The Invention of World Religions: Or, How European Universalism Was Preserved in the Language of Pluralism*. Chicago: University of Chicago Press.

Mathur, H. C. 1998. *Siddhi: The Science of Supernatural Powers.* New Delhi: Shree.

McDaniel, June. 2007. "Does Tantric Ritual Empower Women? Renunciation and Domesticity among Female Bengali Tantrikas." In *Women's Lives, Women's Rituals in the Hindu Tradition*, ed. Tracy Pintchman, 159–76. New York: Oxford University Press.

McLaughlin, Jim. 1998. "Pestilence on Their Backs, Famine in Their Stomachs: The Racial Construction of Irishness and the Irish in Victorian Britain." In *Ireland and Cultural History: The Mechanics of Authenticity*, ed. Colin Graham and Richard Kirkland, 50–76. London: Macmillan.

Mehta, J. L. 1985. "Problems of Intercultural Understanding in University Studies of Religion." In *India and the West: The Problem of Understanding—Selected Essays of J. L. Mehta*. Chico, CA: Scholars.

Moor, Art. 1999. "From Cult Site to Teen Camp: Anything That Can Go Right Will, Young Discovers." *Christianity Today* 43, no. 13: 22.

Müller, Max. 1872. *Lectures on the Science of Religion.* New York: Charles Scribner.

Murphy, Dell. 1986. *The Rajneesh Story: The Bhagwan's Garden.* West Linn, OR: Linwood.

Myerhoff, Barbara, and Jay Ruby. 1982. "Introduction." In *A Crack in the Mirror: Reflexive Perspectives in Anthropology*, ed. Jay Ruby and Barbara Myerhoff, 1–39. Philadelphia: University of Pennsylvania Press.

Nandy, Ashis. 1983. *The Intimate Enemy: The Loss and Recovery of Self under Colonialism.* Delhi: Oxford University Press.

Narayanan, Vasudha. 1992. "Creating the South Indian 'Hindu' Experience in the United States." In *A Sacred Thread: Modern Transmission of Hindu Traditions in India and Abroad*, ed. Raymond Brady Williams, 147–76. Chambersburg, PA: Anima.

Neil, Stephen. 1984. *A History of Christianity in India: The Beginnings to AD 1707.* Vol. 1. Cambridge: Cambridge University Press.

———. 1985. *A History of Christianity in India: 1707–1859.* Vol. 2. Cambridge: Cambridge University Press.

Neville, Robert Cummings, ed. 2000. *The Human Condition.* Albany: State University of New York Press.

———. 2000. *Religious Truth.* Albany: State University of New York Press.

———. 2000. *Ultimate Realities.* Albany: State University of New York Press.

Níelsson, Haraldur. 1924. "Remarkable Phenomena in Iceland." *Journal of the American Society of Psychical Research* 18: 233–38.

Nussbaum, Martha. 2003. *Upheavals of Thought: The Intelligence of Emotions.* Cambridge: Cambridge University Press.

Obeyesekere, Gananath. 2002. *Imagining Karma: Ethical Transformations in Amerindian, Buddhist and Greek Rebirth.* Berkeley: University of California Press.

O'Leary, Paul. 1996. "From the Cradle to the Grave: Popular Catholicism among the Irish in Wales." In *Religion and Identity: The Irish World Wide: History, Heritage, Identity*, ed. Patrick O'Sullivan, 183–95. London: Leicester University Press.

Olson, Carl. 1992. *The Theology and Philosophy of Eliade: A Search for the Center.* New York: St. Martin's.

Oppenheim, Janet. 1985. *The Other World: Spiritualism and Psychical Research in England 1850–1914.* Cambridge: Cambridge University Press.

Orsi, Robert. 2005. *Between Heaven and Earth: The Religious Worlds People Make and the Scholars Who Study Them.* Princeton, NJ: Princeton University Press.

Owen, Alex. 2004. *The Place of Enchantment: British Occultism and the Culture of the Modern.* Chicago: University of Chicago Press.

Paden, William. 1988 [1994]. *Religious Worlds: The Comparative Study of Religion.* Boston: Beacon.

———. 2000. "Elements of a New Comparativism." In *A Magic Still Dwells: Comparative Religion in the Postmodern Age*, ed. Kimberly Patton and Benjamin Ray, 182–92. Berkeley: University of California Press.

———. 2001. "Universals Revisited: Human Behaviors and Cultural Variations." *Numen* 48, no. 3: 277–89.

Paramahansa, Yogananda. 2006 [1946]. *Autobiography of a Yogi.* Los Angeles: Self Realization Fellowship.

Patton, Kimberley. 2000a. "Juggling Torches: Why We Still Need Comparative Religion." In *A Magic Still Dwells: Comparative Religion in the Postmodern Age*, ed. Kimberly Patton and Benjamin Ray, 153–71. Berkeley: University of California Press.

———. 2000b. "The Net of Indra: Comparison and the Contribution of Perception. A Conversation with Lawrence E. Sullivan." In *A Magic Still Dwells: Comparative Religion in the Postmodern Age*, ed. Kimberly Patton and Benjamin Ray, 206–36. Berkeley: University of California Press.

———. 2009. *Religion of the Gods: Ritual, Paradox, and Reflexivity.* New York: Oxford University Press.

Patton, Kimberley, and John Hawley. 2005. *Holy Tears: Weeping in the Religious Imagination.* Princeton, NJ: Princeton University Press.

Patton, Kimberley, and Benjamin Ray. 2000. "Introduction." In *A Magic Still Dwells: Comparative Religion in the Postmodern Age*, ed. Kimberly Patton and Benjamin Ray, 1–22. Berkeley: University of California Press.

Patton, Laurie. 2000. "The Magic in Miniature: Etymological Links in Comparative Religions." In *A Magic Still Dwells: Comparative Religion in the Postmodern Age*, ed. Kimberly Patton and Benjamin Ray, 193–205. Berkeley: University of California Press.

Pearson, Joanne. 2006. "The History and Development of Wicca and Paganism." In *Belief Beyond Boundaries: Wicca, Celtic Spirituality and the New Age*, ed. Joanne Pearson, 15–54. Burlington, VT: Ashgate.

Penvenne, Jeanne Marie. 2005. "Settling against the Tide: The Layered Contradictions of Twentieth-Century Portuguese Settlement in Mozambique." In *Settler Colonialism in the Twentieth Century: Projects, Practices, Legacies*, ed. Caroline Elkins and Susan Pederson, 79–94. New York: Routledge.

Pétursson, Pétur. 2002. "Ragnheiður Brynjólfsdóttir og Harmleikurinn í Skálholti: Athugun á frásögn miðils." *Kistan Fræði.* Þriðji hluti og Fjórði hlutii (Part Three and Four) www.kistan.is 13–22. Háskola Íslands.

———. 2005. "Ancestors and Destiny: Icelanders' Approach to Death and the Afterlife." *Tidsskrift for Kirke, Religion, Samfund* 48, no. 1: 1–15.

Pordzik, Ralph. 2001. *The Quest for Postcolonial Utopia: A Comparative Introduction to the Utopian Novel in the New English Literatures.* New York: Peter Lang.

Prochaska, David. 1990. *Making Algeria French: Colonialism in Bône, 1870–1920.* Cambridge: Cambridge University Press.

Prorok, Carolyn. 2003. "Transplanting Pilgrimage Traditions in America." *Geographical Review* 93, no. 3: 283–307.

Prothero, Stephen. 1996. *The White Buddhist: The Asian Odyssey of Henry Steel Olcott.* Bloomington: Indiana University Press.

Radford Ruether, Rosemary. 1983 [1993]. *Sexism and God Talk: Toward a Feminist Theology.* Boston: Beacon.

————. 1992. *Gaia and God: An Ecofeminist Theology of Earth Healing*. San Francisco: HarperCollins.

Raj, Selva J. 2008. "Being Catholic the Tamil Way." *Journal for the Society of Hindu-Christian Studies* 21: 48–55.

Raj, Selva, and Corinne Dempsey, eds. 2002. *Popular Christianity in India: Riting between the Lines*. Albany: State University of New York Press.

Ramanujan, A. K. 1981. *Hymns for the Drowning: Poems for Viṣṇu by Namālvār*. Princeton, NJ: Princeton University Press.

Rattlesnake-Heaven. 1992. *Economist* 323, no. 7754: April 11.

Rennie, Bryan. 1996. *Reconstructing Eliade: Making Sense of Religion*. Albany: State University of New York Press.

Richards, Shawn. 1998. "Breaking the 'Cracked Mirror': Binary Oppositions in the Culture of Contemporary Ireland." In *Ireland and Cultural History: The Mechanics of Authenticity*, ed. Colin Graham and Richard Kirkland, 99–118. London: Macmillan.

Rickard, John. 1997. "Studying a New Science: Yeats, Irishness, and the East." In *Representing Ireland: Gender, Class, Identity*, ed. Susan Shaw Sailer, 94–112. Gainesville: University of Florida Press.

Rinehart, Robin. 2008. "The Neo-Vedanta Miracle." In *Miracle as Modern Conundrum in South Asian Religious Traditions*, ed. Corinne Dempsey and Selva Raj, 23–38. Albany: State University of New York Press.

Romey, Kristin. 2004. "Flashpoint Ayodha." *Archaeology* 57, no. 4: 48–55.

Said, Edward. 1993. *Culture and Imperialism*. New York: Alfred A. Knopf.

Saler, Bensen. 2001. "Comparison: Some Suggestions for Improving the Inevitable." *Numen* 48, no. 3: 267–75.

Sax, William. 2003. "Divine Kingdoms in the Central Himalayas." In *Sacred Landscape of the Himalaya: Proceedings of an International Conference at Heidelberg, 25–27 May 1998*, ed. Niels Gutschow, Axel Michaels, Charles Ramble, and Ernst Steinkellner. Vienna: Austrian Academy of Sciences Press.

Schüssler Fiorenza, Elisabeth. 1983. *In Memory of Her: A Feminist Theological Reconstruction of Christian Origins*. New York: Crossroads.

————. 1990. "Missionaries, Apostles, Co-workers: Romans 16 and the Reconstruction of Women's Early Christian History." In *Feminist Theology: A Reader*, ed. Ann Loades, 57–71. Louisville, KY: Westminster John Knox.

Scott, Jamie. 2001. "Introduction." In *Mapping the Sacred: Religion, Geography, and Postcolonial Literatures*, ed. Jamie Scott and Paul Simpson-Housley, xv–xxxiii. Amsterdam: Rodopi.

Segal, Robert. 2001. "In Defense of the Comparative Method." *Numen* 48, no. 3: 339–73.

Segundo, Juan Luis. 1970. *Theology and the Church: A Response to Cardinal Ratzinger and a Warning to the Whole Church*. Translated by John W. Diercksmeier. Minneapolis: Winston.

Sekkizhaar. [1985.] *Periya Puranam: A Tamil Classic on the Great Saiva Saints of South India*. Ed. N. Mahalingam. Madras: Sri Ramakrishna Math.

Seligman, Adam, Robert Weller, Michael Puett, and Bennett Simon. 2008. *Ritual and Its Consequences: An Essay on the Limits of Sincerity*. New York: Oxford University Press.

Sen, Amartya. 1993. "India and the West: Our Distortions and Their Consequences." *New Republic* 208, no. 23 (June 7): 27–34.

Sered, Susan Starr. 1994. *Priestess, Mother, Sacred Sister: Religions Dominated by Women.* New York: Oxford University Press.

Shafir, Gershon. 2005. "Settler Citizenship of the Jewish Colonization of Palestine." In *Settler Colonialism in the Twentieth Century: Projects, Practices, Legacies*, ed. Caroline Elkins and Susan Pederson, 41–58. New York: Routledge.

Sharpe, Eric. 1986. *Comparative Religion: A History.* 2nd ed. La Salle, IL: Open Court.

Sheldrake, Phillip. 2001. *Spaces for the Sacred: Place, Memory, and Identity.* Baltimore: Johns Hopkins University Press.

Sherma, Rita DasGupta. 1998. "Sacred Immanence: Reflections of Ecofeminism in Hindu Tantra." In *Purifying the Earthly Body of God: Religion and Ecology in Hindu India*, ed. Lance Nelson, 89–131. Albany: State University of New York Press.

Sigmund, Paul. 1990. *Liberation Theology at the Crossroads: Democracy or Revolution?* New York: Oxford University Press.

Singh, Kuhu. 2000. "Temples in the Grand Canyon." *Indian Express*, July 9. Retrieved from http://www.hvk.org/articles/0700/22.html.

Siquiera, T. N. 1990 [1948]. "Introduction to the Second Edition." In *Sister Alphonsa*, by K. C. Chacko, 6th ed., 19–21. Bharananganam, Kerala: Vice Postulator, Cause of Blessed Alphonsa.

Slemon, Stephen. 1995. "Resistance Theory for the Second World." In *The Post-Colonial Studies Reader*, ed. Bill Ashcroft, Gareth Griffiths, and Helen Tiffin, 104–10. London: Routledge.

Smith, Huston. 2000. "Methodology, Comparisons, and Truth." In *A Magic Still Dwells: Comparative Religion in the Postmodern Age*, ed. Kimberly Patton and Benjamin Ray, 172–81. Berkeley: University of California Press.

Smith, Jonathan Z. 1978. *Map Is Not Territory: Studies in the History of Religion.* Chicago: University of Chicago Press.

———. 1982. *Imagining Religion: From Babylon to Jonestown.* Chicago: University of Chicago Press.

———. 1987. *To Take Place: Toward Theory in Ritual.* Chicago: University of Chicago Press.

———. 1990. *Drudgery Divine: On the Comparison of Early Christianities and the Religions of Late Antiquity.* Chicago: University of Chicago Press.

———. 2000. "The End of Comparison: Redescription and Rectification." In *A Magic Still Dwells: Comparative Religion in the Postmodern Age*, ed. Kimberly Patton and Benjamin Ray, 237–41. Berkeley: University of California Press.

———. 2004. *Relating Religion: Essays in the Study of Religion.* Chicago: University of Chicago Press.

———. 2010. "The Eternal Deferral." In *Hermeneutics, Politics, and the History of Religions: The Contested Legacies of Joachim Wach and Mircea Eliade*, ed. Christian Wedemeyer and Wendy Doniger, 215–37. New York: Oxford University Press.

Smythe, Gerry. 1999. "Decolonization and Criticism: Towards a Theory of Irish Critical Discourse." In *Ireland and Cultural History: The Mechanics of Authenticity*, ed. Colin Graham and Richard Kirkland, 29–49. London: Macmillan.

Sobrino, Jon. 1984. *The True Church and the Poor.* Translated by Matthew O'Connell. Maryknoll, NY: Orbis.

———. 2006. *Where Is God?: Earthquake, Terrorism, Barbarity and Hope.* Translated by Margaret Wild. Maryknoll, NY: Orbis.

Soja, Edward. 1995. "Heterotopologies: A Remembrance of Other Spaces in the Citadel—LA." In *Postmodern Cities and Spaces*, ed. Sophie Watson and Katherine Gibson, 13–34. Oxford: Blackwell.

St. Alphonsa: The First Indian Woman to Be Canonized. 2008. Bharananganam, Kerala: St. Alphonsa Chapel.

Stark, Les, and Mal Harding. 2006. "A Short History of the Big Muddy Area." www.croc. org/events/rogaine2006/Big_Muddy_History.pdf, accessed April 10, 2010.

Sullivan, Lawrence. 1986. "Sound and Senses: Toward a Hermeneutics of Performance." *History of Religions* 21, no. 1: 1–33.

———. 1990. "Seeking an End to the Primary Text." In *Beyond the Classics: Essays in Religious Studies and Liberal Education*, ed. Frank Reynolds and Sheryl Burkhalter, 52–53. Atlanta: Scholars.

Swan, Laura. 2001. *The Forgotten Desert Mothers: Sayings, Lives and Stories of Early Christian Women.* New York: Paulist.

Swatos, William. 1990. "Spiritualism as a Religion of Science." *Social Compass* 37, no. 4: 471–82.

Swatos, William, and Loftur Reimar Gissurarson. 1997. *Icelandic Spiritualism: Mediumship and Modernity in Iceland.* New Brunswick, CT: Transaction.

Taylor, Bron. 1995. "Resacralizing Earth: Pagan Environmentalisms and the Restoration of Turtle Island." In *American Sacred Space*, ed. David Chidester and Edward Linenthal, 97–151. Bloomington: Indiana University Press.

Taylor, Charles. 2002. *Varieties of Religion Today: William James Revisited.* Cambridge: Harvard University Press.

Taylor, Lawrence. 1985. "The Priest and the Agent: Social Drama and Class Consciousness in the West of Ireland." *Comparative Studies in Society and History* 27: 696–712.

———. 1990. "Stories of Power, Powerful Stories: The Drunken Priest in Donegal." In *Religious Orthodoxy and Popular Faith in European Society*, ed. Ellen Badone, 163–84. Princeton, NJ: Princeton University Press.

———. 1995. *Occasions of Faith: An Anthropology of Irish Catholics.* Philadelphia: University of Pennsylvania Press.

Tharakan, Anniyil. 2008. *The Canticle of the Beloved: A Cycle of Poems and an Essay on the Life and Spirituality of St. Alphonsa.* Kottayam, Kerala: Deepika Book House.

Thompson, Judith, and Paul Heelas. 1986. *The Way of the Heart: The Rajneesh Movement.* Wellingborough, Northamptonshire: Aquarian.

Tingay, Kevin. 2002. "Madame Blavatsky's Children: Theosophy and Its Heirs." In *Belief Beyond Boundaries: Wicca, Celtic Spirituality and the New Age*, ed. Joanne Pearson, 239–49. Burlington, VT: Ashgate.

Tromp, Marlene. 2006. *Altered States: Sex, Nation, Drugs, and Self-Transformation in Victorian Spiritualism.* Albany: State University of New York Press.

UPI. 2005. "Hindus, Hawaiians, Agree on Sacred Stones." March 26. www.upi.com/ Top_News/2005/03/26/Hindus-Hawaiians-agree-on-sacred-stones/UPI-70751111817201/tab-listen/March 26.

Urban, Hugh. 1996. "Zorba the Buddha: Capitalism, Charisma, and the Cult of Bhagwan Shree Rajneesh." *Religion* 26, no. 2: 161–82.

Van der Leeuw. 1963. *Religion in Essence and Manifestation: A Study in Phenomenology.* New York: Harper.

van der Veer, Peter. 1992. "Ayodha and Somnath: Eternal Shrines, Contested Histories." *Social Research* 59, no. 1: 85–109.

———. 2001. *Imperial Encounters: Religion and Modernity in India and Britain.* Princeton, NJ: Princeton University Press.

Vanmikanathan, G. 1985. *Periya Puranam: A Tamil Classic on the Great Saiva Saints of South India by Sekkizhaar.* Madras, India: Ramakrishan Math.

Vengaloor, Eliseus, FCC. 2006. *In the Footsteps of Alphonsa*. Translated by Thomas Chavarany. Bharananganam, Kerala: Jeevan.

Víkingur, Séra Sveinn. 1962. *Lára Miðill: Sagt frá Dulhæfileikum og Miðilsstarfi frú Láru I. Ágústsdóttir*. Akureyri, Ísland: Kvöldvökuútgáfan.

Viotti, Vicki. 2005. "A Gentle Collision of Two Traditions." *Honolulu Advertiser*, posted March 25. http://the.honoluluadvertiser.com/article/2005/Mar/25/ln/ln01p.html.

Viswanathan, Gauri. 1998. *Outside the Fold: Conversion, Modernity, and Belief*. Princeton, NJ: Princeton University Press.

———. 2000. "The Ordinary Business of Occultism." *Critical Inquiry* 27, no. 1: 1–20.

———. 2004. "Ireland, India, and the Poetics of Internationalism." *Journal of World History* 15, no. 1: 7–30.

———. 2005. "The State of the World." *Victorian Studies* 48, no. 1 (Autumn): 124–33.

Wach, Joachim. 1935 [1965]. "Introduction: The Meaning and Task of the History of Religions. In *History of Religions: Essays on the Problem of Understanding*, ed. Joseph Kittegawa, 1–20. Chicago: University of Chicago Press.

Waghorne, Joanne. 2004. *Diaspora of the Gods: Modern Hindu Temples in an Urban Middle-Class World*. New York: Oxford University Press.

Wallace, Alfred Russel. [1896] 1975. *Miracles and Modern Spiritualism*. New York: Arno.

Weinstein, Donald, and Rudolph Bell. 1982. *Saints and Society: The Two Worlds of Western Christendom, 1000–1700*. Chicago: University of Chicago Press.

West, Angela. 1990. "Sex and Salvation: A Christian Feminist Bible Study on 1 Corinthians 6.12–7.39." In *Feminist Theology: A Reader*, ed. Ann Loades, 72–80. Louisville, KY: Westminster John Knox.

White, David. 2000. "The Scholar as Mythographer: Comparative Indo-European Myth and Postmodern Concerns." In *A Magic Still Dwells: Comparative Religion in the Postmodern Age*, ed. Kimberly Patton and Benjamin Ray, 47–54. Berkeley: University of California Press.

White, Hilary. 2009. "Pope Warns against 'Deceitful' Marxist-Based Theology to Brazilian Bishops." *LifeSiteNews.com*, December 8, http://www.lifesitenews.com/news/archive/ldn/2009/dec/09120805.

Wilce, James. 2006. "Magical Laments and Anthropological Reflections." *Current Anthropology* 47, no. 6: 891–913.

Wolfe, Patrick. 1999. *Settler Colonialism and the Transformation of Anthropology: The Politics and Poetics of an Ethnographic Event*. London: Cassell.

INDEX